Educational Development

SRHE and Open University Press Imprint
General Editor: Heather Eggins

Current titles include:

Catherine Bargh et al.: *University Leadership*
Ronald Barnett: *Beyond all Reason*
Ronald Barnett: *The Limits of Competence*
Ronald Barnett: *Higher Education*
Ronald Barnett: *Realizing the University in an Age of Supercomplexity*
Ronald Barnett and Kelly Coate: *Engaging the Curriculum in Higher Education*
Tony Becher and Paul R. Trowler: *Academic Tribes and Territories (2nd edn)*
Neville Bennett et al.: *Skills Development in Higher Education and Employment*
John Biggs: *Teaching for Quality Learning at University (2nd edn)*
Richard Blackwell and Paul Blackmore (eds): *Towards Strategic Staff Development in Higher Education*
David Boud et al. (eds): *Using Experience for Learning*
David Boud and Nicky Solomon (eds): *Work-based Learning*
Tom Bourner et al. (eds): *New Directions in Professional Higher Education*
John Brennan et al. (eds): *What Kind of University?*
Anne Brockbank and Ian McGill: *Facilitating Reflective Learning in Higher Education*
Stephen D. Brookfield and Stephen Preskill: *Discussion as a Way of Teaching*
Ann Brooks and Alison Mackinnon (eds): *Gender and the Restructured University*
Sally Brown and Angela Glasner (eds): *Assessment Matters in Higher Education*
Burton R. Clark: *Sustaining Change in Universities*
James Cornford and Neil Pollock: *Putting the University Online*
John Cowan: *On Becoming an Innovative University Teacher*
Sara Delamont, Paul Atkinson and Odette Parry: *Supervising the PhD*
Sara Delamont and Paul Atkinson: *Research Cultures and Careers*
Gerard Delanty: *Challenging Knowledge*
Chris Duke: *Managing the Learning University*
Heather Eggins (ed.): *Globalization and Reform in Higher Education*
Heather Eggins and Ranald Macdonald (eds): *The Scholarship of Academic Development*
Gillian Evans: *Academics and the Real World*
Andrew Hannan and Harold Silver: *Innovating in Higher Education*
Lee Harvey and Associates: *The Student Satisfaction Manual*
David Istance, Hans Schuetze and Tom Schuller (eds): *International Perspectives on Lifelong Learning*
Norman Jackson and Helen Lund (eds): *Benchmarking for Higher Education*
Merle Jacob and Tomas Hellström (eds): *The Future of Knowledge Production in the Academy*
Peter Knight: *Being a Teacher in Higher Education*
Peter Knight and Paul Trowler: *Departmental Leadership in Higher Education*
Peter Knight and Mantz Yorke: *Assessment, Learning and Employability*
Ray Land: *Educational Development*
Mary Lea and Barry Stierer (eds): *Student Writing in Higher Education*
Dina Lewis and Barbara Allan: *Virtual Learning Communities*
Ian McNay (ed.): *Higher Education and its Communities*
Elaine Martin: *Changing Academic Work*
Louise Morley: *Quality and Power in Higher Education*
Moira Peelo and Terry Wareham (eds): *Failing Students in Higher Education*
Craig Prichard: *Making Managers in Universities and Colleges*
Michael Prosser and Keith Trigwell: *Understanding Learning and Teaching*
John Richardson: *Researching Student Learning*
Stephen Rowland: *The Enquiring University Teacher*
Maggi Savin-Baden: *Problem-based Learning in Higher Education*
Maggi Savin-Baden: *Facilitating Problem-based Learning*
Maggi Savin-Baden and Kay Wilkie: *Challenging Research in Problem-based Learning*
David Scott, Andrew Brown, Ingrid Lunt and Lucy Thorne: *Examining Professional Doctorates*
Peter Scott (ed.): *The Globalization of Higher Education*
Peter Scott: *The Meanings of Mass Higher Education*
Michael L. Shattock: *Managing Successful Universities*
Maria Slowey and David Watson: *Higher Education and the Lifecourse*
Anthony Smith and Frank Webster (eds): *The Postmodern University?*
Colin Symes and John McIntyre (eds): *Working Knowledge*
Peter G. Taylor: *Making Sense of Academic Life*
Richard Taylor, Jean Barr and Tom Steele: *For a Radical Higher Education*
Malcolm Tight: *Researching Higher Education*
Penny Tinkler and Carolyn Jackson: *The Doctoral Examination Process*
Susan Toohey: *Designing Courses for Higher Education*
Paul R. Trowler (ed.): *Higher Education Policy and Institutional Change*
Melanie Walker (ed.): *Reconstructing Professionalism in University Teaching*
Melanie Walker and Jon Nixon (eds): *Reclaiming Universities from a Runaway World*
David Warner and David Palfreyman (eds): *Higher Education Management of UK Higher Education*
Gareth Williams (ed.): *The Enterprising University*
Diana Woodward and Karen Ross: *Managing Equal Opportunities in Higher Education*

Educational Development

Discourse, Identity and Practice

Ray Land

Society for Research into Higher Education
& Open University Press

Open University Press
McGraw-Hill Education
McGraw-Hill House
Shoppenhangers Road
Maidenhead
Berkshire
England
SL6 2QL

email: enquiries@openup.co.uk
world wide web: www.openup.co.uk

and Two Penn Plaza, New York, NY 10121-2289, USA

First published 2004

A catalogue record of this book is available from the British Library

ISBN 0 335 21328 6 (pb) 0 335 21329 4 (hb)

Library of Congress Cataloging-in-Publication Data
CIP data applied for

Typeset by RefineCatch Limited, Bungay, Suffolk
Printed in the UK by Bell & Bain Ltd, Glasgow

For Moira, Eleanor, Christopher
and Clarissa

Contents

Acknowledgements

My thanks are due to the educational developers in various institutions who generously gave their time to be interviewed for this study.

Parts of Section 1 were originally published as R. Land (2000) Orientations to academic development, *Educational Developments,* 12 April: 19–23; R. Land (2001) Background to the territory: Orientations to educational development, in C. Rust (ed.) *Improving Student Learning Strategically*. Oxford: OCSLD; and R. Land (2003) Orientations to academic development, in R. MacDonald and H. Eggins (eds) *The Scholarship of Academic Development.* Buckingham: SRHE and Open University Press. Part of Section 2 was originally published as R. Land (2001) Agency, context and change in academic development, *International Journal of Academic Development,* Vol. 6.1, May. Thanks are due to the publishers for their kind permission to re-use material here.

Part of the research for this book was kindly supported by the small grant scheme of the Staff and Educational Development Association (SEDA), for whose generosity I am deeply grateful.

I am indebted to Kym Fraser for coining the term 'Provocateur' and to Stanley Frielick for his apt suggestion of the term for the Discipline-specific orientation in the framework described in the book. I have since adopted this term with their permission.

Glossary of Acronyms

ACORN	Action, Communication, Ownership, Reflection and Nurture
ALT-C	Association for Learning Technology Conference
AQAG	Academic Quality Assurance Group
ASDC	Academic Staff Development Committee
API	Age Participation Index
ASSHE	Assessment Strategies in Scottish Higher Education
C&IT	Communication and Information Technology
CTI	Computers in Teaching Initiative
CPD	Continuing Professional Development
CVCP	Committee of Vice-Chancellors and Principals
DENI	Department of Education for Northern Ireland
DfEE	Department for Education and Employment
EARLI	European Association for Research on Learning and Instruction
EDS	Educational Development Service
EDU	Educational Development Unit
EHE	Enterprise in Higher Education
EIP	Evaluations and Investigations Program
ELT	Enhancing Learning and Teaching
FDTL	Fund for the Development of Teaching and Learning
FSEDA	Fellow of the Staff and Educational Development Association
HE	Higher Education
HEA	Higher Education Academy
HEFCE	Higher Education Funding Council for England
HERDSA	Higher Education Research and Staff Development Association of Australasia
HESDA	Higher Education Staff Development Association
HoD	Head of Department
HMI	Her Majesty's Inspectorate
HRM	Human Resource Management
ICT	Information and Communication Technology

IiP	Investors in People
IJAD	International Journal of Academic Development
ILTHE	Institute for Learning and Teaching in Higher Education
IT	Information Technology
LTSN	Learning and Teaching Support Network
MARBLE	Metropolitan Area Networks Accessible Resource-Based Learning Exemplars
NLP	Neuro-Linguistic Programming
NVQ	National Vocational Qualifications
OECD	Organisation for Economic Co-operation and Development
OFSTED	Office for Standards in Education
POD	Professional and Organisational Development Network in Higher Education
PVC	Pro-Vice Chancellor
QAA	Quality Assurance Agency for Higher Education
QIAS	Quality Improvement and Academic Standards
RAE	Research Assessment Exercise
R&D	Research and Development
SEDA	Staff and Educational Development Association
SMG	Senior Management Group
SRHE	Society for Research into Higher Education
STLHE	Society for Teaching and Learning in Higher Education
THES	The Times Higher Education Supplement
THETO	The Higher Education Training Organisation
TQA	Teaching Quality Assessment
UCoSDA	Universities and Colleges Staff Development Agency
UGC	University Grants Committee
UNICEF	United Nations Children's Fund
VLE	Virtual Learning Environment
WBL	Work-based Learning

‘Be ye therefore wise as serpents, and harmless as doves’

St. Matthew x.16

Introduction: A Catching Fire

Educational development remains a little understood activity, even within the higher education institutions in which it is located. This book arises from a recognition of the under-researched nature of educational development practice, and of educational developers as a professional, or sub-professional, group working in higher education. It draws on a series of 35 interviews with educational developers in a range of UK universities. Its context is principally that of the UK, but the issues discussed in the text, it is hoped, have a useful bearing on practice in other cultures. It examines the historical moment and convergent pressures on higher education systems out of which educational development has expanded rapidly in the last two decades. It then presents a set of 12 analytic categories of practice or 'orientations' to educational development derived from an empirical study of developers within the UK. These categories are analysed further in terms of the perceived stances on educational and organizational change which are held by developers, given that involvement in change processes tends to be a fairly commonly held attribute of this professional group. The book then considers the strategic terrain developers occupy in terms of the organizational cultures and structures against which they both adopt and adapt their strategic approach.

The changing landscape of higher education and the growth of educational development

The growth of educational development as a practice within UK higher education since the 1970s is best perceived not as a linear narrative but as a complex tapestry of interwoven developments. These developments must be viewed as a response to a range of interconnected factors, including global economic and political pressures that have obliged governments worldwide to reduce public spending and retrench in relation to welfare services (Cameron and Tschirhart 1992; Pollit 1993; Clarke and Newman 1997;

Scott 1999; Becher and Trowler 2001). Higher education comes to be seen as operating within what is characterized variously as post-industrialism, globalization, late capitalism, or postmodernity. Whatever the label, the environment is characterized by volatile change, rapid and massive flows of information, uncertainty and unpredictability – particularly in relation to enrolments and revenues. The environment is marked by fierce competitiveness and potential organizational decline unless there is a vigilant drive for innovation and flexibility. This period witnesses an acceleration in the generation and proliferation of knowledge, the transgressing and fissuring of disciplinary boundaries. In order to compete successfully within a globalized economy, there are pressures for the higher education (HE) curriculum to become more vocational, for HE to be more closely linked to the needs of a global economy and employability needs. To create the modernized workforce necessary for such a transition there follows an expansion of the HE system, which entails a widening of access and greater cultural diversity within the student body. There are more opportunities for access for lower-status or previously marginalized groups on the one hand, and an increasing intake of international students paying full costs on the other. An expanded system brings with it calls for greater accountability for the extended government investment as well as increased managerialism to achieve and maintain efficiency and effectiveness through reduced resourcing and higher numbers.

It is against the background of, and as a reaction to, these developments that higher education institutions, particularly in the UK and Australasia, began to establish educational development units (EDUs) as one strategic and operational means of helping academic staff to accommodate and cope with such rapid changes in practice and organization. Though there had been a limited culture of educational development from the 1960s (such as the London University Teaching Methods Unit) focused mainly on practical lecturing and tutorial techniques, and, from the 1970s, a more advanced research culture investigating the nature of student learning in higher education, generally from a phenomenographic perspective (Marton and Säljo 1976; Entwistle, Hanley and Hounsell 1979; Laurillard 1979; Ramsden 1979), it was mainly from the mid-1980s and into the early 1990s that the need for change within the HE sector was becoming apparent in terms of coping with the effects of the changes mentioned earlier. These changes related particularly to coping with increasingly large and more diverse classes with constrained resources, and to the need for flexibility and transferability within the curriculum exemplified by such developments as modularization, credit schemes, and the adoption of Web technologies and virtual learning environments. This was accompanied by a growing emphasis on quality, and on changing pedagogical paradigms which placed greater emphasis on active learning and reflection. There was a focus also on developing new skills to cope with the implications of widened participation, including the needs of students with disabilities, and on enhancing employability (Gosling 1996 and 2001).

It is important to point out that whilst the 'supercomplexity' (Barnett 2000) confronting HE has been the source of important opportunities for educational developers and other 'new professionals' (Gornall 1999), as new academic identities and roles have emerged in response to the spaces opened up in this changing environment, this same environment has, on the other hand, brought tensions and difficulties in terms of competing priorities, particularly regarding the intensification of academic labour and expectations of greater research productivity. The new environment is also characterized by qualities of epistemological contestability (Barnett 2000) and organizational ambiguity (Alvesson 2002) in which developers often find themselves caught, and an increasing sense of borderlessness or the blurring of boundaries – what Bergquist (1995: 11) terms 'boundariless anxiety' – which educational developers find themselves negotiating. It is therefore worth considering particular aspects of the changing conditions of the higher education landscape in a little more detail before we move on to analyse the experience of developers and their varied reactions to such an environment.

Massification

The implications of the steep increases in participation rates occasioned by the changed conditions of HE, particularly in terms of the increased entry of non-traditional students into the HE system, are alone sufficient to have had a profound impact upon the conditions of academic work in UK higher education (Fulton 1989). In many respects Trow's (1974) account of the complex transition involved in shifting from an elite to a mass (15 per cent Age Participation Index) and now more-or-less 'universal' system (40 per cent API) proved prophetic. Trow's account anticipates the elements of crisis that were to afflict HE systems in the UK and Australasia from the early 1980s until the present. These included declining units of resource necessitating stringencies in staff-student ratios and infrastructure, and a much less homogeneous student body. These elements in turn entailed significant changes in student expectations; the re-design of curricula and changed pedagogy; shifts in the balance of priorities for staff in relation to teaching and research roles; and confused public perceptions about the role and status of both universities and their graduates in modern society. Scott (1995: 9–10) emphasizes that the transition from elite to mass must be interpreted not just in terms of the expansion of numbers and ensuing resource pressures but also 'in the context of the restless synergy between plural modernisations – of the academy, polity, economy, society and culture'. Nixon (1996: 93) argues that the 'significant shift' during this period of crisis 'is at the level of values and underlying structures of belief; structures that are in new and vital interplay with emergent forms of professional agency.'

Within a mass system, and even more so within a universal system, we can identify a discourse of access and opportunity, equity and widening participation. In an 'ideal' or pure form, which it is unlikely ever to be, a mass system is one of diversity. It is regulated, accountable, with an emphasis on the culture of the organization. There tends to be an increasingly observable split between teaching and research, with the latter often of an applied nature. Interdisciplinarity is common. The curriculum is usually modularized with a vocational and predominantly utilitarian focus. Staff tend, in the main, to be the less autonomous, more managed 'locals', in Gouldner's (1979) phrase. HE is seen as the servant of the state and there is a prevailing ethos of the strategic. An elite system, on the other hand, in its ideal form, employs a discourse of excellence and selection. It is a more uniform system in which the autonomy of the academic is jealously guarded. Disciplinary culture is important. Strong emphasis is placed on the status and reputation of the individual, the organization and the discipline. Teaching and research tend to be unified within the discipline. Teaching is more course-based with a liberal endorsement of learning for learning's sake. Amongst academic staff there are likely to be comparatively more of Gouldner's 'cosmopolitans' – those entrepreneurial academics whose status allows them a privileged role and greater autonomy within the organization. HE is seen as a critic of the state. The ethos, in principle at least, is more collegial. These characteristics will prove to be important determinants of the practice and subjectivity of developers as we encounter them in Section 1 below, and we will observe there how developers are often caught in the tension between these competing discourses.

Managerialism in higher education

Educational development came into being during a period of radical revision of the modes of governance of HE. After the euphoric arrival of the new 'plateglass' universities of the mid to late 1960s had been somewhat eclipsed by the global recession and worldwide oil price increase of 1974, the mood of HE funding bodies changed to one of critique and reform. This rumbled through the 1970s, surfacing pointedly in the UK in Prime Minister James Callaghan's warning speech at Ruskin College in 1976 that all sectors of UK education should address national employment needs in a more obviously relevant fashion. This hardened during the 1980s under the new Conservative Government into targeted attacks on managerial weakness, wasteful 'dead wood' and lack of public accountability – a sustained critique amounting to what (Ball 1990a) has termed a 'discourse of derision'. Such criticism came to a head with the publication of the Jarratt Report (1985) which recommended reform in institutional and financial management within HE institutions along the lines of the corporate sector.

> The Jarratt Report (1985) attempted to promote management into a self-justifying activity and allowed that it might take on imperatives of its

> own – with the implication that they could be endorsed separately from higher education's primary objectives, and could be distributed hierarchically [. . .] the Report complained about 'large and powerful academic departments together with individual academics who sometimes see their academic discipline as more important than the long-term well-being of the university which houses them', and put its weight behind universities as corporate enterprises to which the component units and individuals should be subordinate.
>
> (Becher and Kogan 1992: 181)

This was followed by a series of policy statements and ministerial interventions enthusiastically advocating the embracing of such private sector-style practices as market competition, rational managerial decision-making and performance monitoring (Salter and Tapper 1994; Miller 1995a). One effect of this new managerialism seems to have been the separating out of teaching from the nexus it formerly constituted with research, a nexus very firmly located within the disciplinary domain. Teaching and learning in this period came to be seen as more generic, as located within the organizational rather than the disciplinary culture and hence more subject to managerial control, and to the influence of educational specialists (developers) rather than disciplinary experts. Technology might be viewed as an effect of this same tendency, to draw the pedagogic aspect of academic practice into a more observable and manageable sphere, and to bring it under the influence of other kinds of professionals who are not located within the disciplinary community of practice. 'In this sense', Sawbridge suggests (1996: 6), 'one can see employer initiatives, including the growth of interest in staff development, as intervening in the collegial culture because it leaves too much to chance at a time of institutional challenge'. In this way the positioning of educational developers (and learning technologists) is rendered problematic, located between discipline and management, and will require careful negotiation. As Lieberman (1989) points out:

> Working in bureaucratic settings has taught everyone to be compliant, to be rule governed, not to ask questions, seek alternatives or deal with competing values. People are supposed to follow orders from those at the top. Working to create more professional cultures in schools, however, calls upon people to engage in discussion to seek a collective vision and the practical means to achieve it. Instead of one leader and many followers, a leader [. . .] works to facilitate leadership and encourage it among entire staff [. . .] Developers, like others in the educational establishment, must define their success not by becoming yet another group of specialists, but rather by engaging in the building of a culture of inquiry and improved learning environments for students and teachers.
>
> (Lieberman, cited in Day 1993: 88)

Accountability

Another major driver for the work of educational developers in HE has been the increasing requirement for institutions to engage in procedures for assuring the quality of education, the growth of the so-called 'quality culture' or 'audit explosion' (Barnett 1992; Ellis 1993; Green 1994; Power 1994; Goodlad 1995). These measures derive to a large extent from concerns with public accountability and making more efficient use of resources. As a report of the UK Quality Assurance Agency (1998: 6–7) explained, 'with the rapid expansion of numbers of students and institutions, the associated broadening of the purposes of HE, and the considerable increase in the amount of public money required, more methodical approaches have had to be employed'.

Not only was teaching quality assessment (TQA) of the total educational experience of students in a specific subject area (rather than of an institution's systems), but the results of TQA came to be linked to the funding of student places. This delegating of accountability for quality in practice to the unit or, often, departmental level, coupled with the inevitable use of TQA outcomes in the educational and national press for 'league table' rankings was throughout the 1990s to provide one of the most powerful motivators for academic managers and their staff to seek the assistance and utilize the experience of educational developers within their organization. It proved to be one of the most salient drivers in enabling educational developers to exert influence within their organizations at both individual and departmental level. TQA also often allowed developers to gain strategic inroads institution-wide when their guidance was sought at senior management level for TQA purposes by a Pro-Vice Chancellor, Vice-Principal (Academic), Dean of Teaching and Learning, or equivalent. Gordon and Partington (1993: 6), in discussing the significant implications of both TQA and audit for the work of educational developers, suggest that professional development for individual staff members remains 'one of the fundamental aspects of the work of staff development for quality enhancement'.

The direct linking of educational development to notions of quality in this way, however, occasioning perhaps a blurring of notions of quality *enhancement* with quality *assurance*, also complicates the operational practice of developers, merging the monitoring of standards with the development of good practice. A typical example of the problematic nature of this accountability factor is the still controversial issue of the accreditation of academic staff in terms of teaching and learning, recommended in the UK by the Dearing Report (Dearing 1997). Whilst many developers have become involved in the promotion of membership of the Institute for Learning and Teaching in Higher Education (ILTHE) – now the Higher Education Academy – in the interests of enhanced provision to students, others are wary of being seen as aligned with management and government agendas to do with the regulation and domestication of academic practice. As we will see in later sections, quality assurance and accountability are issues on which developers will take different stances. As one remarked about the professional and institutional position of his own educational development unit, 'We strive hard to be seen as the social workers, not the police' (Respondent 21).

Learning technology

Any consideration of the growing role of educational development in higher education has to be set against the continuously dynamic state of technological development during this period. During the last two decades information and communication technologies have been developing at an unprecedented and increasingly rapid pace. The processing power and storage capacity of computing technology has been doubling at an exponential rate, roughly every 18 months, and the cost of the technology has been falling proportionately. The use of the Internet, the World Wide Web and, increasingly, virtual learning environments (VLEs), has revolutionized communications and is causing radical developments in the ways universities and colleges enable their staff and students to find and create knowledge and interact with each other (Land and Bayne 2004).

Assisting academic colleagues in getting to grips with new learning technologies at the levels of skills development, electronic courseware and materials development, design and delivery of online programmes, and strategic aspects of implementing learning technology at institutional level, has been a major strand in the multiple narratives that constitute the rise of educational development in UK higher education. The increasingly powerful presence of information and communication technologies (ICT) has provided both opportunities and tensions for the educational development community. ICT has often been a lucrative source of additional institutional funding from which EDUs – traditionally the Cinderellas of funding support within institutions – have benefited. A range of funding initiatives has also drawn in many academics who would not otherwise have engaged with pedagogical aspects of higher education. These latter have tended to operate from a disciplinary focus rather than the more generic approach adopted by more mainstream educational developers, or have been technological specialists drawing on distinctive cognitive psychological theories of learning. Learning technology has helped spawn a plethora of educational development funding initiatives, coordination activities and networks during the last decade, and in many institutions educational developers have been recruited into the production of e-learning strategies.

Marketization and consumerism

The implementation of new national systems of quality assurance – requiring institutions to undergo academic audit, and the assessment of both teaching and research quality at unit level (Trow 1993) – has come into existence within a climate of increasing institutional competition and consumer-oriented marketization (Williams 1992). As Foucault (1975) has observed, once a measure has been established to mark variance either side of a regulatory norm, then a powerful discipline can be exerted to observe and regulate the practice of social groups, which in turn often develops into self-regulatory behaviours and regimes. Through the discourse of excellence, manifest in such initiatives as National Teaching Fellowship Schemes, and their internal institutional equivalents, Centres of Excellence in Teaching and Learning, the research excellence gradings of the Research Assessment Exercise, and the various league table rankings published in the national press, such regulatory practice can be identified. The positioning of developers *vis-à-vis* such regimes is complex. It often falls to the educational development unit within the institution to promote and organize the proposals or bids for such external and internal competition, and by necessity collude with the discourses and practices that sustain them. For those who might be inclined more to the critique of such practice, this often entails complex identity management in relation to the ways in which they might be perceived professionally by senior management on the one hand and the academic staff with whom they are collaboratively engaged on the other. It similarly can require careful translation or management of meaning between different groupings and across competing discourses within the organization, a skill in which many developers learn to become proficient.

Such competition operates in tandem with the marketization and incipient consumerism that has become an increasing feature of higher education during this same period. The debate concerning the charging of variable tuition fees that has exercised various governments is one salient aspect of this trend. Leaving aside the issue of whether students are indeed positioned as consumers or are, conversely, the product of higher education, or whether other stakeholders – employers, government, parents – are the consumers, there has been an observable *commodification* of the higher education curriculum and student experience. As part of this process, the curriculum in many HE institutions during recent decades has simultaneously undergone a process of *modularization*, often as part of a credit accumulation and transfer framework. This has been for a variety of reasons including student subject choice, increased flexibility of access to HE, efficiency gains or administrative convenience. As Darby (1995) points out, though the technological capacity for flexibly delivered provision has been in place for some considerable time, the key catalyst of such developments is the eventual combination of learning technology *with* modularization through provision of virtual learning environments. However the many tensions that modularization has brought into matters of course design, assessment and teaching/learning methodology in higher education has been a further factor in increasing demand for the specialist services of educational developers within higher education institutions. Again, as recent research indicates that increasingly consumer-oriented provision might be fostering a culture of passivity and non-criticality within students seeking a trouble-free acquisition of knowledge (Naidoo 2003), this leads to interesting stances in terms of whether developers, in their assistance and guidance in the design of such flexible and packaged curricula, perceive such offerings as located within the discourses of flexibility, access, meeting of student need and widening participation, or whether they find themselves awkwardly positioned between these discourses and the competing discourses of market economics.

Pedagogic and epistemic change

A final and significant factor in the rapid growth of educational development activity in the last two decades has been a radical transformation of the higher education curriculum. Barnett (1994: 47) offers a notion of 'epistemic change' as an explanatory theory for this perceptible 'paradigm shift' within the higher education curriculum:

> Higher education has begun to show a paradigm shift in reorientating its knowledge functions, its research projects, its curricula and its wider mission towards the wider society. 'Paradigm shift' is becoming an empty phrase, used all too readily to describe the first signs of any social change. It is justified here since there are indications of academe, in its most intimate recesses, thinking explicitly of the world beyond in framing and delivering a curriculum. Being a historian is no longer a sufficient *rites de passage*; higher education hears from society that an academic framing of knowledge is an inadequate preparation for the life ahead. Now 'transferable skills' have to be imparted to students before they pass on to find their way in the labour market.
>
> (20)

Barnett represents this turn within the higher education curriculum as a shift from disciplines to 'action', from a curriculum driven mainly by declarative or propositional knowledge to one incorporating considerably more procedural knowledge.

> Knowing how to do things as well as knowing that such is such is the core of this epistemic change; and this change is affecting our sense of what the academy is for. Enabling students not just to know things but also to do things: this is the new order.
>
> (47)

Barnett's perspective follows a line of analysis similar to Weiner's (1981) study of how English educational culture, including higher education, has until recently perpetuated a dispensation (largely inherited from the nineteenth century) in which the Platonic, 'classical', rural and clerical concerns of an elite landed class remained privileged over matters urban, industrial and commercial. Maxwell (1987) in distinguishing the acquisition of 'knowledge' from that of 'wisdom' has pointed to the over-emphasis within academic practice on the cognitive problems inherent within disciplines, a somewhat solipsistic and narrow tendency towards problems of the academy's own making rather than those emanating from the needs of the wider society. Becher (1989) has explored 'tribal' academic ideologies of the pure intellectual. Barnett (1994) writes with a conscious awareness of such traditions and perspectives.

> The term 'paradigm shift' is often overplayed, so it is employed with some caution here. But we are entering a climacteric in which the long-held sense (since the late nineteenth century, at least) of propositional discipline-based knowledge can no longer capture the high ground of the curriculum [. . .] Terms such as 'experiential learning', 'transferable skills', 'problem-solving', 'group work' and 'work-based learning': these do not just point to new teaching methods but are illustrative of the changing definitions of knowledge that are taking place.
>
> (46–7)

Barnett's concern about a possible drift towards 'operationalism' (47) gives rise to discussion of epistemic change.

> The framing of the curriculum necessarily contains an epistemology. A curriculum is more than its knowledge components; much more [. . .] the medium *is* the message.
>
> (45–6)

The German philosopher Habermas (1978) has differentiated between instrumental and non-instrumental forms of reason, arguing that in many of the human transactions of modern society – bureaucratic, technocratic and generally strategic transactions – instrumental reason has become the dominant form of reason. As a consequence the educational institutions of modern society are likely to reflect this same purposive nature and to incorporate instrumentalist forms of reason within their curricula and working practices. Following Habermas' line of argument, it is possible to view the increasing curricular gravitation in higher education during the 1990s towards the use of outcomes, programme specifications and competence statements as predicated on a sense of closure that emanates from instrumental reason. This can be associated with the rise in managerialism in higher education discussed earlier (Trow 1993; Jary and Parker 1994; Miller 1995a; Clarke and Newman 1997), which has been one significant factor in determining orientations towards educational development in higher education.

A number of tendencies can be detected as evidence of this curricular shift and of changing perspectives on teaching and learning in higher education. The last two decades have witnessed an unprecedented burgeoning of research literature and staff development activity in relation to the pedagogic aspects of higher education. Much of this work has emphasized the value and effectiveness of an *active learning* approach that requires learning by doing, a task-based focus and the interactivity of the learner with tutor, peers or materials. Such approaches have been found to foster a 'deep' or transformative approach to learning (Entwistle, Thompson and Tait 1992).

Higher education in the 1990s has also been characterized by a concern for the development and assessment of wider core skills or personal transferable skills to help graduates prepare for employability in an increasingly competitive world of work. The Dearing Report (1997) renewed the call for a more systematic and concerted approach to the development of employability within the higher education curriculum. 'Transferable skill' remains an elusive term but one bearing much rhetorical potency in the various agendas of institutions, employers, funding bodies and government departments. It has, probably for the latter reason, become a significant area of curriculum development, and one in which many educational developers have invested considerable effort. Employability remains for many academics, however, a discourse that is located outwith their discipline, in the managerial or organizational space of generic teaching. It can be viewed as a form of troublesome knowledge, an alien discourse, and threshold concept (Meyer and Land 2004) engagement with which entails a repositioning of self, a shift in academic identity which many academics are unwilling to undertake. In this way developers again find themselves caught in competing discourses, in what will be termed below as 'domesticating' agendas, and are again called upon as translators, to manage often difficult meaning across boundaries. It is to the professional identity of these educational developers, their ideas about change, and the cultures of the organizations in which they work that we now turn.

1

Orientations to Educational Development

> Use of the word 'development' . . . brings with it much that we could do without. In some ways it is a cursed word, and one we could be well rid of.
>
> (Webb 1996a: 65)

The interviews with practising educational developers that were undertaken for the purposes of this study reveal a fragmented community of practice. What emerges from the narratives of individual developers is the many-faceted aspect of their agency. They have different academic and professional identities, inscribed within different discourses and drawing on different metaphors to represent the issues they face and the contexts in which they work. Their differing orientations can be viewed as variations on practice. Marton (1999) has argued that variation is a crucial dimension in our understanding of the nature of skill and expertise. Schön makes a similar point:

> The distinction between reflection- and knowing-in-action may be subtle. A skilled performer adjusts his responses to variations in phenomena. In his moment-by-moment appreciations of a process, he deploys a wide-ranging repertoire of images of contexts and actions. So a baseball pitcher adapts his pitching style to the peculiarities of a particular batter or situation in a game. In order to counter an opponent's changing strategies, a tennis player executes split-second variations in play. We can say, in cases like these, that the performer responds to variation rather than surprise because the changes in context and response never cross the boundaries of the familiar.
>
> (Schön 1987: 29)

How should we explain this variation? Stones (1996) has spoken of 'agent conduct analysis' and 'agent context analysis' as ways of understanding practice, and the agent's 'strategic conduct' and 'strategic terrain' as means of characterizing the site of practice. If we consider the agency of educational developers we might perceive their context and strategic terrain as the organizational forms, academic cultures and subcultures within which they have to practise. Their strategic conduct can be characterized by what I have termed their *orientation* to educational development. Orientations are analytic categories that include the attitudes, knowledge, aims and action tendencies of educational developers in relation to the contexts and challenges of their practice, but they are not innate personal characteristics of developers, and are not fixed. Rather the term *orientation* is chosen to imply a way of making sense of a given situation or set of tasks that subsequently informs and influences action. In this definition a practitioner may (and indeed does from the data available in this study) adopt differing orientations in different strategic contexts. Hence it is inappropriate to talk of an individual practitioner as say, a 'Romantic developer', but rather 'a developer with a Romantic orientation'. It is perhaps more useful to think of them as aspects of their subjectivity, constructed and brought into being by, or in reaction to, the social and historical contexts in which developers find themselves situated. Being *constructed*, they are rendered more or less stable, dependent on the strength of dominant discourses within an organization. These subjectivities are constructed within, and in relation to, cultures and discursive practices and are at the heart of ways of thinking and practising. The central argument here is that there are multiple orientations to development deriving from the multiple cultural configurations and competing discourses to be found within academic organizations.

Looked at in this way, certain orientations will constitute a part of the identity of a developer. Such identities, like any identities, are constructed partly by the flows of influence and power in which the subject, in this case the developer, finds him or herself enmeshed. One such influence is the discursive function of language, in its capacity to bring about the things of which it speaks, and the effects of a discursive text 'to mask the contradictions and incoherences of the ideology that is inscribed in it' (Codd 1988: 245). Clarke and Newman (1997: 39–40) draw attention to the normalizing function of discourses:

> Discourses seek to mobilise – to build alliances and support for specific social projects. They aim to establish themselves as normalised 'truths', the self-evidently correct frameworks of thought and action.

Other commentators emphasize the social functions of discourses, in particular 'their ability to close off possibilities' (Abercrombie et al. 1994: 120). The effect of the discourse, it is argued, is to determine the boundaries of what can be thought or said, and by whom. In this respect their function is almost ideological. 'That is, a discourse, as a ready-made way of thinking, can rule out alternative ways of thinking and hence preserve a particular distribution of power' (120). ' "Development" ', suggests Webb (1996a: 65), 'may be viewed as a site for contest: *it is not a unitary concept* for which, one day, we will provide a model. The very meaning of the word "development", how it is constituted, the kind of activities it implies, are all discursive, and can be interpreted according to various ontological and epistemological standpoints.' In a stance owing much to postmodern approaches to educational research, he argues that there is no 'super-standard' from which we can judge these positions, and our notions of development are 'of necessity a site for encounter and dispute'. As we will see, discourses may overlap or complement each other, but they may also conflict. For example, some of the discourses of development will serve an emancipatory function whilst others will serve to domesticate. Some will be systems-oriented and some oriented to the person.

From this it follows that within the community of practice of educational developers, indeed within individual EDUs, we should expect to find competing discourses of development. The idea of a 'community of practice' (Lave and Wenger 1991; Wenger 1998) emphasizes that everyday learning is *situated*, implying that learning is a function of the activity, context and culture in which it occurs. In this respect it differs from much classroom learning which often involves abstract and non-contextualized knowledge.

> Social interaction is a critical component of situated learning – learners become involved in a 'community of practice' which embodies certain beliefs and behaviours to be acquired. As the beginner or newcomer moves from the periphery of this community to its centre, they become more active and engaged within the culture and hence assume the role of expert or old-timer. Furthermore, situated learning is usually unintentional rather than deliberate. These ideas are what Lave & Wenger (1991) call the process of 'legitimate peripheral participation'.
>
> (Kearsley 2000: 1)

Though respondents in the accounts given below occasionally discuss systematic and intentional research or reflective activities, it would appear that much of the professional learning that takes place within the educational development community of practice is of a similarly situated nature. Diversity and difference in the various 'tribes' (Becher and Trowler 2001) that constitute this community soon become recognizable from the testimony of respondents in the study:

> I remember once – fairly sharply, I suppose – saying to someone who said to me 'Oh, you're an educational developer!' and I said 'No, I'm not!' (*laughs*). And I think that was because I didn't see myself as – and you know I could have put up some names of people – and I just thought 'But I'm not really like them'. Because I didn't come from that type of background and base. Couldn't figure out what that really meant – 'academic development'?
>
> (Respondent 14)

It is necessary now to engage the reader in some deconstructive unpacking of various development discourses and try to indicate both how they serve to construct the identities and orientation of developers and how, as Webb suggests (1996a: 65), they are all discursive, and 'can be interpreted according to various ontological and epistemological standpoints'. From the analysis of qualitative data in this study 12 orientations to practice emerged, which are analysed and illustrated below.

Managerial

Developers with a strong managerial, or human resource management, orientation reflect this concern in the views they hold concerning the need for strong strategic leadership in institutions, seeing this goal-oriented approach as more professional and effective. 'The main area where change is needed is to develop progressive and coherent systems of CPD', suggests one respondent, 'There is a need for professionalisation at all levels and we need much more and better-founded management development in HE' (Respondent 28).

> I think the issue here is the need to develop strategic leadership. There are two distinct tracks and traditions in UK higher education. The ex-polytechnic institutions have always accepted the need to have competent academic managers and have sought to put them in place, and not only that but they have rewarded them and paid them as such. There is a new compulsory CPD element in the new universities. Then there is the other tradition, in the old universities, of rotating the role of leadership. I can't help but feel that this is a less successful approach. It leads to a reluctance to commit. And the problem is particularly felt at Department and Faculty level. The major issue is at HoD level. Above that level it's not as acute.
>
> (Respondent 28)

When people have been through a specific management cycle twice, in an area such as, say, teaching quality assessment, they begin, he suggests, to start thinking about some of the issues. But when staff manage on a rotating basis, as they tend to do in more collegial cultures, then they are 'not really willing to commit' and are waiting to get back to other agendas such as research. At the faculty level, leadership is seen as remaining essentially voluntary or 'amateur'. This might be reflected symbolically or stylistically in matters of dress where there is an issue of staff not wishing, through the adoption of codified formal dress, to be identified as 'management', and no longer regarded as *bona fide* researchers.

> This is a problem for the old universities who are trying to balance these conflicting demands. The basic problem, I suppose, for these kind of people is that they can't distinguish between managerialism and effective management. They can't see the difference between being business*like* and being a business*man.*
>
> (Respondent 28)

The same respondent's location within a strong managerial discourse becomes apparent in the emphasis on clear 'institutional signalling':

> I think institutions can also become good at institutional signalling. They can do this through contractual requirements, performance review, putting appropriate policies in place, applying resource constraints. These are all levers for change that can be used but all the levers must be pointing in the same direction, and this leads us back to the need for clear strategic direction and management.
>
> (Respondent 28)

The use of a metaphor of levers here in itself suggests an assumption both that change can be managed in some directive fashion and also the likelihood of some centralized agency – the signal box. It's interesting to note how this respondent's concept of development as 'transition management' also reflects a rational planning view, with defined outcomes. Development becomes increasingly teleological, a doctrine of final causes, almost, in which developments are due to the purpose or design that is served by them.

> Development mainly implies change, but you need to consider the term from the perspective of both its denotations and its connotations. In its denotative sense it means change towards something, but in its connotative sense it implies change for the better, that progress is being made. But I think I would define development as transition management, basically getting from where you are now to where you need to be. And that's a cycle that will need to be repeated over and over again as time goes on.
>
> (Respondent 28)

Asked whether educational development could be seen as a profession another respondent replied:

> I don't think academics see it that way.
>
> *The Interviewer: Do you see it that way?*
>
> I think it sort of meshes with the discipline of Change Management. Or even Human Resource Management.
>
> (Respondent 1)

A respondent who had decided that his unit would be involved in implementing the University's decision to achieve 'Investors in People' status (IiP), a staff development approach originating from the commercial sector and Human Resource Management (HRM) theory, sees the process as a question of the 'right approach' and 'the right words' and realizes the powerful lever of Quality Assessment:

> I do not think we will have a big problem if we use the right approach and we use the right words and we do it the right way, in getting the

> overwhelming majority of folk that we're going to be briefing for the IiP thing to want to represent the University in a good light, and fairly. You know? That is a gigantic culture change. I mean if I went back (*pause*) sixteen years to when we had a UGC institutional visit and I led the non-professorial side in that visit. And the Secretary of UGC said to me then that academics, on all of the visits they made, you only needed to put a smallish number of them together in the same room and in no time at all they'd be squabbling amongst each other. They could not adopt a reasonably common line. That the students always hugely outperformed the academics because the students would sort out what issues they were going to prioritize and the line they were going to take. And the academics wouldn't. So that's a culture change that has been a big culture change. I'm not saying [name of institution]'s unique. I think that things like Quality Assessment actually have been an important ingredient in changing that climate, because departments were put on the line in Quality Assessment and, because people love their subject, most of them were not going to hurt their subject and most of them actually kind of cottoned on to what this was all about, and realized that actually, you know, this was not a clever game.
>
> (Respondent 14)

This developer's unit has aligned its departmental priorities very closely with those of the institution. The unit appears to be working very much within an institution-wide plan for organizational development, taking its lead from senior management:

> The University's set itself some ambitious priorities in its Strategic Plan 1997–2001. They've picked out five priority areas and the first one was the Quality of Education. Second one was really changing the Teaching and Learning Process. Third one is Research. Fourth one is Investing in Human Resources, which in effect is IiP. And the fifth one is Strategic Alliances. And these are the big [priorities]. We are trying to set our priorities to match the institutional priorities. So we're trying to deliver our support in progressing these institutional priorities. The University's trying to get every department to do that, and, to be honest, making reasonable headway.
>
> (Respondent 14)

The increasing size and complexity of some universities appear to oblige some educational developers to recognize the inevitability of a managerialist or systems-based approach:

> It's a huge organization and many of its functions are technical, bureaucratic, managerial, administrative, whatever. It's like a cross between a conventional university and the Abbey National, frankly, because it's got to have systems and procedures to the nth degree, for student registration, for the whole production side of things, for the whole assessment side. You're talking about marking a million pieces of work a year, or

> more. You can't change your mind at the last minute and ring up a couple of students, or email them, and say we'll do it differently this time. There have to be systems.
>
> (Respondent 27)

Such systems, in large universities with complex course structures and long planning cycles, may well resemble those of modernist or Fordist production lines. Emphasis is on quality, efficiency and the market, and some educational developers, in attempting to improve practice, see themselves as working within such an agenda:

> But it may be starting to confuse slowness with quality. It may be in danger of confusing elaborate systems and procedures with quality. It has to find a way of being as good, faster. I think it's got to find ways, for example, of developing and running smaller courses. The typical course is 60 points, and I think it's got to find systems for running 30s and 15s on a greater scale because I think that degree of flexibility is what the market wants. But the course production handbook refers to the first years of presentation of a course as 'P' year and the course production handbook processes start in 'P' minus 7. Not a lot happens till about 'P' minus 5 but things are really rolling by then. We managed to get a course from cold start to presentation in about 20 months. It can be done. And that's not the speed record either. I think 'time to market' needs to find ways of reducing substantially.
>
> (Respondent 27)

It can be seen how a managerial orientation to development moves with little impediment to the adoption of a managerialist discourse and to prioritizing institutional needs or those of students-as-consumers. As Parker (1997: 15) points out, the defining metaphor of the modernist or positivist tradition of education is the production line, and this can be reflected in the experience of educational developers:

> And we kept addressing the question of where do we want to do this from? And it always came back to [name of institution] because it was the only possible place to do it from. Because it was the only place which had this industrial strength approach to course development and production, which had the absolute commitment to quality and which could deliver courses around the country in a way in which no other institution credibly can.
>
> (Respondent 27)

In establishing a new programme for the training of university teachers, to be offered largely through open learning materials, the systems-based and whole-institution approach is seen as crucial:

> It was in our business plan, because we are working on a business plan here, and we've got to do this to make the numbers come out right in order to stay alive. So there is a clear financial imperative here. We did it

with substantial co-operation from across the university. We were initially only part of Student Services. They did not have a course presentation infrastructure and systems. The University was therefore willing to set up a new academic approvals system or process for our courses involving a fairly high-powered Committee, – it probably *was*, chaired by the Pro-Vice-Chancellor (Academic), the Pro-Vice Chancellor (Courses) – and set up a steering group with Deans and people on it to guide the academic development. And once the production system kicks in and accepts your schedule it will do what is humanly possible to deliver on time. So we did it in an unusual way just by deciding we were going to, and asking for help and getting it. That's the mixture of procedure-based operation and principle-based operation which is [name of institution] at its best. The procedure is, it takes four or five years, the practice is 'OK, you've set yourself a more ambitious schedule, how can we help you to achieve it?' It's amazing, it is amazing, it's wonderful.

(Respondent 27)

However, as this respondent points out, though educational developers may find themselves operating within a managerial system this may well sit above a quite different residual institutional culture which the educational developer simultaneously has to accommodate:

So at one level it's a gigantic – I think relatively efficient – machine, bureaucracy, necessarily. But it's also fiercely collegial. We have appointed Pro-Vice-Chancellors, usually for fixed periods of time and the Deans and heads of School are, to my knowledge, elected, in some sense. So it combines those two very, very different cultures and that's not easy.

(Respondent 27)

Some developers of a managerial orientation ally themselves fairly firmly with aspects of the institutional mission, almost to the point of devising institutional systems that will render the educational process teacher-proof.

Teachers have an obligation to teach well. Institutions have an obligation to make it possible for teachers to teach well. They actually have an obligation – I haven't thought of this before – they actually have an obligation to make it difficult or impossible in the medium term for teachers to teach badly. And staff developers have the role of helping all this good stuff happen. And that's where I locate myself in the grand scheme of things.

(Respondent 27)

The somewhat anti-collegial view of this respondent may not be too surprising. It is appropriate to hypothesize that a strong managerialist imperative in modern higher education institutions is to increase managerial scope and range by breaking the traditional hegemony of the department in collegial organizations. Emphasizing the (increasingly consumer-aware) needs of the student clientele sits very well with managerial missions. Bender (1997: 30), in his review of American higher education, notes a remarkable continuity in the structure of universities since the 1920s in that 'the department remains the basic organisational unit'. We recall also the view of a respondent cited earlier that 'the problem is particularly felt at Department and Faculty level. The major issue is at HoD level' (Respondent 28).

The managerial orientation also raises issues of a phenomenological nature. For example, another respondent, as part of his institutional responsibilities as Head of Educational Development, sits on a 'Human Resource Task Force' with the Vice-Chancellor, Pro-Vice-Chancellor, Head of Personnel and Chair of the Governors. When asked whether he felt his senior management saw his unit as an instrument of their policy, he replied:

> Well, I think, judging by the sorts of things the Vice-Chancellor sends me and expects me to respond to, then I think he does see us as fulfilling some functions like that. But the critical reflection and research area is something personally we would be more committed to, and we do have [name of colleague] who has specifically responsibility for the MA, but also for what we call [name of research group] which is the Research in Educational Development Network. And he tries to help people get published, he runs seminars of a more critical reflective kind than the more pragmatic 'How to do assessment' or 'How to lecture effectively', which we also have to do.
>
> (Respondent 6)

There are competing discourses here, and multiple, complex and to some extent fractured identities. Though seemingly identified as a management instrument by the head of the organization this is not the preferred self-image or identity of these particular educational developers. When academic colleagues accuse them of collusion or complicity in managerial agendas, this perception from a second vantage point within the organization is similarly rejected:

> Some people would regard us and have called us (when there's name-calling going on) 'managerialist' or part of a managerial tendency, and that's coming mainly from Social Sciences.
>
> *The Interviewer: But they call everybody managerialist!*
>
> That's right. (*laughs*) But, I mean, to take this student retention example, some people would say 'Ah yes we're involved in that, that's managers trying to persuade us that we should be doing x, y and z, and EDS is part of that so we are a tool of managers.' But given that management is rather weak here – I don't think we can be accused of that too much.
>
> (Respondent 6)

As was seen above when developers were asked whether managers themselves viewed the unit as an instrument of their policy there emerged what appears to be a degree of cognitive dissonance amongst the developers regarding the ways in which the unit might be represented to colleagues within the university. This raises the problematic issue of what we might term 'complicity' in the work of educational developers, in which developers often find themselves negotiating meanings between institutional managers on the one hand, who regard them as part of a managerialist agenda and a human resource management mechanism to effect particular change, and 'front-line' academic colleagues on the other, who may wish to confide in developers in relation to personal anxieties, resentments or radical changes in their practice. These situations require developers to be able to manage multiple perceptions of their role and to interpret practices and meanings upwards and downwards within organizations. In this regard they may exercise some of the 'discretionary power' of 'street level bureaucrats' reported by Lipsky (1980) in his study of public service personnel. This can be a stressful boundary that developers have to patrol, requiring substantial skill and leading to ethical and procedural dilemmas. Bergquist (1995: 11) argues that in modern organizations boundaries served as 'containers of anxiety'. However, in the postmodern condition these boundaries are eroded and there is a 'spilling out of anxiety'.

> To survive, most postmodern organizations have had to formulate clearer mission statements, in part because they can no longer retain clear boundaries. In the modern world, boundaries (and identities defined by roles and rules) served as 'containers' of anxiety. In the postmodern world we must look to a clear sense of mission and purpose (both organizational and personal) to overcome this boundariless anxiety, the sense of living on the edge.
>
> (11)

Deleuze (1992: 3) similarly has used the term 'enclosed environments' to describe territories which are circumscribed within organizations 'to concentrate; to distribute space; to order time; to compose a productive force within the dimension of space-time whose effect will be greater than the sum of its component forces'. Taylor (1999: 11) suggests that terms such as 'boundaries' and 'sites of enclosure' are used 'to describe attempts by institutions to create contexts – enclosed territories – in which only the occupants define the particular rules and practices which govern internal operations. This intention is often expressed in terms of a need for operational cohesion.' However all three commentators regard such attempts at enclosure as failing within postmodern organizations. Out of Bergquist's state of 'boundariless anxiety' (1995: 11) often appear what Deleuze terms the 'boundary riders' whose task is to try and contain anxiety, to maintain 'operational cohesion, stability and autonomy' and who 'never cease announcing supposedly necessary reforms' (1992: 4). The term would seem an apt descriptor of the work of many educational developers with a Managerialist orientation or, at least, those who are obliged to assist institutional managers in their own attempts to make what Deleuze calls 'tidying' responses.

Political-Strategic

Where the Managerialist orientation seems to be predicated on the notion that change in educational practice is to be achieved through the identification of goals and outcomes, on rational planning and activity designed to accomplish the furtherance of such goals, other educational developers appear to operate more from a belief that strategic action depends upon the operation of influence and power relationships within the micropolitics of higher education organizations. From this perspective, as educational development is often perceived by some colleagues as a marginal, vulnerable and (because of its centralized 'top-sliced' funding) somewhat 'parasitic' operation, it behoves educational developers to keep a wary weather-eye on shifts in organizational power relations, and to seek strategic alliances or support from wherever they may be gained. The need for effective positioning of an EDU within an organization in order to maximize advantages of power becomes paramount.

> Personally I have a sort of philosophy about it, which is that educational development is absolutely at the heart of an educational institution. If it wants to be a learning community then educational development is crucial. I have a sort of theory of how it works which is a 'sandwich' model. I think that educational development has to be in the middle between development and innovation on the ground where people are working with teaching and learning, and policy development and management at the top. And I think educational development has to be right in the middle there and be able to work from one to the other as a communicator and as a conduit. Upwards and downwards, yes. Because of that I think educational development is vulnerable because I don't think it belongs at the top *per se* or at the bottom *per se*. It's in the middle and because it's a sandwich it can get squashed very thin!
>
> (Respondent 17)

One respondent who held office at a fairly senior level pointed out that whilst EDUs have always been quite good at producing operational leaders they have not always been as good at producing strategic leaders who understand the importance of appropriate organizational positioning and who can invest educational development resource and effort where it is most likely to yield effective returns.

> Again, there is a need for strategic leadership. For units there is an important question to be addressed, which is 'What kind of beast do you want to be?' Are you a training unit operating at that level and offering skills courses on, say, how to use the Web, or do you see yourself as being

> about R&D, as part and parcel of the executive arm of the institution? And there are EDUs in universities in this country, as we know, who are spread right across this continuum. But it comes down to this question of what kind of unit you think you are. And where you are located within the organization is an important part of this question. If you have a relatively short reporting line to say a PVC (Academic), and can make recommendations there, then you are in quite a different position than if you are a training unit located much further down the institution. And this is one of the dilemmas for EDUs, and it is beginning to cause differentiation within the development group.
>
> (Respondent 28)

Developers of a Political orientation see informal personal contacts or networks, and the identification of powerful champions for an organizational cause, as more effective bases of strategic action than more formal reporting channels.

> I must be honest it's only in the last eighteenth months/two years I've used the going-around-and-having-a-cup-of-coffee-and-a-word-in-the-right-ear. I was very naive and thought you could do it all sort of by the book, and a few committees. Doesn't work. It's more important I think to have influential people on your side, and informally dropping something out and saying 'I've done this. I'll send you a copy.' If the person's fairly important, you know.
>
> (Respondent 1)

The positional power of potential clients or collaborators is uppermost in the minds of such developers in terms of their value 'in strategic terms'.

> You can talk about change in an individual – well an individual changing themselves because of your interventions. But in strategic terms if that individual is a lowly unimportant person it doesn't really matter. It's not going to change your department. So what you really need to ensure is that there is a change occurs in the minds of people who can influence more people than just themselves. Now sometimes that can come about from the things you do with the department or sometimes the change can come about by their recognition of a need themselves. Again it depends on the department.
>
> (Respondent 1)

This recognition of positional power is picked up by another developer who describes what tends to help the process of her own work:

> Well what supports it is the converts in influential positions – heads of school or deans or individual course directors. What hinders it is other prevailing attitudes.
>
> (Respondent 5)

As well as containing military metaphors (strategies, alliances), the discourse associated with a Political orientation also draws on financial metaphors. Notions of 'investing', of calculating the risks of any adopted line of strategy, also emerge as features of this orientation.

> *The Interviewer: Have there been other interventions which have nose-dived?*
>
> Probably not. I probably haven't taken enormous risks. I don't normally sort of invest in things which are doomed to failure – only things that have a reasonably good chance.
>
> (Respondent 5)

It would appear also that educational developers are not averse to employing coercive measures where it is deemed appropriate – for example, in situations where there is external pressure on the institution, such as a pending Teaching Quality Assessment inspection, and the institution's public standing may in some way be at stake.

> The other ploy we tried as well, that didn't lead anywhere incidentally. We had a chat and the person just felt that I couldn't be allocated to the department. This person had been given the job of preparing the framework document, on their own. And so what we did was we rang the Teaching Support Unit, told them the situation, and said 'Put the scarers on them!' We decided. The Director [of Staff Development] and I decided. I talked to her about it and we decided we needed some action. So we rang the Teaching Support Unit and said 'This is the situation. You know? Nothing is happening. Yes?' So they rang and said you really must ring the Director of Staff Development and she said well you need to book us quick or else you won't be able to book us at all. So we were booked. It's a case of trying several [. . .] it's power-brokering.
>
> (Respondent 1)

When taking a strategic view of policy implementation, other developers however, perhaps more commonly in older institutions with an overtly collegial culture, see it as counter-productive to engage in confrontation with departments or to force their colleagues' hands, preferring a 'softly, softly, catchee-monkey approach' (Respondent 22).

> In every thing we do there are tensions. One of the things, for example, that we can claim we caused to happen was to put in place a programme for the training of research supervisors in the University, to get that accepted as a policy, and to get it developed. We got it accepted as a policy but then there was really a considerable brouhaha, especially with some of the faculties, who considered that they should do it themselves. (And to be honest a member of my staff, I don't think, basically would share that view.) But I've learned long, long ago, it's much wiser to get the policy in place and say look you can either do it yourself or we can do it jointly or we'll do it for you, and let that evolve, than to try and ram it down their throat. So that's how we progressed. And all you do after that then, of course, is really just from time to time nudge the process, first of

all to see that it's happening, and then to see whether it seems to be effective. And then just to move it forward and enhance it. And that just has to be the intelligent way forward. Otherwise you run into this territory that really is not productive, where you get some people fighting you on the grounds that you don't have a nuclear physicist on your staff so how do you know anything about nuclear physics? It's barren territory. It's really not worth it.

(Respondent 14)

At times, however, there appears to be strategic mileage in using institutional reporting mechanisms to quietly 'drop a department in it' (Respondent 21) by drawing the attention of a Dean or similar figure to a department's non-involvement in staff development activity:

We find it quite easy to get volunteers to work with us, departments to work with us, but there are also some reluctant debutantes, in other words there are some departments which, when you look, they have remarkably little contact with you. What I've found quite productive in the last couple of years is simply to say to the Advisory Group, in reporting, these are the kind of departments we're working with and they've said well you don't seem to have very many from our faculty. And I've been able to say well, yeah, you're right. And then you've got, kind of, 'Oh, I'll have a wee word with somebody about that'. (*laughs*)

The Interviewer: Strategic embarrassment!

Yes.

(Respondent 14)

Certain Political-Strategists can also see that even adopting an institutional policy that may not be overtly popular across the institution may nonetheless prove strategically useful in the longer term by providing entrées into particular departments:

We had had a kind of strategic look at ourselves in [name of department] about just a year ago and had decided that what we should do was marry our priorities to the institutional priorities. So I was able to say well, you know, the institutional priority is to follow IiP because the Principal has decided we're going to do that. So here's an institutional priority, we're being asked to help out. And that was a sensitive one because really a lot of folk thought eeuurrrgh! Nobody's going to like all this jargon and terminology. They're not going to like it. And also it's going to take a lot of time and work and effort and so on. We talked it through and we did it. I think it's going to pay off because I think it has actually led to a kind of change of perception within the institution. Now whether we get huge praise out of that or not is a separate issue. But it has let us go and work quite closely with some areas, which has been quite helpful. And people have admitted, Heads of Department admitted at Senate, that although at first they didn't like some of the

> language and all that sort of stuff, that actually they found bits of doing the process quite useful.
>
> (Respondent 14)

The same respondent, however, is under no illusion as to the need to win the support of influential middle and senior managers by 'creating bridges':

> One of the things that came up in the [name of department] Review was that the group that thought least well of us were Heads of Departments and Deans. That students thought tremendously of us and generally that staff thought extremely well of us, including staff that we were not responsible for, including secretarial staff and so forth, because we ran some events for them, just out of the kindness of our hearts. And they were so grateful for that that they thought we were wonderful.
>
> *The Interviewer: Was this the top-slicing factor?*
>
> No. I think Heads of Departments and Deans hadn't a clear enough picture themselves of what they were supposed to be doing in staff development and what staff development priorities were, to really see how that matched in with what we were doing. So they were having a problem making a connection with what we were doing and we were having a problem making a connection with what they wanted. It was a kind of two-way problem!
>
> (Respondent 14)

One solution appears to be to 'create better bridges at strategic levels':

> Most Heads of Department, if they came to me at all, came to me for one or two reasons. They came to me to change an individual – you know, can you remedy X? – which is always highly problematic. Or they came because they had a bigger change agenda, which wasn't so problematic, other than sometimes it was quite difficult for them to recognize the scope of that bigger change agenda. And that's been tricky but it didn't come with the broader raft that really you would expect. Now *that* I think is changing now. People are realizing that there is a much wider raft of things in that sort of way. So I think we're starting to create better bridges at those strategic levels.
>
> (Respondent 14)

One approach to creating bridges seems to be gaining an influential position on high-level committees.

> And therefore creating our bridges, you know, is really extremely important.
>
> *The Interviewer: How do you 'get in'?*
>
> The Deans are not so difficult – well actually the easiest are the

> Vice-Deans. My main bridge – I mean I know all the Deans personally well and get on fine with all the Deans – but my main bridge is with the Vice-Deans (Academic), because I chair that committee [Academic Quality Assurance Group] and I have a lot of dialogue with them. And that works extremely well and we've got extremely productive relationships through that.
>
> (Respondent 14)

However, this strategy was found not to work so effectively at Head of Department level where a different strategy is required:

> Heads are a different matter. After the [name of department] review I tried, because I discussed with the Pro-Vice-Principal at the time 'What do we do?', and we agreed that what I would try and do would be to go to Faculty Boards or Committees and speak with Heads that way. Didn't work. Didn't work at all well. I mean I was really saying to them 'Can you give me some ideas what you're interested in? What you want?' You know, obviously I was speaking Hindustani or something because they really didn't come back with terribly helpful answers.
>
> (Respondent 14)

The successful approach with this group of stakeholders is not individual 'schmoozing' (Respondent 21) through individual conversations but using larger-scale initiatives as a wagon on to which to hitch staff development activity:

> I didn't do what [another developer] did at [a university nearby] – maybe I should have done but I didn't, partly because I didn't have the time – which was to go and try and have individual conversations with them. You know I just didn't do that. But what we're finding now is that other things are happening to help us create these bridges, and kind of planks. Like IiP is helping us to do that. What I'm doing is trying to use initiatives as the focus rather than trying to do some sort of three-year visit-everybody-and-have-an-hour-with-them.
>
> *The Interviewer: A kind of opportunistic thing but in a more strategic way?*
>
> I would confess that actually I tend to operate that type of way. I actually think that's the only realistic way you can operate, because there are just too many change factors. The Heads change, you know, and other things change, that if you've got some vast plane it's probably not going to go anywhere anyhow. So [. . .]
>
> (Respondent 14)

Other developers taking a Political-Strategic view had come to appreciate the strategic value of internal champions for educational development.

> In terms of the managerial, and where we are, we were set up about five years ago by a Pro-Vice Chancellor who has since left. So I suppose

> in that sense we're slightly vulnerable now in that our main champion at the head table is not there any more. I now report directly to the Vice-Chancellor and I have monthly meetings with him. And in some ways that's positive because it means he knows what we're doing more than he did before. It's less positive than it might be because I get very frustrated with his failure to drive things forward in a very directed way.
>
> (Respondent 6)

The issue of 'complicity' was discussed earlier in relation to educational developers' accommodation of managerialism, usually in more collegial cultures. Political developers appear to take a more phlegmatic view of the need to exploit senior managerial 'muscle' when necessary, in order to achieve aspects of their own change agenda with less tractable colleagues.

> Unfortunately – and this is where educational development needs the support of champions in order at some point or other maybe to say to some of the diehards 'You gotta do this guys'. I think that's overtly political and I think that educational development has always been a political process and some of us I suppose have continually delayed the day in which we have least knowingly been accomplices in a kind of manipulative strategy of change.
>
> (Respondent 2)

One respondent spoke from bitter personal experience on the matter of losing a champion for educational development:

> We wouldn't have arrived the way we did if we hadn't had internal champions. And they are extremely important. In a previous life my internal champion left the University nine months after I arrived, before I'd developed any others, if you like. The unit limped on and when the financial crisis hit it was broken up and I was made redundant. I do know about the importance of internal champions from bitter first hand experience. The early departure of the champion was a disaster for me, because I hadn't yet built up sufficient other links, other connections, in a university whose culture seems to be powerfully resistant to the idea of development.
>
> (Respondent 27)

The respondent provides a vivid example of the kind of attitude at senior management level that is often interpreted by developers as resistance to development:

> I was doing my tour as a Head of Department in a previous institution – a kind of introductory tour – and I was seeing one Head of Department and one of his senior members of staff bounced into the office to ask him something. And the Head of Department introduced that person to me, and she looked me up and down and said 'Ah! You're the one who's come here to tell us all how to teach are you?' I managed to respond

'You only have to ask', but that was indicative of the culture which I was up against there.

(Respondent 27)

This respondent had learned the bitter lesson that implementation is a much harder nut to crack than initial policy formulation, and that 'implementability' should be a guiding criterion in the business of policy-making in the first place.

When I went to the previous institution, I came into it – my first management job – thinking that the really tough part was to get the policy established and once you'd got the policy set everything was OK. I subsequently discovered that getting policy established is hard but getting it implemented is much, much harder. You see universities have that rather compliant, squishy kind of culture in which the fact that it goes through all the committees does not mean that it will happen. So it's totally naïve, but this came as a terrible shock to me, and I never quite recovered actually. What I discovered is you've got to take it all the way through. I discovered that implementability has to be a criterion for choosing which policy to go on in the first place. It's all tied together for me now. I wish I'd discovered this twenty years ago! But it's as well I've discovered it now.

(Respondent 27)

A procedures manual for implementation is recommended as one practical way forward, but at the end of the day even this is vulnerable to institutional will and support.

'No policy development without a procedures manual' would be the kind of extreme position I'd take at the moment. Don't say 'Oh wouldn't it be nice to . . .' Let's have a policy for it! If you can't work out how you're going to do it, don't get it approved. Because you'll get it approved and fail to do it. So one element is just implementability and you can check that easily by writing the manual for it. But the other thing which buggers up implementation is not whether it's technically possible; it's whether people actually want it or not. People will sign up for something because it's parenthood and apple pie and difficult to vote against, but then in practice there will be a thousand reasons why it can't be done.

(Respondent 27)

A number of commentators have analysed the relationship between policy and implementation. Reynolds and Saunders (1985: 200) talk of the 'implementation staircase' at the various levels of which the original policy purposes get 'rinsed' through. Trowler (2002) illustrates the way in which policy necessarily changes during implementation through local 'resistance and reconstruction' and through signs being read in different ways and hence readings becoming difficult to predict. Ball (1990a) suggests that

'Most policies are ramshackle, compromise, hit and miss affairs, that are reworked, tinkered with, nuanced, and inflected through complex processes of influence, text production, dissemination and, ultimately, re-creation in contexts of practice.' Taylor (1999: 75) points out that implementation is 'a mutually adaptive process' in which both intentions and practices change. 'Thus, cultures and traditions are also changed, and always at the local level' (75). A head of unit in a large new English university reports the same difficulties firstly with implementation of policy:

> When I first came here I discovered it wasn't anything like a staff development policy. We had a one-line policy which was that staff development is the responsibility of the line manager. (*laughs*) So, you know, Deans were meant to be responsible for their Heads of Department, and down the scale. And I thought this was totally inadequate, and I argued long and hard that we needed a proper policy. And we went through various drafts. It went to various committees. Personnel drafted one and people didn't like that it was too 'Personnel-ly'. I redrafted it to make it more academic-friendly and it went through. It was called a Personal and Professional Development Policy. And it makes all the right noises I think in terms of, you know, (*mock pompous voice*) 'Every member of staff, whatever their grade or status, is entitled to appropriate development' and this sort of thing. We gave examples of different forms of development because we didn't want people to see it just in terms of attending courses, conferences and workshops. Work-shadowing, mentoring, all these sorts of thing. Lots of different things. And we had a lot of debate about how do we know people are doing it, whose responsibility is it? What proportion of the budget should be allocated to staff development? And eventually we got something quite nominal put in. But even then people said they couldn't afford it.
>
> (Respondent 6)

and then with the monitoring of the policy:

> And then the other part, which was contentious, was the monitoring of the policy. How do you know people are doing it? Does anybody in the centre need to know? What power do you have to enforce it and so on? And I tried to do what I thought was a very user-friendly kind of reporting process which essentially asks people what are the main objectives of your staff development work in your department? Essentially, what did you do last year, in summary? We asked them to provide some statistics, but very few. And then what are your plans for next year, so it was a kind of rolling programme. Where are you at? Where do you want to get to? What have you done? And what are you going to do next? I didn't think it was very bureaucratic but nevertheless we have had two difficulties. One is that not every department complies. And as soon as some don't comply the word gets round and it falls into disrepute. And secondly,

even the ones who did comply – what do we do with the report? What happens to it? What's the point?

(Respondent 6)

The issue of non-compliance is a distinctive feature of academic organizational life, particularly within cultures that might be characterized as collegial or anarchic. This respondent, though of a marked Political orientation, despairs at the frustration of not being supported in such a culture by senior management and hence, recognizing this as a bad investment, with little or no return for the effort of the educational development section, lets matters 'drift'.

So really when I look back I've almost just let this drift because we were running up against problems that we couldn't really deal with. The Committee, as I've said, went out of existence, so I'm not quite sure who would receive these reports now. The lack of compliance I think is a real problem. But I think the whole policy really is not being followed up. And I think the main issue is, it's not really supported from above.

(Respondent 6)

A female respondent comments on the capriciousness of senior management views and of male power networks.

I've talked about the support of the big committees, but I find that the iterations I have to go through to get a paper through – you know, go to this group, let them have a look at it, go to that group, let them have a look at it. Actually when I was in EDS it was just a matter of 'Oh we'll do this; we'll have this Large Groups Network', and I would do it. Now, because I'm working at a strategic level, I have to actually be more strategic, and I have to actually consult more people, and on a couple of occasions I've been set off on doing things and I've put hours of work into it and then I've been told by the Deputy Vice-Chancellor actually it's not really what we want. And it's not that I've done it badly it's just that he changed his mind. And it's quite capricious. In the University there can sometimes be: 'Oh, no, we've changed our minds, we're going to do that. Oh, no, stop doing that, do this.'

The Interviewer: Someone's been talking to someone..?

Yeah, in the gents' toilets usually.

(Respondent 3)

One strategy for obviating such capriciousness seems to be the time-honoured political expedient of pushing matters through at a time when it is calculated that objectors will be absent.

So that was the downside. Now the energizing, exciting side is we can actually make a difference in this unit. We can actually change things. So, for example, with the key skills initiative, we want things to happen.

> I've got a paper through QIAS, and I must be getting smarter. I chose the time when I knew people were away that were going to cause me any bother, and I've got it now, if you like, on the statute book. You've got to now, on the Faculty Quality Committees, check every course coming up for review to make sure that there's key skills in there. You've gotta do it, it's there!
>
> (Respondent 3)

This respondent also recognizes the leverage and binding nature of decisions that have been backed, and recorded, by the 'big committees' (and internal champions):

> We're in the p-words. Power. I'm not a power freak, but I do like being able to . . . well, it's not now just a matter of 'Why don't you?' it's 'I really think you should'. I won't get involved in heavy aggressive confrontations or things like that because it's not my style, but when the chips were down it was very nice in this nasty confrontation I had where this guy tried to bully me – sat here in my own room and tried to bully me – and I just said I think if you go back to the QIAS papers you'll find I'm right. And we were able to quote chapter and verse and I was backed by the Dean, and I was backed by the Pro-Vice-Chancellor, and I was backed by the Registrar. When the chips were down, the guy hated it but he couldn't get out of it.
>
> (Respondent 3)

Deans, it appears, can sometimes be champions of educational development, but at other times, in other institutions, they can constitute a political threat to an educational development unit's operation by challenging the central funding on which its existence usually depends. A respondent from a large new English university describes:

> A kind of carping, shooting-from-the-boundaries approach of some Deans and Heads of Department. A downplaying and undermining perhaps of the value of one's work. Matched by, sometimes, (maybe used as an excuse for), a failure of quite a lot of academics, especially if they have research leanings, to engage in educational innovation.
>
> (Respondent 2)

The respondent speculates as to whether such carping is just political posturing to keep a unit from being an effective player, or whether it is based on a disparaging view that educational development doesn't have any substantial research base or disciplinary pedigree.

> I think it's both. For some Deans and Heads of Department it's the former. It's all part of a political game anyway, and seeing central departments taking resources that you'd like to come to your department is on its own sufficient for you to want to undermine their credibility. For those of a research inclination it's the latter. That is, as far as they can see, there's no real substance to educational development. It's

all fly-by-night, fly-by-the-seat-of-the-pants kind of work. It's not empirically tested. It's not founded on rigorous theories. There's a sense that it's unscholarly and that it simply doesn't measure up to the kinds of rigorous tests that they would apply in their own world.

(Respondent 2)

The strategic awareness of educational developers in a new university in which a large educational development unit had been entirely dismantled and its members dispersed to other functions, or retired, was of particular interest. The following respondent's account reveals a shrewd political insight, if a somewhat bleak sense of institutional *realpolitik*, when it comes to the vulnerability and expendability of centralized operations such as educational development.

The Interviewer: EDS had a high reputation; it was an exemplar. Why was it disaggregated?

Well, actually just a few things. Firstly, a new Vice-Chancellor came into post before a new Pro-Vice-Chancellor took over. The Pro-Vice-Chancellor had no sense of ownership of what the previous Pro-Vice-Chancellor, to whom we reported, had instigated. That former person had championed EDS and, as I said, when he retired I knew we were going to be vulnerable, because not only had he championed EDS but before leaving he tried to get a scheme agreed whereby the position of EDS would have been consolidated. It would have merged with another central department, but the implication was that EDS would be even stronger. The incoming guy didn't want any of that and didn't feel any obligation towards the existing model of things.

(Respondent 2)

The respondent's strategic perspective is that a unit has to be 'locked into' the management structure – in effect, a managerialist view, which, ironically, many educational developers eschew on the grounds that it compromises their neutrality. In this instance, according to the respondent, the lack of it led to their demise.

The new Pro-Vice-Chancellor and the new Vice-Chancellor both share, in my view, though in different ways, a relatively managerialist view of things. EDS was not locked into the management structure. They wanted it to be. They wanted it to be the implementation of policy. That's what its function was meant to be. And so that didn't fit either. The institution was reaching a point where financial problems were becoming noticeable. The institution's always been cautiously run in terms of its accountancy; it was never going to be, you know, like Westminster or whatever, on the edge of financial viability. So cuts needed to be made partly to finance this new campus. So where were they to be made? Well, a range of areas were to be considered, but how does a new Vice-Chancellor first of all demonstrate a determination to

> cut, and then persuade Deans to accept cuts in the Faculties? Start at the centre! Where do you start at the centre? Well you can't cut much in terms of the Registry. External Relations is the 'big thing'. You don't cut External Relations, and not when you're projecting all these images. By a process of elimination there were only two departments that could really bear the brunt, EDS and Unilink, which was a kind of curriculum innovation.
>
> *The Interviewer: But the Dearing agenda was looming over the horizon; this was pretty bold, brutal managerialism? Rather two-fingerish?*
>
> Yes. It was up to the University – largely meaning the Vice-Chancellor and the Governors – to decide how the Dearing agenda would be addressed. If they wanted to do it with a different structure it was entirely up to them to make that change.
>
> (Respondent 2)

Sound political calculation, of course, depends on reading the direction in which an institution seems to be moving. Such sense of direction, however, is not always easy for an educational developer to read, and can lead to 'tension' and 'disquiet', as one Head of an EDU attests:

> I think the institution has a problem in that I'm not sure that it does have a clear image of itself or of its vision. Although we are very strongly committed to things like widening access, student participation, multi-ethnic community, serving the region – I mean those are the things that would be trotted out in any kind of mission statement and so on – there are also strong elements within the University that want us to have a strong research element, that want us in a sense to be more like a traditional university. And there's quite a lot of tension. Certainly two of our Deans are very keen on that. So I think there's a bit of a mixed message, and one of the reasons for the current disquiet that I was referring to is the fact that there isn't a clear vision, clear sense of direction about where the institution is going.
>
> (Respondent 6)

However, many educational developers see the influencing of policy and direction as an important and legitimate part of their practice and strategic role. Indeed, some view it as a feature that distinguishes the practice of educational development from that of 'lower-level' activities such as Staff Development.

> *The Interviewer: Do you see yourself as influencing policy?*
>
> Certainly, yes I do, definitely, and I think that's a big difference between the way we conceive educational development as opposed to, if you like, a lower level Staff Development role, in that we do try and influence policy and that is part of our mission statement and part of our objectives.

> Now whether other people necessarily like us trying to influence it is another matter but we're all playing the kind of political game. And we would put things through Committees. Some of those major papers that go to Quality would then go on to Academic Board. So we do have a route through to Academic Board, which is very important.
>
> (Respondent 6)

Again the use of the 'big committees' is identified as important:

> Although, obviously, we don't like to lose as it were our main Committee, if that Committee is slightly sidelined, slightly lacking in status and power, then I think in some ways it's better for us to go through the Committee which is obviously recognized as being the Main Committee on Quality matters, and for us to have a direct input into that. I'm not actually too unhappy about that particular change because when I was putting through any kind of major proposal I found that I probably had to put it to Quality Committee as well as Educational Development in any case.
>
> (Respondent 6)

Equally important is aligning the work of the unit with currently fashionable developments.

> But then I suppose I also influence policy by being actively involved in developments that happen to be current at the time. So, for example, because of the under-recruitment last year we've got an action plan looking at student retention and progression. Now I have a function in that action plan, disseminating good practice and contacting departments, checking what they're doing and so on. So I'm pretty active in driving certain elements of policy.
>
> (Respondent 6)

However, too close an alignment with issues that smack of management agendas, of 'employer-led' staff development as Sawbridge (1996: 6) terms it, or the 'Quality' agenda, is deemed to be risky in terms of the way educational developers may be perceived within the organization. In political terms this would be to align the unit too closely with activities that are unpopular.

> And I do sometimes worry about whether we are too closely associated with what some people might regard as Quality Assurance functions. I think we are quite closely associated with Quality Assurance and that doesn't always do us a favour. The trouble is they don't like Quality Assurance! (*laughs*)
>
> *The Interviewer: Are you seen as part of the senior management apparatus?*
>
> I think by some people, yes, definitely. Some people would see us in that way – as just adding extra obstructions and bureaucracy. We produce these guidelines and people just think 'Oh, one more thing to do.' That is, no doubt, an issue that we have to deal with.
>
> (Respondent 6)

The obvious counterbalance to this therefore is to be seen to be working with, and in the interests of 'the troops', the 'front-line' academics (Respondent 21) in the departments, as a means of demonstrating one's usefulness.

> One of the things we did was we had a full-day conference/exhibition last year and a keynote speech and 200 people visited the exhibition – mostly our own staff. It was mainly an internal thing and that was a big success. It was a huge effort. So we realized in that one day we'd got to people in a way that all the other little bits of effort we'd been able to do hadn't done. That convinced me that these events are worth doing, although they aren't the things that make the difference. Actually, it's all the work that went beforehand that makes it possible. People think, 'Oh!', you know, 'Goodness, look what they're doing'. It's odd, that's not what we're doing, but they see that's what we're doing. That's the thing that gets you the credibility. This year it's a one-day conference and next year we hope to host the Staff and Educational Development Association (SEDA) conference. So it's kind of the growth thing, it's kind of a developmental push.
>
> (Respondent 17)

Another avenue to gaining credibility is through supporting departments in preparation for Subject Review.

> We however also try to work at grass roots level helping individual lecturers, helping individual departments. The influence of TQA [Teaching Quality Assessment] Subject Review has been quite large on our lives in that we're now very actively involved for a period that starts about two years before the visit. Working with the departments, we do observations of teaching for them or we help them do it on a peer basis, so we're very much working at grass roots level in a way that we hope demonstrates our value and our usefulness.
>
> (Respondent 6)

This raises 'the important issue for educational development units about how much you want to make an *impact*, as opposed to how much you want to be seen as having a *presence*' (Respondent 28). One experienced developer, now in a senior position with a national professional body, points up the different political significance of these factors depending on whether developers are trying to promote technical innovation 'across the whole university' or whether they are trying to engage the interest of 'institutional opinion-moulders' in the innovation.

> And if you're working with the former group then you need to have presence. If you're dealing with the latter then you have to have impact. You can develop a useful quadrant in order to measure where you are positioned in terms of two axes of high to low impact, and high to low presence.
>
> (Respondent 28)

This can be represented as follows:

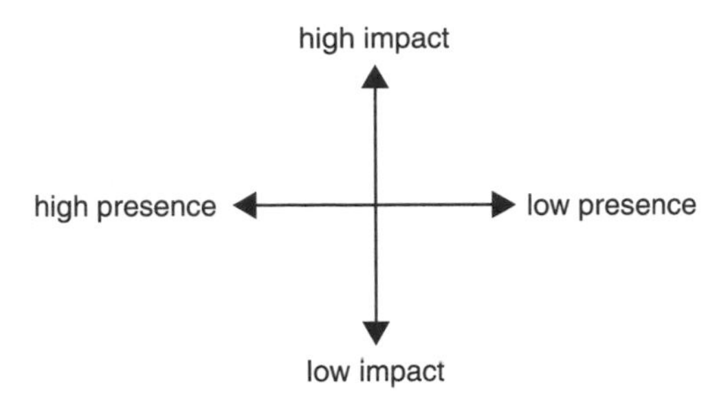

Very often, suggests this respondent, educational development units spend much time and effort attempting to be 'a kind of educational Kleen-Eezy Man, trying to get a foot in the door of various departments, selling brushes and trying to have a presence'.

> We've all been there and we know what it feels like when they are not interested in buying brushes, or that particular kind of brush. But many units in this respect are *structurally* behind. The best units work on both axes and develop both high presence and high impact. You often need high presence for political reasons.
>
> (Respondent 28)

This last point is significant and was picked up by other respondents, namely that a 'front-line' or 'grass-roots' involvement can not only lead to an improved institutional profile or presence but, through a policy almost of 'infiltration', can be an effective means of influencing policy. One head of an EDU describes her own approach:

> I've recently discovered that I need to use a more political strategy for things because I am finding that it's difficult to get decisions at the level of ESMG [senior management group]. So one strategy I'm beginning to use is grassroots politics.
>
> *The Interviewer: And are you well placed to do that, in a sense?*
>
> I'm extremely well placed because I'm a central place. I'm a 'Web'. Yes, extremely well placed to do that.
>
> (Respondent 30)

Developers of a Political orientation often recognize, astutely, the way in which decisions about policy matters, because of the complexity, volatility and protean nature of the managerial task, tend to get delegated or simply left unattended for other interested parties to pick up and make the running with. In this way developers find themselves in a position to influence policy. This situation is much in keeping with Lipsky's (1980) analysis of the discretionary power with which 'street level bureaucrats' often find themselves endowed, save that in this case the decision-making returns upwards from street level to institutional policy level.

> Because management thinking is more focused at senior levels, then it has not the time or possibly the interest to think about everything and so those things that senior managers don't have the time or interest to think about, they delegate. So, for example, in relation to the two last consultation papers from the Planning Group for ILTHE, effectively that job has been delegated to me. And as far as I'm aware, certainly the first response went through from the institution unaltered. And the second response might get altered because it's a bit more strategic – I don't know, we've just submitted it to the Deputy Vice-Chancellor. I think that in many cases senior managers are very keen to be given hooks to hang ideas on. So long as they are not wildly at odds with the ideology that drives them, or what they regard as the political realities, then they'll be more than happy to go along with them. In other respects, where their purposes are clear, I think they'll be looking for implementation rather than shaping of policy.
>
> (Respondent 2)

Another respondent, working in an ancient university and sitting on major committees, makes the following observation.

> When it actually comes to the meat of the proposals being discussed in committees, you don't have any sense that some of the most senior people in the University are aware of the strategic plan. And since they have agreed to it they just have it carried forward. Suddenly it is just an intellectual issue. As though they were just anybody, you know. As though they were the lab technician. '*I don't know engineering!*' But they *have* to be aware. The lab technician isn't going to get on Senate or something like that. So that really is a problem. On the other hand, it is quite easy for, not so difficult for, people to drive through particular initiatives that other people don't see as threatening to them. You know, 'We have got to do something about this! We have to produce a response to this government document!' So somebody has to pull all that together. If people don't see that as really threatening them materially, then they are quite happy to see it happen and go forward.
>
> (Respondent 22)

When the objectives of developers are in alignment with those of their managers, when, as one respondent quoted earlier put it, the levers are all pointing in the same direction, this can constitute a substantial convergence of interests:

> It's very tricky but some of the contradictions are that sometimes managers – or more likely managers in response to external pressures like the QAA – will want to initiate or support initiatives that are absolutely in line with what educational developers would like to see happen. So

> there is often a happy coincidence of goals, if you like. Motives might be different (*laughs*), the goals might be similar.
>
> (Respondent 2)

But when there is a divergence of goals, a political impasse inevitably arises:

> Sometimes of course there isn't that coincidence, and so in the mythical university where the Vice-Chancellor came in one Tuesday morning and said we're going to become a 'competence' institution, enforcing a particular approach to teaching and learning on staff – (it may be that educational developers will feel there's something to be said for key skills development and so on, but they may not want to go down an exact kind of competence route) – then what do you do?
>
> (Respondent 2)

In such situations one response of political developers may well be the 'grass-roots' option already noted. Some developers report a strong awareness of the limitation of policy-driven approaches:

> I think probably in my first couple of years here I was a bit too confident about the value of policies and guidelines and putting them through committees and then somehow thinking that would influence people. I've become much more sceptical about those, although that's not to say occasionally we don't still do that. I mean our student feedback policy was an example; we did that last year.
>
> (Respondent 6)

They prefer to work 'bottom-up', infiltrating at departmental level, the nodal element, after all, of collegial cultures.

> I think we work much more effectively by working with departments we know are active, then trying to get some examples out to other people. They see that it works and then we try to bring them on board. Because this is not the kind of institution, as I said at the beginning, which really drives things from the top. So we can't really expect, unfortunately, any strong strategic direction. So in a sense we're forced to work the bottom-up. But it isn't entirely bottom-up in the sense we're not working only with lecturers. I mean, as I've said, we work at the Committee level, we work with Heads of Departments, with Deans.
>
> (Respondent 6)

The volatility of policy development in a complex organization and a rapidly changing external environment is another headache faced by developers:

> But you've got this almost apocryphal situation where the Vice-Chancellor goes off to a conference and someone says something to him and he latches on to it and it becomes the year's overriding project.
>
> (Respondent 2)

To ensure an informed response to these unstable situations, respondents point out the need for comprehensive 'intelligence' of the organization's activities and concerns.

> We're into everything. We're in everywhere and every angle is covered and it's not necessarily by design but it's by numbers, critical mass. I mean Jean [Head of Department] is on the important AQAG and Academic Practice committee. I'm on three of the Faculty Committees that are concerned with teaching and learning. Peter [a colleague] might be on the Postgraduate Committee. Kim [another colleague] might be on something else but nothing can happen in this institution without us knowing about it. So we're everywhere and involved with everything. I think the thing that Tom [a colleague in a neighbouring institution] found surprising was how much access we have to departments and how easily we can get in and out of departments and be there and see how things are happening, sitting in classes or whatever it might be. And Jean has her role in that because she is good at fighting the political end.
>
> (Respondent 12)

However, the same respondent discusses 'the sheer volume of and involvement in so many things' that this form of comprehensive intelligence-gathering and response requires. It is 'a difficult balance really to achieve' and 'it creates the tensions in educational development units. I think it creates divisiveness there unless it's really co-ordinated by a strong leader and good strategic planning' (Respondent 12).

A number of politically oriented developers report disillusionment with the level of support, clear policy direction and general vision provided at senior management level.

> I attend one (what you might think to be a high-level) Committee, which is just the Vice-Chancellor, Pro-Vice-Chancellor, Head of Personnel, myself and the Chair of the Governors. And that's called the Human Resource Task Force. And you might think that there one could drive through the Staff Development Policy. But there's no direction. The V-C's not that interested really. So it tends to occupy itself more with 'How do we deal with underperformance?' and the more kind of 'union-y' sort of issues than human resources.
>
> *The Interviewer: There's no bigger picture there?*
>
> No. Personally I don't feel supported at senior level, and neither does the Head of Personnel.
>
> (Respondent 6)

An experienced developer, nearing retirement from a traditional university, looks back on the psychological resilience required of developers working in the 'rough house trade' of organizational politics.

> It asks for public exposure. It asks for taking flak and it asks for – what is the word? – *engagement* in nitty-gritty politics. The rough house trade which professionally we have here. Events shape your subsequent responses to pressure and what you are prepared to work with, to work *in*. You choose your territories, your defence, if you are cautious. You are aware that if the pressure comes on you might not be able to carry it. So there is a tendency to say, you will stick with what you know you are good at and avoid other things. That may be a bit hard but that is how I see it.
>
> (Respondent 18)

Several evince a tendency towards what Taylor (1999: 152) has termed 'self-interested self-management' or 'the value of a self-knowing form of self-interested activism'.

> And I was trying to persuade the Vice-Chancellor and others that we needed a strategy for learning technologies. You know, this is the new world around us, we can't ignore it, if we don't we'll fall behind etc. But there's a certain amount of nodding and 'Yes, I suppose so, but we haven't really got a lot of money,' and then in the end nothing really happened. So that is a real frustration. We can get so far by this kind of working with people. It's less easy to get something that really goes right across the board. But maybe we shouldn't worry too much about it.
>
> *The Interviewer: Yes, even if you have that strategic policy.*
>
> People resist it anyway! (*laughs*)
>
> *The Interviewer: Yes, so maybe you probably have to carry on with your initiatives anyway?*
>
> Yes I think so.
>
> (Respondent 6)

Taylor distinguishes between 'plan-driven change', which he associates with managerialism, and 'action-driven change', the flow of which, he argues, most academics are willing to go along with, and which, he suggests, is a more effective strategy within academic cultures.

> The rise of managerialism within universities has accentuated the reliance on plan-driven change. It has also led to attempts to guide both change and sensemaking through the use of benchmarking, performance indicators and similar concrete measures of outcomes rather than abstract principles and purposes, or even assumptions. This has the effect of emphasizing a form of rationality that sees grieving as self-indulgent, and privileges action over purpose, and information over negotiation and dialogic conversation. It also locates the decision-making processes and actions as separate, unconnected or poorly connected activities. The irony here is that the subjective and non-rational

> are being banished at the same time as the flexible and open are sought.
>
> (Taylor 1999: 150)

Taylor, furthermore, recommends that academics in future do not align their interests too directly with the interests of universities. 'They have more opportunities than they recognise to resist the intolerable. They are freer than they feel to explore new possibilities.' This advice would seem to be shared by some of his politically oriented development colleagues in the UK system. He advises involvement, scepticism and 'qualified optimism' rather than commitment. Using the analogy of a breakfast of eggs and bacon, he points out that the hen is involved, whereas the pig is committed.

> That is, there are good reasons for academics to disentangle their professional career paths from those of the institutions known as universities, especially when both are under pressure to change.
>
> (158)

Entrepreneurial

It would appear that the challenges generated within the external environment of higher education are increasing, whilst the operational windows within which organizations have to respond to these challenges appear to be shortening. However, Altbach (1997), in a study of the North American professoriate, found that most academics appeared fairly oblivious to these pressures:

> In general, there is little sense of crisis among academics; most seem unaware of the magnitude of the problem facing American higher education [. . .] The average full-time American professor remains largely insulated from the broad trends taking place in higher education. Not only that, the professoriate seems to have little understanding of these trends.
>
> (Altbach 1997: 330–2)

Taylor (1999: 50), working in Australian higher education, suggests, similarly, that 'academics are "programmed" to ignore "external" trends and issues related to higher education more generally' as a result of their strong disciplinary acculturation and immersion in their own research agendas. This reflects Becher's earlier (1989) observation that research-oriented academics often have a much stronger loyalty to their disciplinary peers, or 'guild', than they do to their employing institution, and that too enthusiastic a regard for non-disciplinary developments might be interpreted as research stagnation or lack of commitment. In contrast, Taylor found, as part of the Evaluations and Investigations Program (EIP) study, that academic managers were 'very aware' of external trends.

> More importantly they had, in a range of ways, initiated responses to those trends, responses which were discussed in terms of institutional needs and priorities. These included issues like funding, competitive pressures, market share and the like. These managers weren't experiencing 'future shock' – they were showing entrepreneurial flair.
>
> (1999: 50)

As with the academic managers in Taylor's study, educational developers in this study were found to be significantly different from their academic colleagues in this specific respect, in that they too appear to be sensitive to the impact of external trends. One respondent from a new Scottish university describes his watching brief as 'that role when you go out and see what's going on around the country. That's important – environmental scanning.' The borrowing of this term from the discourse of corporate business suggests an awareness of competitive pressure and rapid external development, as does his later use of the term 'industrial espionage'. The role is seen as a crucial but enjoyable part of his work.

> The other thing which is useful, and it's, I think, a unique privilege in people like us, is to work across the institution with a range of people from the Vice-Chancellor, all the team at the top but through to the newest, youngest members of staff both in the academic side and in the support area and also outwith the institution. I'm going to [University A] on Friday. I haven't really been there before but the opportunity is part of the environmental scanning role to see what's going on elsewhere. I found it refreshing down at [University B], eye-opening, being part of their quality procedures last Wednesday. I would do that job for nothing because its professionally useful for me, and that's almost like industrial espionage to see what they're doing, but also in terms of the process that they go through to ensure the quality of distance learning material and the lessons that they learn and are adopting from their first cycle in doing that.
>
> (Respondent 10)

A developer in a Welsh university makes a similar observation:

> There is also this other dimension, which is that in some senses we've become a kind of intelligence unit and I don't mean in a kind of 'James Bond' way – more scanning the environment and briefing the Vice-Chancellor, Deputy Vice-Chancellors and the Deans, and so forth. Intelligence within and outwith the institution. We sometimes have the brief to develop an initiative within the institution and bring it to committee in the first place. We'd be looked at as very much change agents.
>
> (Respondent 11)

Certain developers tended to have a particularly outward-focused orientation which might be described as 'Entrepreneurial'. Interestingly, several of the respondents indicating such an orientation tended to have moved into educational development work through previous involvement in the Enterprise in Higher Education Initiative (EHE) which had funded projects within their institution. The EHE Initiative was to some extent transformed and transfigured by its academic stakeholders somewhere in its ascent or descent of what Reynolds and Saunders (1985) have termed the 'implementation staircase'. This shifted the initiative away from a more strictly business-oriented interpretation of the concept 'enterprise'. One respondent, a former Head of an EHE unit, drew on her experience to conclude that 'It could have been more accurately described as the *Innovation* in Higher Education Initiative' (Respondent 1). But many of the values and *modi operandi* of Entrepreneurial developers appear to have been carried over into their subsequent educational development roles. The development orientation they exemplify is characterized by a number of related qualities, including: a strong focus on incorporating graduate employability factors within the higher education curriculum, such as transferable skills; involvement in the development of partnerships with external agencies, both locally and internationally; concern with access and equity issues, particularly in relation to the needs of mature students; and involvement in community development. One Head of Educational Development perceives his university in the following way:

> Its culture is really geared towards employability in all shapes and forms and goes beyond the idea that we're going to produce business studies graduates. So even with the media, arts, communication type approaches there is still an eye on graduate employment. There's a culture that is geared towards friendliness and high-quality teaching provision. There isn't so much of a research culture. And there's a growing cultural commitment to the community again in all shapes and forms. That is how it's seen by members of staff provided you accept employability in its widest definition. And there's occasionally a misunderstanding that it's all about producing entrepreneurial business studies-type people. But if you dig below that there's a commitment by everybody towards us. And I should add also a tremendous commitment to adult learners and that includes mature students who are full-time on campus as well as part-timers.
>
> (Respondent 11)

The preferred operational approaches of these developers appear to be strongly project-driven, both internally and externally:

> The teaching and learning advisor network is part of the teaching and learning strategy; every department has one. We have 10 key individuals. The advisors are responsible for collecting the bids for projects. We have an annual fund that people bid into which is managed by EDU. That allows us to support colleagues with various projects. £5000 is our limit but then we expect departments to match that. In effect, it's £10,000. We have about £35,000 a year but occasionally extra money becomes

> available through Government funding council initiatives. So sometimes we're suddenly given £100,000; this has got to be dedicated to widening access. The network across the institution come up with a proposal and this is why the teaching and learning strategy is just vital to everything we do.
>
> (Respondent 11)

They are frequently active, and often successful, in pursuing opportunities to acquire funding for policy-related projects.

> I think that the focal point for project work is important. I mean we've been fairly successful over the years in utilizing externally funded projects to initiate change by bringing money and support from elsewhere, but very rarely or never really doing it to do something that we wouldn't want to do anyway. There's the dissemination aspect but there's also maybe the implications for, say, virtual campus development or online assessment or student support mechanisms or electronic point of contact for all student enquiries on a pilot basis. If that proves to be successful in the pilot, there are implications to be carried forward. Then it ceases to be a departmental project. It becomes a university project.
>
> (Respondent 10)

They tend to be entrepreneurial also in the more traditional sense of engaging in income-generating activities or finding novel ways to optimize available resources. The following account provides one such example:

> The advantage of having a substantial externally funded project was that we had one additional member of staff. What it meant was we had parts of the brains of three people to apply to the development of the Centre's courses and parts of the brains of three people to coordinate the [name of project]. So by increasing the range of activities you don't make a profit on externally funded research, but what you do is you enlarge the team. You don't enlarge the total resource available to your academic work but you enlarge the pool of people on whom you can draw. And by quite explicitly fractioning the [name of project]'s work and the Centre's work we had access then to three people rather than two. The figures are rather greater now. So that's a strategy for the outside world – getting work which will have a good effect and increase not the total resource but the range of talent open to you in the Centre.
>
> (Respondent 27)

Entrepreneurial development projects often have an international dimension:

> Now it has to be said that some of those priorities are engaging. That to become part of an international, or more international, university is exciting. Goodness gracious, who would not want that? The notion of, you know, helping to be someone who establishes links between different countries, different parts of the planet is something that one would

> want to do, most people would want to do. Most people enjoy meeting others, learning about new cultures and working overseas. I love it! And I'd like to do more of it. So for the University to say, as it did about two years ago, we shall become much more focused in developing our international links is something that provides a rationale and a reinforcement for people who may have wanted to do that anyway or were already beginning to.
>
> (Respondent 2)

Or the projects have a community dimension:

> And then we have this massive Community University project where we're doing all sorts of things in the community and summer schools and so forth but our own campus lecturers would not always know about that.
>
> (Respondent 11)

Such projects tend to be characterized by the related dimensions, mentioned earlier, of employability, partnership arrangements, access and equity. The discourse through which these ideas are represented tends to differ from that of conventional business enterprise in that it has a certain social and moral dimension of, say, international fraternity, of community responsibility or social inclusion.

> Community University, in the [name of region]. Starting from nothing. So all of our part-time education people had to come to the campus. Or the business school would be doing something with a specific company or firm and they'd go to a training room. But they'd always have to go to a campus. Either our campus or a further education franchise. Then we'd lift it off, this programme where people could just do one module for pure enjoyment and they get a credit transcript if they successfully complete it. Or, they'd do something for pure enjoyment and get no credit at all, it wasn't even assessed. Using community annexes, locking into premises used by community groups, leisure centres, setting up a video conferencing network, establishing teams of part-time tutors, running study skills modules in secondary schools. All of this was community linked and we within three years went from nothing to 2000 people a year. A number of things explain this. One was definitely the commitment from the top at every opportunity. We're going to be a community university. Another was commitment from the bottom in that I never, ever had an argument from a lecturer or a student about why we're doing this. There was immediate acceptance that this was a good thing. Almost a moral responsibility to the area. It coincided with national policy on community widening access.
>
> (Respondent 11)

This development exemplifies the high-energy, high-achievement determination of Entrepreneurial developers to instigate new initiatives, establish them, then pass their steady-state operational maintenance to other agencies within the organization whilst they pursue the next opportunity. A relentless search for the new.

> You needed a central driving unit to work across the departments and to work with the communities and that was our role. Start it, produce the papers, drive it. We got the funding for it from the Funding Council. Then, and this is why I'm picking this as an example, it's reached maturity. We're now in the fourth year of operation so we spun it off. I'm still involved if it's anything new but it's an administrative team now that's gone to a department of student recruitment and marketing that actually are responsible for the student enrolments.
>
> (Respondent 11)

The discourse is inscribed with a certain urgency, touching on the evangelical, which valorizes innovation, enthusiasm, energy and action, as opposed to, say, research, scholarship, scepticism or reflection. It is also a discourse of freedom, risk and appears fundamentally anti-bureaucratic. The following Entrepreneurial developer, when asked what qualities he would seek in a member of his team, placed high priority on commitment, energy and the search for innovative practice. There can be a degree of impatience with those who don't share these values:

> Basically we'd be looking for a love of innovation. I can only describe it as a 'love'. There's got to be a passionate commitment to the fact that somebody wants to develop something. We've had a few ugly secondments where people have been pushed our way. 'Passengers' is the word because it's actually slowed down everyone else. It's a bit like introducing a disease into the community. There's this love for change, love for innovation, an ability to enthuse – not necessarily at a professional level but just to show that there's excitement to other colleagues.
>
> (Respondent 11)

The following account typifies the fairly widespread encouragement that Entrepreneurial developers often receive from senior managers, as many of the more entrepreneurial projects align well with institutionally strategic priorities. However, the expectation that this kind of development will also be self-financing to a certain degree is also not unusual, and can be an unwelcome pressure.

> We are in a position where we can generate a lot of our own work. Clearly we can submit bids for funded research, but also I've had quite a lot of support from the institution for links I'm developing in South Africa, for example. That was entirely initiated by me, and I've had nothing but encouragement.
>
> *The Interviewer: So there's a kind of entrepreneurial spirit to this?*
>
> There is, yes.

The Interviewer: Do you enjoy that?

Yes I do and I get the support from senior managers in the Faculty.

The Interviewer: Do you get brownie points?

I don't know about brownie points. I mean the downside is – or it's a kind of downside – we have to earn enough income to pay for some of our posts. Which is something that Shirley [a colleague in a different unit] doesn't have to do, at least not so directly. And so that's a kind of cutting edge.

(Respondent 2)

The freedom to initiate, mentioned here, seems to be a valued element within this orientation to development. One head of unit described her own approach as 'essentially one of creative disobedience' (Respondent 35). There is a preparedness to take risks, which, of course, any innovation entails. The approach seems to be to seek forgiveness rather than permission.

I suppose emotionally our agenda comes from what we see as being necessary through our interaction with Schools. So we've carved out where we are, or we are constantly carving out our own niche, because, whatever the set agenda is, we're actually fairly free agents, and that is something that I am keeping as my ace. So although there is a spelt agenda and there is a framework, because of the way the university has been managed, that is exploitable. And, although I've tried strategic methods to get things done, what I've also discovered is that it's possible just to go ahead and do things and present them as innovations. Yes.

The Interviewer: So there are creative possibilities in this?

That's right. And so you wait for people to say to you 'Oh, you shouldn't have done that!' But it hasn't happened yet. Well, it did happen once!

The Interviewer: So you've taken calculated risks?

Yes.

(Respondent 5)

Another Head of unit describes it this way:

One way is what could be called the entrepreneurial spirit route, which is you create an environment, you encourage this sort of entrepreneurship and you let people run with initiatives and you just try and do a bit of tidying up from time to time. And actually [name of university] has been pretty good at doing that over about ten years. I think that approach is, currently, a wee bit out of fashion, and is undervalued. I think it is far better as a method than a lot of people understand.

(Respondent 14)

This unleashing of the 'entrepreneurial spirit', however, often runs against the grain of existing administrative procedures and practice, which come to be perceived by developers of an Entrepreneurial orientation as inflexible and obstructive to innovation.

> Accountants can't comprehend it because they just can't get their mind round it. Accountants cannot get their mind round something like that because they cannot believe that that's an efficient use of resources. There must be waste and duplication – their tidy minds tell them that that's bound to be so. You cannot get them to comprehend that there's always going to be waste and duplication, but the benefits may outweigh the waste and duplication. It's not a simple equation like that.
>
> (Respondent 14)

Another respondent working in a new university complains, similarly, of the 'bureaucratic impediments' encountered in the management of an entrepreneurial project.

> We have not managed in this institution to substantially reduce the bureaucratic impediments to innovation. In fact, in some ways they get worse because we've drastically cut our administrative staff, which means that academics do more admin., or are required to provide more data, more returns to the Centre and so on. So it gets worse and there's that constant sense, especially financially, having to account for every pound that you spend. You can't be entrepreneurial and be preoccupied with saving every single receipt for every sandwich you buy. Or the equivalent of that. The way you have to account for expenditure, on a monthly or quarterly basis. The way that if you secure an externally funded project or consultancy that devotes so much money to hospitality, you can only order hospitality according to the University's pricing system. So you have important people coming here from across the country to participate in something and you have to give them a sandwich – you know, that kind of nonsense.
>
> (Respondent 2)

One of the most powerful and straightforward incentives to engage colleagues, which developers who worked originally in well-funded EHE units came to appreciate, was to use project money to buy departmental services. Some of these developers came into development when typical EHE operational budgets were in the range of one million pounds over a four to five year development period. Such operational methods still tend to function through internal bidding or when other external resources can be accessed.

> Offer money? For them to do something? Yes. We do, yes! It can be done, yes!
>
> (Respondent 1)

However, Entrepreneurial developers have been largely responsible for effecting one of the most radical and significant shifts in areas of the higher education curriculum in recent years, which is the increasing adoption, mainly in newer universities, but increasingly in particular areas of older institutions, of work-based learning (WBL). In this approach to curriculum design universities still determine what is acceptable, but the content of the curriculum is not predetermined but negotiated. Employers tend to support work-based learning because 'it directly advances the enterprise' (Boud 1999: 1). The enterprises involved may be private, public or community organizations.

> Students negotiate their learning with a faculty member and a work supervisor. Guidance on learning how to learn and work-based learning skills are provided. Work is the foundation of the curriculum. Work *is* the curriculum. Work is a site of knowledge production. The curriculum is unique for each person and context.
>
> (1)

Entry can be at any level according to prior qualifications and experience. Exit is at the level of learning demonstrated. There can be a variety of starting points for students through the use of recognition of current competencies via portfolio development strategies. Students also make use of reflective devices such as journals, learning partners, action learning sets, which enable students to maintain 'reflective distance from the particularities of the workplace' (1).

> Students do not choose from a university menu. Students create their curriculum, negotiating the curriculum through three-way learning contracts between learner, employer and university.
>
> (1)

Work-based learning provides a salient example of the kind of paradigm shift towards an action-oriented curriculum that Barnett (1994: 20) has discussed. It would appear to be a curriculum development that will continue to spread, particularly since the endorsement of such approaches by Dearing (DfEE 1997), and is likely to be a significant legacy of educational developers working in this particular area. Some units are now formally establishing educational programmes in this area to enable academic colleagues, and students, to gain expertise and skill in the conceptual bases and management of such approaches. Such programmes can gain credibility and status for educational development units.

> We now run work-based learning for the University, and this is something that derived from Stuart's [a member of the EDU] Enterprise days. It was a particular thing that he wanted to do. We now have a MA/

MSc in work-based learning. We have an administrator out there, and we are the central organizing unit for work-based learning and we intend for it to go both up to PhD and down to at least final year undergraduate. So that's something again where I think a lot of people are around who support us. It's very strongly supported by most of the – Social Sciences is the exception again! – by the other Deans. They thought this was absolutely great and so on and EDU were doing it. And that I think was very helpful.

(Respondent 6)

Romantic (Ecological Humanist)

A quite different orientation from those considered so far is one that is directed principally towards supporting the academic as an *individual* practitioner, towards his or her personal development, growth and well-being.

It really is important to go home at night with that feeling inside that you have been effective, and the most important way that I know that I get that feeling is when I work effectively and see an individual, see change or enabling change with someone, in a context which is concrete, and where someone is going to try something that you have hoped to lead them towards, or support. Or even better, when you get feedback from it and someone has been successful. I think that is just *rich*. It is terribly important.

(Respondent 18)

This raises the issue of the *organizational levels* at which educational development should operate, and who the stakeholders are that it should address.

My approach to work has been to help colleagues here by supporting individuals with initiatives they take. And this at times has been very personal and it goes back to my perception of how an EDU works. I believe the mission if you like of educational development has to be carried out at different *levels*. There is strategic level; it is influencing policy. There is personal level, influencing personal practice. And there are a lot of steps in between those poles. You talked earlier on about a unit being a change agent unit. If it is to be effective, it has got to be effective at different levels. There is no one route to take. I have always taken the view in this Centre that what we have to do is try and ensure that people from different strands make their contributions in different forms.

(Respondent 18)

The intra-organizational levels of educational development tend to be the institutional level (relating to strategic policy or cross-institutional *functions* such as course leader, director of studies), the departmental or disciplinary level, and the personal level of the individual academic. Some developers see the most effective aspect of their practice, and their major contribution and skill, being at the personal level, working on a one-to-one basis.

> If you come down to my own level of working it is in the same mould. If I work with an individual I never represent myself as an expert; it is always the *enabling*. If you like, the counselling, rapport, enablement of other people to find within themselves. It's heavily influenced ultimately by Carl Rogers, to provide freedom in structures and, in the case of counselling theory, freedom of space for individuals to explore their concerns and their resources in their own way. Now, that whole thing about how you work, working within [name of EDU] to support people where they are at, and when they want, has always been for me a very important part of practice. Actually I don't know of anything that has been written anywhere about this personal learning.
>
> (Respondent 18)

Approaches that appear initially to be concerned with more strategic or operational issues may well turn out to be matters relating to personal concerns.

> I felt the strength of [name of EDU] was that it intervened at every level. That it was represented on committees, on the one hand. That it advised the Deputy Vice-Chancellor, and that anyone, virtually, not just academics, could ring up [name of EDU] and say will you help me with this? And some of that was very close to the counselling model I mentioned earlier. Some people come along and they say 'My head of department sent me along because I have real trouble teaching large groups of two hundred students'. And it wouldn't take long to discover that what was happening was a crisis of confidence. It was stage fright. So you could talk about some techniques that might help, but you couldn't help but address issues a bit more personal than that. And to some extent I felt qualified to do that. I've got a Counselling Certificate but I'm not a qualified counsellor in any professional sense.
>
> (Respondent 2)

The influence of a counselling approach is strong within this orientation. Respondents who reflect this preferred mode of working cite the work of Carl Rogers as a major influence. Rogers' person-centred, non-directive approach to counselling (Rogers 1942, 1961) was later developed into a model of learning (Rogers 1969) within a framework of humanistic psychology, and predicated on a notion of 'unconditional positive regard' for the client/learner. Rogers (1969) stressed an essentially open-ended and client-centred approach to learning and development, with no predetermined outcomes, with the traditional tutor's role transformed into that of facilitator or catalyst.

> If I look at some of the heroes that I would acknowledge, Carl Rogers for me would be someone who has a great influence on the way I view

> student-centredness, in the way I operate. And although I don't operate at that level in terms of teaching and learning, I know, running workshops in particular, that it's a very useful tool to have used. I've done two stages of the counselling skills course and have been able to recognize when you actually have to stop talking and see if there's a bit of pain there. And if you really want to let off some steam then that's been a useful technique for me as a trainer, undoubtedly. And there's a whole range of books up there on the psychological front, even more back at home in the office there.
>
> (Respondent 16)

For Rogers, knowing in advance where a learning session would lead was in effect to deny the possibility of 'significant' learning taking place. The purpose of all sessions was learning, not teaching, and this applies as much to the facilitator as the rest of the group. The session is to be a journey of self-discovery for all participants.

> I approach any educational development event which I undertake now with a number of questions, one of which is 'What am I going to get out of this?' I've become a selfish developer over time. I don't do things which I won't learn from, because life's too short. It has other pedagogic benefits, does going in prepared to listen, which are too obvious to be worth telling, but I do it for primarily selfish motives now.
>
> *The Interviewer: Didn't Carl Rogers once say that he wasn't interested in any learning event in which he knew what was going to take place from the outset?*
>
> I'm just an ageing hippy, that's all Ray, influenced by Rogers, substantially, in the eighties, when I was working in Independent Study. I got off on that quite a lot. It's obviously gone deeper than I realized! Thank you for pointing out that connection, that was useful.
>
> (Respondent 27)

The open-ended, client-focused characteristics of this conception of development are clearly not immediately congruent with the more strategically driven and mission-directed approaches that would be favoured by Managerialists. In this orientation the emphasis, in quasi-counselling fashion, tends to be on the individual's development and on the importance of trust and integrity. The prevailing discourse relates to (personal) 'growth'. Organic metaphors are rife.

> I think staff development is about supporting staff to grow, and I've mentioned this before, to grow and develop as professionals and I am delighted when I see someone say 'Gosh, I write so much better now' as a result of having been through this programme. 'Gosh, you know I never thought I'd be here six months ago!' That gives me the biggest thrill, to actually see the face and feel I made a contribution.
>
> (Respondent 30)

It is an orientation that privileges the practitioner's own subjectivity and self-esteem.

> There's 'development' on a number of planes. I'm very concerned myself about the person's development. An individual's development. And I think my job's to do with the development of individuals, to be concerned about the development of students in their role as students in an institution like this. I think my focus has to be on their development and how that happens. Development is at the heart of education you see. I don't think you can learn without developing, almost kind of want to put the word in the same box, and say that actually you only really learn if you have developed – it's almost the same thing.
>
> (Respondent 17)

Again, there is a moral dimension attributed to the notion of development:

> Similarly, for staff, I don't believe that you can be a good teacher without being in some sense a good human being. The two things are kind of congruent? One encloses the other. In order to be a better teacher I believe you have to become a better person. I think it's something to do with your interpersonal skill, and your ethical concerns for people, as well as the techniques that you use. And there's a point at which you can get so far with technique and then you can't get any further until you hit some barrier in your own personal make-up that stops you getting that technique better.
>
> (Respondent 17)

This notion of 'betterment', of personal *improvement* as opposed to becoming technically more *competent*, of an implicit faith or optimism in the perfectibility of the human spirit, unspecific and essentially personally contracted as that might be, links the orientation to a historical line of educational thought running from the educational philosophy of the Romantic period such as that of Rousseau, through Arnold and Dewey to Rogers and the individualistic projects of the 1960s 'Deschooling' movement. It is a conception of development that is mobilized primarily through discourses of improvement, of the 'progressive' and the 'emancipatory'.

> Management is exactly the same in my view. Personal development and practical skills of teaching. I think I am optimistic, probably too much, but I think that the role of educational development should be about improvement. I think you have to have a notion about what improvement means. And you are dealing with individual people.
>
> (Respondent 17)

This conception of development takes as axiomatic a holistic view of the practitioner, and a humanist, unified notion of subjectivity. 'I think the essence of this,' suggests one developer, 'is that I don't think you can ever compartmentalise people. People have to be seen as a total persona' (Respondent 18). This perspective puts considerable value on emotion, affect and the *non-rational* aspects of academics' experience. Notions of 'improvement' may well imply some amelioration of the practitioner's affective state and sense of well-being rather than mere technical accomplishment in skills-based development.

> I know what I would see as better or worse. I think there's such a thing as 'life-enhancing'. So, like inside courses for staff, I've got a strong view that what we should be doing is helping someone to enjoy teaching, feel better about teaching and do better at it, but not just by saying 'this is a hoop, jump through this'.
>
> (Respondent 17)

This emphasis, and the influence of a counselling model, become most apparent in the developer's concern for the stress faced by colleagues as they struggle to cope with the current challenging work conditions of higher education.

> I've always felt it's very important to be aware, in this business, of helping individuals to change. Many of the individuals we work with are at the margins of psychological demand and stress. And I've always felt, and I've never seen it referred to in the literature ever, that *we* might be perceived by academic staff as one of the stressors.
>
> (Respondent 18)

This particular developer has reservations about overly ambitious or too rapid strategic advances in educational development which might neglect the psychological well-being of individual colleagues, of 'people's individual locus', or 'staff as staff'.

> And that's always cautioned me about how fast you would move or seek to move and I've always been worried about – hopefully not pejoratively because I recognize it's important to have it – but the strategists who want to push institutional change quickly and get change on the grand scale. I don't think it works like that and I think we have more than enough evidence that any academic staff, if we look sensitively at what comes through in the Times Higher and the literature . . . a lot of our colleagues are at breaking point on all sorts of fronts. That's part of my worry about moving to the IT thing. It's too distant from people as people. Yes it can provide information and I'm not taking issue with that. But I think if we lose contact with staff as staff, where they're at, what they're carrying, what Sarah Smith on a Wednesday afternoon is actually thinking, and feeling, I think we're in danger of becoming too distant from them. I think we need to be aware of people's individual locus. And I'm very, very struck by how often on our induction course in September we have colleagues who are very, very close to [. . .] they're coping with too much transition, too much change, too many pressures, too many uncertainties, too many insecurities and actually we're then asking them to talk about self-development, and frankly that's not best

> done unless you're feeling a strong sense of self-esteem. And I think there's a very, very big area here which we might actually, helpfully make a research focus over the next four, five years. I think it's an important area.
>
> (Respondent 18)

This 'caring', almost therapeutic approach is applied to the psychological well-being of one's colleagues in the EDU also.

> Let me give you a very simple example of the delicate tread and balance we have been doing with Jenny [a colleague in the unit, recovering from an accident] over the past six weeks. When a person is injured and defensive how can you help that person without being a stressor? So the odd telephone conversation with Jenny. We had a Vet Medicine Faculty workshop a fortnight ago and she was taking the session here. Genuinely we could do with her expertise. 'How do you feel if we provide a taxi? Is it an intrusion? Mentally could you cope with 45 minutes?' Could we insert her into a session? She is great and it spoke entirely to me, it was about keeping her in with the fold at a time when she feels in danger of falling out of the fold. There is an awful lot of developments going on here at the moment which suddenly, as a result, she is not involved in. It is that crucial feeling of holding and bringing people together which for me is an absolutely critical . . . It is never *seen*; it is about a *style*, but it is critical.
>
> (Respondent 18)

Other developers who don't share this orientation nonetheless recognize it in colleagues, though not always uncritically. A respondent with a predominantly Researcher orientation commented:

> You know I look around at my colleagues and a lot of them have a kind of 'nursing' model of educational development. They make a big thing of wanting to help people. They seem to want to show that they 'care'.
>
> (Respondent 24)

The discourse of care here appears to be mistrusted as seeming to offer support whilst masking a power relationship which renders the recipient dependent upon the support of the provider. Macintyre (1985) has commented on this kind of role in modern organizations, which he refers to as 'therapist':

> MacIntyre's thesis is that positivism is the dominant culture of modernity and that its self-conception is embodied in its metaphors and, in particular, the metaphors which are the *characters* of the manager and the therapist. One way in which the thesis is made visible is through current fashions of educational inspection, the practices of which are easily accommodated within the vocabulary described above [. . .] educational inspection – such as that presently carried out in the UK by HMI and Ofsted in schools, colleges and universities – is grounded in a

technical-rationalist framework whose values are those of the bureaucracy and whose cultural characters are the manager and the therapist.
(Parker 1997: 17)

Foucault, similarly, compares such therapeutic approaches with the confessional as a form of control (Ball 1990b). Theoretical support for the approach taken by Romantic or humanistic developers, however, may be found in the work of Taylor (1999). He has drawn upon the research of Weick (1995) to argue for the importance in educational development of helping colleagues engage more deliberately in the task of 'sensemaking'.

> Sensemaking conceived in this way involves choice, and therefore values. Issues of significance, or attention, of expectation are based on individual values. This, in turn, hints at the importance of the *non-rational* in the sensemaking process. Issues of choice and sensemaking are too often presumed to lie in the terrain of the cognitive and the rational. Academics value the rational, the intellectual – it is how they make sense of and contribute to the formal knowledge which is their stock-in-trade. But they often misrecognize change-focused learning as *necessarily* based on informed and rational processes. It may be, but it is more likely to be a form of rational sensemaking structured around a particular set of criteria – one's values.
> (Taylor 1999: 9) [author's emphasis]

Emotion and the non-rational feature strongly in Taylor's argument. 'Sensemaking', he argues, is framed by 'expectations, intentions, desires whose achievement is "anticipated" more at an emotional than cognitive level.' The process of sensemaking often involves the 'creation of meanings that allow individuals to feel good/better/disappointed rather than to see more clearly' (9). This process requires a considerable effort of critical introspection, suggests Taylor, but is an important factor in enabling academics to cope with the challenges of change. There is a need:

> to acknowledge and deal with *issues of loss* associated with change, and with the importance of the *non-rational* in the sensemaking process, and in any other engagement with change. What is seldom acknowledged is that change is always *from* something, not just *to* something.
> (8) [author's emphasis]

Taylor cites Craib's work *The Importance of Disappointment* (1994) as a source of insight into the processes of 'articulation' and 'internal arguments' in which individuals must engage to cope with, and allow for, ambivalence and indecision when choices are limited but individuals are condemned to choose:

> The most important aspect is the toleration of the arguments, the recognition that when I am thinking or feeling one thing, I will be thinking and feeling something fairly different shortly [. . .] Such judgements are never purely rational, but they are surrounded by rationality: they need

> to be thought about, argued about internally and externally. The toleration of argument and the making of choices both require sacrifices and their attendant disappointment.
>
> (Craib 1994: 171–2)

Romantic developers, it might be argued, are a principal means of support to individual practitioners in this process of 'external argument', in helping them engage in sensemaking, choices and 'attendant disappointment'.

> I have a young colleague on the course from [name of department] who said to me 'These four walls [the educational developer's office] are the only place in this University where I can even talk about these ideas. If colleagues in my department heard me discussing these things they'd – well they wouldn't even know what I was talking about – but they'd think I was mad or something. There's no-one I can talk to there about this. We just don't have those conversations about education.' He described our tutorials as his 'therapy'. He's now publishing these ideas in educational journals.
>
> (Respondent 21)

We recognize here a lack of personal and discursive space in which anxiety or unease can be discussed and addressed. However, this is not to suggest that the academics Romantic developers choose to work with tend to be those pathologized by change, or lacking agency, being 'pawns' rather than 'players' in Taylor's parlance (1999: 155). Indeed, Trowler (1997) has commented on the preparedness of academics to contest the meaning of specific institutional change. He found a variety of responses, broadly characterized as 'sinking', 'using coping strategies', 'policy reconstruction' and 'swimming'. Nonetheless his research, too, endorses the need of individual academics to engage in organizational 'sensemaking' and, hence, the value of educational developers interacting with them at a personal level.

A further significant feature of the Romantic orientation is the sense of *trust* in the response of participants. Here an experienced developer attributes the success of a particular development event to this particular quality:

> It was outstandingly successful and if we say let's look at why was it successful. What we took to it ourselves was our own professionalism but I think one of the central things was the sense of *trusting* the participants and I think there is a very interesting issue here. Essentially it is about having the strength for self-esteem, trust itself, having the strength to trust somebody else as a facilitating partner and co-leadership but, most critically, have the sense of trust in participants that they will work with a professional integrity for their own development. Now we think in that programme we got a lot of this right and it was wonderful.
>
> (Respondent 18)

This trust is related to another Rogerian notion, that of *positive regard* for the client:

> We are working at the highest quality of academic staffing. Fine. So if you see that as a resource base, you could trust it. That is my view and I never, ever have a problem with that, and that helps the work. I also think that partly personal persuasion and partly personal qualities . . . I do think I come over as non-threatening and I also think I can inspire people to trust themselves.
>
> (Respondent 18)

The idea of 'inspiring people to trust themselves' is an example of the humanistic principle of *empowerment*.

> I believe in the idea of empowerment you see because – and I suppose there must be something that I'm connected with in that – because I've worked internationally with UNICEF on country-wide development projects. But I think, in higher education, there must be a context from my working with people, and that context is to improve the educational experience.
>
> (Respondent 12)

It is not surprising also to identify the concepts of self-awareness and self-esteem – concepts derived from psychotherapeutic settings or Rogerian counselling theory – as they arise within the Romantic orientation to development.

> I do think that there are factors within myself I have. It is difficult to say this with a sufficient degree of self-awareness but also humility. I prefer to claim for myself what I know by experience works for me, that is towards *self-esteem*. I have a good sense of self-esteem inside and I don't have unrealistic ambitions, put it that way. I have a good strong sense of myself and I knew that was very helpful. I have a self-belief. So that is the most critical thing but I also have, I think, a trusting awareness and it has grown again with observation and fact, but the quality of stuff we work with is very high [. . .] and that helps me in workshops [. . .] to trust.
>
> (Respondent 18)

In further keeping with the principles of humanistic psychology, Romantic developers endorse the notion that valid learning and personal change can only be achieved through personal motivation, when the need to acquire learning makes sense to the learner, or is perceived as significant. Going against the grain of this is seen as counter-productive. A developer in a traditional university in the north of England describes her approach this way:

> I can provide opportunities for that to occur. But it's the individual who [. . .] I can provide opportunities for people to develop. They can only develop themselves. You can't change someone. They can only change themselves. You can point out areas where they might want to explore, and having explored will decide to see things

differently, but I cannot make that decision for them. Does that make sense?

(Respondent 1)

A developer working in a traditional Scottish university takes a similar view:

It's all to do with finding an angle first of all, finding a motivation. You see you've got to apply your own principles to your own work and when you're dealing with human learning you've got to use all of those principles. What was the motivation for anyone to want to buy into this? You can't go into a department and say 'Throw out all your practices! I know better'. You go in and you *listen.*

(Respondent 12)

Some developers are uncomfortable with the term 'development', with its implications of a perceived or known direction or end-point of change, and prefer terms such as 'growth' or 'support'. But again the emphasis is on the learners' self-directedness.

But you're not pushing people to do something. In a sense you're allowing them to take the running. I think that mostly they're doing the running, you're providing the service so maybe that's why some people would say it's a support, but at the same time you are a kind change agent in the institution so you're opening up things that other people haven't thought of. You're introducing something into the system which is new as well that they can take on board and maybe do better things with it than you can and that can be an interesting thing as well.

The Interviewer: It could be catalytical?

It could be.

(Respondent 12)

The orientation also has much in keeping with the perspectives found in theories of adult learning such as andragogy (Knowles 1978, 1980; Jarvis 1985; Brookfield 1986) with their emphasis on the adult status of learners and acknowledgement of the learners' experience, their problem-orientation, and focus on immediate professional and personal roles. This can extend to developers' work with students:

When I talk to undergraduates in the medical school, certainly with postgraduates but even with undergraduates – I mean most of the undergraduates we see are 20, 21 – they have got the vote, they are in training for a profession. I would even talk to undergraduates as colleagues and say so, and use that terminology, and we would always make informal use of first names. The notion of staff member/student simply doesn't figure any more in my mind. It is not something I grasp at all. I transfer the staff development approach down to students now. Fine. I

> think of them as adults. I have always taken the view that they have a vote, they have political power in that sense, in the sense that all of us have and actually I suppose you could say it works really off adult theory. I don't think you can empower students if you align them as 'students'. . . it is about adults and a view I very genuinely take. I think it is respected.
>
> (Respondent 18)

The same respondent recounts a telling incident, which underwrites the value of demonstrating positive regard:

> I have seen, in asking for names on forms, cards – which I always do with the 235 medical students – and I have had a girl break down in tears as being the first time anybody – she was in her 5th year – the first time anybody asked for her name in the five years of her undergraduate experience. If you think about that! Especially when she was 23 years old.
>
> (Respondent 18)

In relations with both students and academic colleagues this approach can be seen to exemplify the humanistic concern with *empathy*.

> I think integrity, sense of integrity, humility, a willingness to accept we can only make haste slowly. And that is not because others are resistant, it is because others' priorities deserve due recognition. Research workers in medical sciences, for example. We have colleagues in there who are on deadlines holding research grants for £3 million. Now it is a great idle luxury to say they should drop some of that and come into a staff development workshop. I mean, we have got to be realistic.
>
> (Respondent 18)

In relations with educational development colleagues the Romantic orientation translates into a marked preference for 'working with people' – teamwork, co-leadership, and peer support.

> I think there are probably some base lines, things that you can't do without. Maybe optimism is one of them actually because it's a job of hard knocks. You get the cynical people to deal with. I think you cannot afford to be cynical yourself. I think the cynical educational developer's had it, basically. You have to have a certain degree of love of people in terms of liking, working with people because you tend not to have too much to do that's yourself. You work with and for and through other people so there's some sort of interpersonal skills usually required.
>
> (Respondent 17)

Such peer support can sometimes be done in a somewhat self-effacing, yet nonetheless assertive manner – 'a soft hand on the tiller'.

> I love the classroom but when you come back to staff development I really love the supporting role with colleagues and that is the joint

leadership. I mean the co-leadership with A [a colleague] on Friday but also with B [his Head of Department]. There are times when B desperately needs support. There are times also when – it is not common and it is best that it is not needed – but there have been times when it has been very important to have somebody next to him to hold him back because he gets carried away with his performance and there have been times when it is needed to take his hand in a corner and say 'Hang on a second!'. That role is actually extremely important because it is doing something for the face of staff development if you like, the contact face of it. Without oneself being in a lead role, it is very much more a soft hand on the tiller. A supporting hand, restraining. But it is very important and there have been very, very many times when I have felt that was a very important and significant contribution, and I have enjoyed making it because, . . . it's the person can't *see.* And I have often actually with, funny one should say this without being, hopefully, too strong-minded about it, the number of times I have seen people running workshops and leading sessions like that who need somebody to do that and you can see that it is not going to happen. And you know that the value of the session is going to be lessened because of it. It is very common. So I think there is a role for co-leadership. I enjoy it; it is something I have gained a lot of insight myself from. So in a sense I like the teamwork. I think that is basically what I am saying.

(Respondent 18)

This tendency to a low-key development approach, somewhat self-effacing and behind the scenes, can however have lasting and powerful effects:

Some of us [educational developers] like parading ourselves around, giving keynotes at international conferences, publishing, attending big national committees and generally being fairly loud mouths. And you need publicists for the cause like that. But there are others in our community who have a quiet word here and there with colleagues, one-to-one, who keep a very low profile, almost like outreach workers in the social services, but they can be the ones who you hear colleagues talk about years later saying 'You know once [name of colleague] showed me a particular approach and you know it was the most useful thing I ever learned in this place and I've been using it ever since.' And it's then that you think, yeah, that's development being *really* useful, and valued.

(Respondent 21)

An earlier respondent in this mode provides his own summary of his philosophical position, and provides an alternative definition of this orientation as 'ecological humanist':

There was a very formative time for me after a divorce about 20 years ago and then I was right back to first principles. I did a lot of reading about values, a lot of reading about purpose and I came to a very comfortable position at the time to define myself as 'ecological humanist'; that would

> be broadly the position that I stand in. And that carries with it some over-arching sense of what the purpose of everything is about as an individual. What is the purpose? And I am fairly clear that for me it is about – I know it sounds trite but it is true – it is something about the full sense of trying to nurture and move forward yourself. It is about the valuc of thc full potcntial in all sorts of different aspects of living. So there is unrealizable limit to the potential we have. None of us know what our potential might be. So I don't see life as about coming to a comfortable status. There is always more, and that more can be what you know, how you know it, how you relate to other people, what you can do for other people. And if we make this more restrictive and narrower and, say, in the role of a member of our community as a university, then that is about as far into and moving towards the full potential development of professional standards. That is the way I would look at it.
>
> (Respondent 18)

The respondent was not happy with the term 'Romantic', feeling it implied a certain quixotic quality, whereas he saw his preferred definition of 'ecological humanist' as accommodating pragmatism.

> It is a very pragmatic issue, it's essential. It is about being at peace with yourself, it is about, if it is anything, it is about feeling that, as human beings we can't always be in the state of 'could do better'. I know that. I am quite well aware of that. But to feel that you are actually trying to *do* that. To go home in the evening and feeling that the spirit today is trying me. It is something about the importance of our sense of self-worth, self-belief, strength of character and goodness. Now, I don't see that as 'Romantic', I see that as being the essence of psychological good health. I think it is important to go home each day feeling like that. I know that, if I don't, that something is not right. Now, I don't think I can say anything more.
>
> (Respondent 18)

The term 'Romantic' has been used here in its philosophic sense of indicating concern with the individual and the emotional self. Any suggestion that Romantic developers might be quixotic or unworldly, however, is firmly to be dispelled by the emphasis placed upon realistic expectation and sound self-knowledge.

> You and I know the pressures on people's time, the research emphasis, these people have limited time. I therefore don't, for myself or for others, have unrealistic expectations. I am very, very realistic. I like to think that I have a sense of realism about the context for working with my feet on the ground.
>
> (Respondent 18)

The pursuit of a Romantic, or Ecological Humanist, model, however, is often compromised by more pragmatic needs to satisfy managerial demands or to exploit the 'big drivers' of change in an Opportunistic fashion. As the following respondent, working in a small college, points out in relation to the objects of a Romantic orientation, 'the world doesn't let me do that'. It is interesting to note also here a mild aversion to technological development, a characteristic noted elsewhere in the accounts of Romantic developers.

> *The Interviewer: Does that imply that it is also about personal development?*
>
> For individuals?
>
> *The Interviewer: Yes, rather than an institutional push.*
>
> I think that's a very difficult question for me because I do actually work at lots of levels and I think it's about balancing all of those so I have a different approach depending where I am. I've also seen that role as being someone who's here to support individuals if they're having difficulties. I've had a member of staff who's had great difficulties settling into a department and I'm the person who she comes to see because she doesn't have anybody else to talk to so what I see as very important is trying to make sure that that member of staff finds a way of settling in to the culture of her department. So I do see that as being very important and I guess personally, I would feel that that's probably where I would prefer to work with individuals or groups of individuals and to see them doing something interesting, but the world doesn't let me do that, so I have to get on with these other things which I don't find quite so fulfilling, personally, so I know that I have to drive forward certain things as far as the college is concerned and I think IT's one of these because I'm not completely convinced that IT is the be-all-and-end-all, and I'm very ambivalent about IT and I think that's one area where I actually find it difficult to make a personal commitment. But that's the way the college wants to go so I think in this job, dealing with ambivalences is quite an issue, personally.
>
> (Respondent 30)

Ultimately, it's about finding a workable balance between the competing needs of different stakeholders:

> I do have to react to the way the senior management wants to drive the institution, so I have to react to that, but on the other hand, I also have to help to support the staff, both to meet those needs of the institution, but to address their own individual growth as well.
>
> (Respondent 30)

Opportunist

There was a clear orientation arising from many of the interviews undertaken with practitioners towards the need to remain vigilant for opportunities, either within the institution or within the wider higher educational environment.

> I think that our unit works by opportunism in many ways and it's the opportunism of individuals, but there are obviously some people it suits.
>
> *The Interviewer: Does that suit you – by default?*
>
> Yes.
>
> (Respondent 12)

One educational developer uses a metaphor of predation to describe this tendency:

> I think it's like most things in educational development. You alight on some shiny substance, raven-like, and if it's really nice you kind of fly off with it and show it to as many people as you think might be interested or something.
>
> (Respondent 2)

A Head of a large EDU in a new university in England uses a metaphor of surfing waves to describe her own vigilance for change:

> I think because it's a change agency, it can't afford to stagnate in anything it's doing so the agenda has to constantly change. You have to be responsive to what's there but you have to be proactive as well. And that means that you have to ride the waves and I think that it's a very good educational developer that can be fleet of foot enough to keep on riding the next wave. What is in this particular focus of educational change at the moment which we can use to embed good practice about teaching and learning?
>
> (Respondent 17)

Another points out that 'anything' can serve as an entrée to getting staff drawn into educational development activity.

> I suppose I would argue that anything could be the vehicle for development. Almost anything that interests or motivates people, to some extent engages, could be a vehicle. So you know it could be done a variety of different ways. I mean there are hundreds of ways of doing it.
>
> (Respondent 12)

This ties in with Berg and Östergren's (1979) concept of the organizational 'cracks' that appear when organizations find themselves in states of dynamic change. The developer, here acting as change agent, is alert to the emergence of such cracks and the opening up of possibilities for change. One developer talks of the need to exploit the 'mega-drivers' of change, such as a set of 'Writing for Publication' workshops geared to assisting the institution's performance in the UK Research Assessment Exercise (RAE):

> The writing for publication one, I'd say we had, what, 5 per cent of our staff who completed that programme but it has definitely made an impact and because of course it's very focused on the HE agenda – it's about the RAE.
>
> *The Interviewer: Yes, well, that's one of the big drivers isn't it?*
>
> You can't negate these mega-drivers. If I was trying to run a programme about computer-based assessment, I'm not so sure I would get that kind of commitment.
>
> *The Interviewer: So are you opportunistic in that sense – hitching your wagon on to these big drivers?*
>
> Well, I think I have to be, because that's what's driving the college. Because I sit in this position where I have the college overview, and I have to react to the way the senior management wants to drive the institution, I have to react to that.
>
> (Respondent 30)

Teaching Quality Assessment (TQA) is often cited by respondents as a major opportunity for various kinds of developmental forays:

> And the biggest agent for change for us at the moment is preparing for QAA Subject Review, because in helping people get ready for that we are actually helping them to start talking about teaching and learning, to get them thinking about learning outcomes, get them doing observation of teaching for each other, all that kind of stuff. We're pushing on an open door.
>
> (Respondent 3)

TQA can present a powerful opportunity to augment both the impact and the presence of an EDU.

> The influence of TQA Subject Review has been quite large on our lives in that we're now very actively involved for a period that starts about two years before the visit. Working with the departments, we do observations of teaching for them or we help them do it on a peer basis, so we're very much working at grass-roots level in a way that we hope demonstrates our value and our usefulness. Certainly the two departments that've gone through reviews this year were very supportive and very welcoming of our support. Because they feel slightly threatened and desperate when they're faced with this, they're glad to have help.
>
> (Respondent 6)

A Head of Educational Development also talks of hitching the unit's activities to promising passing juggernauts, but emphasizes the importance of timing in such opportunistic incursions.

> One of the things I have learned in doing the job over the years is that timing is everything. And I think now lots of people do realize just exactly that. If your timing is wrong and people don't see the need to do it there and then, even though you might be right and you've diagnosed it absolutely 100 per cent, it'll not happen. They're busy, they've got a lot to do, and if they don't think it needs to happen tomorrow, basically they're not going to do it. You'll get enthusiasts doing it but you'll not get widespread change. You can get them to address it when they all kind of recognize it's now becoming an imperative. The obvious coming imperatives are the next RAE, and the new Quality Assurance arrangements. These are absolute coming imperatives. Everybody will focus their mind on those issues because they're up in big neon lights in front of them (*laughs*).
>
> (Respondent 14)

A senior developer in a research-intensive university describes how, although one large initiative – Enterprise in Higher Education (EHE) – was being opportunistically exploited through the use of Departmental Educational Coordinators, nonetheless this development was undermined within his institution by its unfortunate coincidence with the most intensive phase of a yet more dominant initiative, the RAE.

> Instead of them working in the department and creating things in the department they did individual innovations and everybody else in the department said 'Right that leaves us alone – let him get on with it'. And it didn't spread. And everywhere else I've come across, it spread.
>
> *The Interviewer: And how would you explain that difference?*
>
> Because they were research-oriented. There is an important point here. Pure timing. Our institution got into Enterprise as the last institution and by then the Research Assessment Exercise was very dominant. About two years before I had noticed that people were saying 'Well, I'm sorry but I can't go on with this. I've got to write my papers.'
>
> (Respondent 7)

Coincidence, even senior management whim, is cited as an important possible condition of opportunism. But the need to be prepared, as well as vigilant, is stressed.

> I think it's really hard to make change from the bottom. I think it's really hard. I think you can try, and this Centre is proof that you can do it, but you have to work really hard and a lot of it is just coincidental. I think that you might have been trying to push through a policy on access or personal academic tutors or something and nothing happens until all of a sudden the principal goes and meets some other principal who says 'We've now got a policy' and she wants one too!

The Interviewer: So a kind of a contingency in that sense?

Yeah, but I think you actually have to be ready for those kinds of events. So if you haven't got anything on the table you miss your opportunity and there's where the opportunism comes back.

The Interviewer: But it's prepared opportunism?

Yes, exactly.

(Respondent 30)

Developers quite openly admit the fashionable appeal of certain topical developments (again drawing attention implicitly to the appropriacy of timing). One experienced developer uses the metaphor of flotsam to describe this tendency. 'What surfaces is what you work with.'

> Well you focus, you focus on the issues of the day, don't you? Five years ago I was mostly talking to people about teaching large groups. They haven't gone away, but now the heat's off, and now we're talking more about ways in which we can support learning through learning resources and particularly IT. So it's with the fashion. You kind of float (if we're using the watery metaphor). You hang on to the bit of old door that you can and try not to get too swept away and actually what surfaces is what you work with. It's quite a good metaphor really isn't it? But it's true. What surfaces is where you focus your attention. And that's not to say the other stuff isn't all there underneath and isn't going to pop up any minute, but we can't do the whole thing all the time.
>
> (Respondent 3)

However, as a developer in one of the ancient Scottish universities sardonically points out, not all the effort invested in opportunistic excursions is rewarded.

> In this line of business you have to cast an awful lot of bread on an awful lot of water. And sometimes what you end up with is just a lot of soggy bread.
>
> (Respondent 15)

Researcher

> I'm still very turned on by the research thing, particularly where the research turns into action research where people are actually researching how they are developing. I want to make sure that I still keep publishing, particularly start publishing on the management of change, which is a big focus for me.
>
> (Respondent 17)

Attitudes towards the nature and status of research within educational development circles vary considerably. Some practitioners, mainly those working in older research-led universities, adopt a somewhat Luther-like stance of 'I can't work any other' (Respondent 7). In these older guild-influenced collegial environments there is an assumption amongst those with a Researcher orientation towards educational development that the use of educational research findings is what influences research-minded academic colleagues.

'The thing is,' argues one developer with a strong Researcher orientation, 'I think the power of ideas as a change mechanism – I think that's the thing that is critical to the development process. That academics will respond to the power of ideas.' He goes on:

> Sometimes their attitudes will make them not respond, but if you can really marshal together a compelling idea then people will find it hard to – and some of them may still resist it – but people will come on board because they will see the logic of it. I mean they haven't spent their whole life trying to understand these things, but, as long as they've got a modicum of the attitudes [. . .]
>
> (Respondent 12)

He argues the need to bring into play three interlocking factors in the educational development process, like Venn diagrams. These are a motivational effect, a cognitive element ('which is maybe the ideas') and a social process. These then constitute 'the dynamic of the action research process':

> You have to build your relationships, you have to find the motivational interest and you have to have a depth of ideas in order to engage people. So I think that that model could be applied to staff as well as students.
>
> (Respondent 12)

The same respondent also finds the distinction between theory and practice unhelpful. It is a question of enabling colleagues in other research disciplines to have ownership of educational research and to realize that 'there is research out there all the time'.

> I see my role really has a lot to do with the interface between theory and practice and trying to apply the research to pragmatic problems, but then using that application and going back and looking at theoretical models. I can't see these as being separate. They are just so intimately related together. I go into a department like Marketing and they have their set of problems but I'm looking at the research and I'm coming back with some solutions but I'm trying to push the boundaries of what they're doing outwards, and I'm trying to make the research something that they kind of have ownership of in some way. And I try to make them realise that there is research out there all the time.
>
> (Respondent 12)

However, a head of unit in a new university is not so convinced that the use of research evidence is always so compelling in terms of professional development. Research is only one effective way of undertaking development

> I don't think research actually changes practice. I don't think research is the same as educational development but I think it's a good basis. I don't think we necessarily need to deal with research first but I think educational developers *should* research. But I don't think it's the only way of being a good educational developer. I think there's an increasing amount of specialization as well.
>
> (Respondent 17)

But it is felt that a research involvement adds *credibility* to the educational development function.

> I think you want some sort of level of experience that would give you some credibility with the people you work with. Whether that's because you're a teacher yourself or whether you've been a researcher in the areas of student learning. I feel that in the UK we have fewer of the latter (the researchers) and I think that's a shame because I think that there's a way in which having done some research on student learning gives you a scholarship behind what you're trying to do.
>
> (Respondent 17)

A well-established researcher in a prestigious English traditional university cites what he considers a telling study in terms of such credibility:

> There was a piece of evidence that was very telling but people don't know about it. In Australian universities educational development some 15 years ago had a very high profile and it was very accepted. And then as money became scarce they cut back on their research work, they became more 'service', and down it went. More recently they've come up again with research and up in prestige. The fact that academics don't respect you if you don't do research I think is being demonstrated very clearly.
>
> (Respondent 7)

This respondent ran a unit whose official remit was for 'research-driven support to teaching and learning'. This was in a traditional university which 'is not interested in any research that doesn't get at the very least a 5, if not a 5 star, and that therefore it must move towards that kind of excellence in its research'. Asked whether in the light of that his unit could not then function as a support service, his response highlighted a dilemma faced by educational developers working in research-led collegial cultures.

> That's a very difficult question to answer because a year ago the College decided to establish a complete Division of Support for Teaching and Learning (and Division is a very big name here, there are very few of them and they are very important). And therefore it includes all the IT,

and the Library, and the educational development units which are [name of own unit], Staff Development and Continuing Education. And now, from that point of view the support role has become much more dominant in the rhetoric. Because the person in charge comes from IT, and in IT there is a support role and virtually no research role, and he is worried, possibly rightly, that since we are top-sliced we will be criticised for spending – frittering away – our time on research. My reaction to that is twofold: one is that if we do not do relevant research then our support will suffer very rapidly and the other is that we will not be respected if we are not researchers.

(Respondent 7)

A developer working in a large civic Scottish university shares this view of the need for credibility amongst peers.

I think in the kind of job we do credibility is everything and I think that when you go into a department you have to be credible. These people are experts in Physics. They've been studying Physics all their life. They're sharpened minds and you have to be able to show them that this discipline has something to offer.

(Respondent 12)

But, he goes on, educational developers are in a privileged situation, institutionally, in that they have an institutional, and often a national, purview of developments to which their disciplinary colleagues do not have access:

It can just start with a simple thing like you can give them a way of looking at something in a procedure for something that they haven't thought of before, and that can be an inroad. But you need credibility and you need to be taken seriously and that means you need to have knowledge and you need to have some kind of experience that you can draw on. The job can give you that because you're travelling across the institution, you're seeing lots of things.

(Respondent 12)

But it is not just educational developers in older universities who have research remits. 'I keep emphasizing', says the head of a unit in a large new university in the North of England 'that our prime function is not to run that course, or those courses, our prime function is externally funded research' (Respondent 2). Within EDUs it is not uncommon to find individual developers pursuing their own research track. Here, in a large new university in the English Midlands:

I'm rather different from my colleagues. There are all kinds of tensions in our unit. I've heard them say about educational development 'This ain't rocket science stuff!' They like 'tips'; they're 'tippy'! But I do think there should be a theoretical basis to what we do.

(Respondent 24)

This dissatisfaction with a pragmatic emphasis on 'techniques' at the expense of a more theoretical approach often marks educational developers with a Researcher orientation.

> And yet I've come to feel that there is a strong need for us to have a theoretical base that has some kind of consistency. OK, I don't believe in the single big model. I think that most subject areas have abandoned that.
>
> *The Interviewer: Postmodernism won't let you do that!*
>
> But no doubt the pendulum will spring back to post-postmodernism, or post-post-post or something. And I have to confess that I have got to the point of acute irritation at the publication of yet another book of 'How to Do It' tips.
>
> *The Interviewer: There are a lot on that shelf over there!*
>
> I know! (*laughs*) And we have a lot of disagreements about that. But not often – we just accept our different positions. And if I contributed more substantially to the research or theoretical basis I'd be in a stronger position to argue it.
>
> (Respondent 2)

A developer with a background of applied research, and now working in an ancient university, finds herself adopting a research-based rather than a research-led approach.

> My first job was working on research and consultancy projects in equal opportunities within a higher education unit that worked for external organizations. It was mostly applied research projects that I worked on. Coming into staff development was actually something quite new for me and I suppose my approach to staff development was to try and ground it in research. So rather than doing a 'do's and don'ts' presentation skills course, I went off and looked up Psychology stuff about memory and attention span and all that kind of compelling evidence to persuade people. That's the kind of stuff I'm handing over now. Many of the courses that we do now, not just because of me, but generally, because of changes elsewhere, are grounded – not necessarily research-led – but they have some sort of basis in research and I could see more of a need for that on the teaching and learning side.
>
> *The Interviewer: Do you feel the staff here expect that?*
>
> Yes. I think it does need to be research-led, not just research-based, but we do not have the research to support research-led development work be it through courses or mentoring or whatever.
>
> (Respondent 9)

Other developers, however, point up the value of 'practice-related' research. 'I use it as a drum to beat for my case,' says one developer, emphasizing the usefulness of applied educational research as a tool of persuasion with colleagues:

> The literature I'm most familiar with is the assessment literature, and I use a combination of my own practice together with what I've read other people have done. And I would say I'm reasonably familiar with the assessment literature. So I think there is a body of research, but it ain't quantitative. It's qualitative. 'Here's five things we did and these were the three things that worked best. And these are the two things we're now going to work on, we're going to do it differently this time.' That's interesting to me. That's pragmatic, that's practice-grounded. That's something that's about learning from practice.
>
> (Respondent 3)

She draws attention, however, to the fundamental problems of using research drawn from a field of education (and a particular methodological tradition) with academic colleagues whose disciplinary culture steers them to a radically different perception of what constitutes research and compelling evidence.

> But we won't ever, I don't think, get the old Bio-medical Sciences people to recognize that as real research. However, in this University, the person who used to most preach to me about this was the Head of the Department of Chemistry, and they got a 2 in the research ratings, and the sector I went into got a 3a! So we have some right to just say 'Well yours isn't the only model of research and maybe some of us do some quite good stuff!' 3a for a former poly is a good place to be!
>
> (Respondent 3)

Others have also commented upon this underlying issue within educational development of the use of different discourses.

> I think there is a discourse mismatch and I think the reason why we haven't got so far into the Physics disciplines and the Science disciplines, which I pointed out are less developed, is that whoever's been going into those disciplines has not been speaking and acting the right way. I think that I personally (and this might be arrogant) could go into the Physics and Science disciplines and make inroads, but I've never actually focused on them because I've had other things to do, too many other things to do (*laughs*).
>
> (Respondent 12)

An eminent professor in an ancient university who has an international reputation in educational research notes that:

> Our colleagues in other disciplines will say 'Come on you've got to show us the evidence as to why we should adopt this particular approach to

teaching and learning'. If you present your findings in a relatively simple and accessible way they'll say 'This isn't proper research. This is Mickey Mouse stuff!' But if you then present fairly rigorous empirical educational research to them they say 'But this is Social Science stuff! Why do you have to use all this educational jargon that we don't understand? We're not Social Scientists!' But the problem is, of course, that in education we *are* working in the Social Sciences and we use the discourse of Social Science. And to make matters more complicated the discourse of educational *research* is a rather different discourse from that used by educational *developers*.

(Respondent 29)

One head of an EDU sees her role in this respect as that of 'translation':

I think it [educational development] has to be research-based but I don't think it is about making other people 'educationalists'. I don't particularly favour the kind of courses which try to be so theoretical as to make everybody think and talk in educationally informed ways. Our role rather is to be 'translators', to be scholars in the research ourselves so we give to people a practical view of what the implications of those theories are. And that's a hard job, all of that.

(Respondent 17)

The net result of this discourse mismatch can be a certain frustration on the part of developers with a strong Researcher orientation and a recognition of the need to exercise a certain restraint in the use of educational research evidence when 'making inroads' into other disciplinary settings.

I can go into any department and I think, you know, I could potentially make a contribution but sometimes you can't make the contribution because people are not ready for that. You can be sitting in a meeting in the faculty and they're talking nonsense but there's no point you stepping in and saying 'Listen, you're talking nonsense here!'. You just have to say – and that's a hard thing to do because you know that they're going down the wrong path, but you know you may have to let them – to just bite your lip.

(Respondent 12)

The research undertaken within educational development units can occasionally be of a large-scale, empirical and quantitative nature when funding is available, such as the Scottish ASSHE study of changing practices within assessment (Hounsell et al. 1996) or the large-scale investigation of undergraduate learning environments being undertaken by the UK ELT project (ELT 2004). But for many individual researchers working on modest or virtually no research budgets more qualitative approaches are utilized, and defended.

There is a view isn't there, that I've come across quite a lot, that the only kind of research is scientific research – the supposition that there is an

> answer to something and all you've got to do is set out and prove it. It's actually quite towards the quantitative end. But I quite like the more postmodern approaches to research which are enabling you to listen to the story and interpret. Now it will always be a Social Sciences soft kind of approach, but it's what I'm most interested in. I'm most interested in analysis and interpretation.
>
> (Respondent 3)

There is a growing interest in the kind of research often presented by developers at seminars and conferences which emphasizes narrative and interpretive approaches:

> Yes, you know the 'Tell the story of . . .' approach, which is quite basic. I'm quite interested in the interpretive styles of research which say 'Here is the data. For example here is the tape of this interview. Now there's different ways of reading this. Let's think about what one can read in and what one can read out.' Now up the Social Science-y end of research is this whole domain. So that's the kind of research I'm interested in.
>
> (Respondent 3)

And there can be recognition of the inappropriateness and lack of explanatory power of 'faux' scientific research – quantitative research undertaken within development settings where the samples are far too small and generalizability is limited.

> I'm interested in telling stories but I'm not interested in research in teaching, learning and assessment of the kind I have seen – that I don't value – which says something like, 'Well there were eight students and they were involved in peer assessment and here are the raw scores and here's the meaning.' And you think what the hell has that to do with anything? There were eight students studying. Well! you know? If you could do it with 500 students, you might get something meaningful, in 24 institutions or whatever, but I'm not really interested in, if you like, *faux* scientific research. We can't do it for real because it doesn't work like that.
>
> (Respondent 3)

Other developers bring their Researcher orientation from their own original disciplinary background before they entered educational development, and this is often a branch of the social sciences.

> *The Interviewer: Are you a research centre as well as a development centre?*
>
> Yes, I think that's one of the complications of being a service unit. I think that without a doubt we are all involved in research in quite a deep way and there is no project I work on that I don't read the research and try to understand and try to interpret the research in terms of practice. My background is Cognitive Psychology, so I see myself as being in a very cognate discipline that really looks at how

people think and how they learn. That's my area, so I think I feel that I'm kind of locked into that.

(Respondent 12)

Another developer in a research-intensive university also considers cognitive psychology a source of more rigorous scholarship, as is, in her opinion, the educational theory derived from research in the secondary sector.

The Interviewer: Do you consider that there is a 'body of literature' on educational development that compares with that in other discipline areas? If so, do you draw on it? How do you rate it?

I'm not that inspired by what research has gone on in higher education teaching and learning. It's OK, and I will refer to it, but it doesn't kind of grab me, because it's not rigorous enough. It just tends to be by two lecturers in the university of so-and-so about a specific course and it's a bit descriptive. I go to research about adult education, generally to Cognitive Psychology, to research about teaching at secondary school level, partly because my D.Phil. is based in the Department for Educational Studies and I think there's a lot in the professional development of teachers that is quite transferable, but the depth and the theory that is there is useful. For example, for this teaching skills seminar that we just put together, I adapted a model of pedagogical content knowledge. I didn't call it that in the seminar obviously, I called it 'Preparing to Teach' but it's taking content knowledge seriously.

(Respondent 9)

Webb has commented on the powerful influence that a very small number of theoretical approaches has exerted for some considerable time in educational development communities in Commonwealth countries (Webb 1996a, 1996b). The hegemony still wielded in Commonwealth countries by action research and phenomenographic approaches emphasizing concepts of deep and surface learning, and, in the USA, by constructivist approaches, can be seen as instances of an insufficiently contested domain of theory. Dissatisfaction with this state of affairs occasionally emerged from research-led developers within this study.

We're very much strangle-held by the surface and deep paradigm which is not a very good explanatory paradigm – it doesn't tell you anything. This surface/deep thing doesn't really deal with the details of how you actually work on . . . what kinds of strategies you would use to develop thinking like multiple representation . . . integrating how you would get people to integrate ideas together into a range of something like 13 elements. It doesn't really tap into the expert/novices studies. I mean there are people in here, a few, who know about it, but not many.

(Respondent 12)

Other developers took issue with the influence exerted by cognitive psychology to the exclusion of other perspectives. This raises the interesting notion that different orientations to educational development might be predicated on different strands of the educational literature, or on other research literatures. Managerialists and Entrepreneurs, for example, seem to draw heavily on the literature of organizational change and development. Romantics are influenced very much by the literature of humanistic psychology or adult learning. Those with a Professional Competence perspective (see following section) make considerable use of the educational development literature devoted to techniques and practical tips. Reflective Practitioners, we will see, often draw on the literature associated with experiential learning and critical reflection. Those of an Interpretive-Hermeneutic orientation may employ philosophical perspectives including postmodernist and poststructuralist writing. This can lead to tensions across teams. Here, for example, a Managerialist speaks of the Researcher orientation of another colleague:

> I'm not a cognitive psychologist. I do think every area like this does need someone actually with that background, but preferably no more than one. That's about as much as you can bear! (*laughs*) I'm sorry if you're a cognitive psychologist, Ray! (*laughs*) I can unintentionally insult people and I don't mean to! But honestly there just can't be more than one of that type in your team. If you've got too many of them it just drives everybody else to despair. They have a valuable input but they tend to think that everybody else is a cognitive psychologist. It really does help that you taught a kind of normal discipline and you know how people approach that view of the world, and everybody else here comes from that background. They taught a normal discipline and they know what that was like and they did it for quite a long time. So, therefore, yes I do read the teaching and learning literature – probably actually more widely than my cognitive psychologist, despite what he thinks. I can read very fast.
>
> (Respondent 14)

This respondent's Managerialist orientation is reflected through his own preferences in the literature:

> But also I read management literature, human resource literature, organizational development literature. And I'm active in all of these areas and I write. I've written in all of the areas, although the balance would probably sit more with staff development and organizational development, than straight teaching and learning stuff. And I think we have to span those fields.
>
> (Respondent 14)

Research-led developers tend also to be dismissive of the practice of their fellow developers who, in their opinion, adopt pragmatic approaches lacking in scholarliness.

> I'm always disappointed at staff development conferences because I feel that the level of debate is low, and it's like 20 years of research went on,

> even in school education, and people just forgot it and started again. They don't even read it.
>
> (Respondent 12)

There can be similar impatience with the perceived excuse of colleagues that their priority has to be 'service'.

> I'm not trying to pretend I'm the most productive person, that I have the biggest writing or anything like that, but I would certainly write a lot more than some folk. I think you would have to search hard and long to find some publications from some folk. And that's just telling you something about the nature of the field. Now partly they would defend themselves, I'm sure, by saying that actually in their organization they're considered to be a service and they've just got to operate in that way.
>
> *The Interviewer: Gouldner's 'Cosmopolitans' and 'Locals'? Some just operate in a localized sphere?*
>
> But we've got to have a reasonable number of cosmopolitans or you can't have a field. My feeling is we haven't got enough.
>
> (Respondent 14)

But even experienced research-oriented developers admit that there are still significant areas of teaching and learning, and educational development practice, that are very much under-researched and under-theorized.

> The research is only useful up to a point. The research hasn't worked out the solutions to all sorts of problems. People talk about group working but they don't know what it means. How do you develop group working over a four-year period? What would it look like in year three as opposed to year one? What would the developmental process be? Areas like assessment – completely under-conceptualized and under-researched – feedback, and so on.
>
> (Respondent 12)

One developer voices a concern that as the research base of educational development grows against a background of RAE pressure, developers will pay less attention to getting colleagues involved in practice-based workshops:

> My big anxiety and fear is that we will end up *talking at* people and we will get them to stop doing enough practitioner work. So the real tension and, I think, the real challenge for staff involvement is as we become research-based and more expertise-orientated. More aware that we hold the hands, the cards, the information. How do we keep engaging others, bringing them into effective workshop contexts? It is a big challenge. All the kudos is going to be on us as *knowers*. I think that is a subtle and tricky issue and indeed a fascinating one because it *can* be done. It is an interesting issue.
>
> (Respondent 18)

As will become evident in the following section there is a certain tension amongst practitioners between the merits of *research-led practice* and *practice-related research*. However, for developers at the more extreme end of this orientation, those tending to work in collegial cultures and more traditional universities, the value of educational research is seen as being to dispose colleagues to take a more critical and informed perspective on key developments in higher education that are influencing their practice. Elton (1994: 24), for example, points out that there are groups of scholars all over the country 'who would not make a decision about the shape of a leaf or the derivation of a word or the author of a manuscript without painstakingly assembling the evidence' and yet are quite content to make decisions about 'admissions policy, size of universities, staff/student ratios, content of courses and similar issues, based on dubious assumptions, scrappy data and mere hunch'. Barton (1996: 6) holds similar views, recommending that 'They should adopt a questioning or critical approach in general, and particularly in relation to concepts such as "quality", standards, or academic freedom, which are part of a professional discourse whose terms are often unexamined in the debates on higher education.' Rowland (1996: 19), a practitioner in this area, envisages the function of academic staff development as being to 'bring teaching and its evaluation into a public domain which is informed by a shared commitment to teaching rather than by bureaucratic demands for accountability'. A programme of academic staff development with these aims, he suggests, 'would be more like a research forum than an instructional course on teaching methods' and would reflect 'the interdisciplinarity, negotiative and socially aware aims of the programme'.

The essential tenets of a fairly 'pure' Researcher orientation to educational development are in keeping with critical models of development based on concepts of perspective transformation (Mezirow 1981) or adult learning theory and andragogical approaches (Brookfield 1986). This orientation emphasizes 'the shortcomings of functionalist and technocratic approaches, which, on this view, have sustained hegemonic social structures – not least of an anti-feminist kind' (Gosling 1997: 214). With its discourse of transformative potential, perspective transformation, understanding, critical reason, contextualization, critique, relativities, and Habermasian notions of social transformation and emancipation (Habermas 1970), it is clearly a competing code with the Managerialist orientation. Self-evidently the direction of any development programme based on this orientation cannot be pre-specified. It cannot even presume that the programme would have any utility in terms of improving practice or achieving any organizational goals, but it might have more credibility with academic specialists in a collegial culture. Enquiry might very probably critique the institution, its strategies and policies, and it often has. In this respect it clearly runs counter to, and is capable of subverting, goal-oriented human resource management strategies for staff development. In the Researcher orientation:

> The task of the educator becomes that of encouraging adults to perceive the relative, contextual nature of previously unquestioned givens. Additionally, the educator should assist the adult to reflect on the manner in which values, beliefs and behaviours previously deemed unchallengeable can be critically analysed.
>
> (Brookfield 1986: 284)

Professional Competence

Unlike the Romantic orientation to development with its holistic conception of the practitioner, its concern for his or her well-being and need for 'sense-making', 'articulation' and 'internal argument', other developers appear to focus more on the achievement of technical and professional *competence.* In this orientation developers seek to build academics' confidence by enabling them to demonstrate achievement of a prescribed set of learning outcomes for professional practice. The emphasis lies predominantly on 'classroom' expertise, the technical aspects of practice, and competent performance in other predominantly teaching and learning-related professional settings.

> And what they're saying is 'We want a qualification'. They don't give a damn about us, initially. I mean we are the route whereby they can gain a qualification. And when we show them the materials and talk to them about the course and talk to them about how it works, and talk to them about how it's 100 per cent routed in their *practice,* and they don't have to write essays on educational theory – all they get to do is teach, think about teaching, use the literature to develop ideas for teaching better. In other words as long as we bang on about it being a totally *practice-based* course – informed by theory, but practice-based – then the enthusiasm grows, and they get quite keen, because they know it will help them in the rest of their lives.
>
> (Respondent 27)

This orientation is the approach most identified with a concern for accreditation and certification, as a means of credentialling the expertise of academics in teaching and learning and of demonstrating accountability to the learning needs and expectations of students.

> Accreditation is the real issue. Work-based learning and CPD are beginning to be taken seriously now. Then when that starts happening the pressure for accreditation will follow. But the main area where change is needed is to develop progressive and coherent systems of CPD. There is a need for professionalization at all levels. And we need much more and better-founded management development in HE.
>
> (Respondent 28)

This orientation has been particularly identified with the professional activity of 'grass-roots' national associations such as the Staff and Educational

Development Association (SEDA), which has sought to raise the profile and status of the teaching dimension of academic practice. SEDA has developed over the last decade a number of outcomes-based schemes for accreditation of higher education teachers and support staff working in higher education. SEDA is often identified with the competence-based approach, though its programmes are not narrowly predicated on the NVQ and training standards model as some of the staff development programmes devised for non-academic staff in higher education have been (for example, those approved in the UK by THETO, The Higher Education Training Organization).

> At one end of the spectrum are competence-based approaches. In New Zealand, the polytechnics have adopted an extensive list of competencies, right down to the details of using an overhead projector. But although such approaches are relatively common among Cert.Ed courses for further education lecturers, it is unusual to find competence-based programmes in higher education. The NVQ [National Vocational Qualifications] and training standard movements have not been widely adopted by the sector.
>
> (Gibbs 1996a: 22)

The SEDA programmes have prescribed objectives but also require evidence of some critical reflection and demonstration of commitment to professional underpinning values. SEDA also offers an accreditation scheme for educational developers themselves, in the form of the SEDA Fellowship, an accreditation programme for staff and educational developers offered by the Staff and Educational Development Association and examined by submission of a portfolio and by viva (SEDA 1997). A strong feature of the competence orientation is the notion that as professional life becomes more complex, more pressured and more responsive to demands for public accountability, lecturers are unable to carry out their duties effectively without specific training. This was a key point of the SEDA submission to the National Committee of Inquiry into Higher Education (SEDA 1996) and, as the following respondent's comment implies, assumes that a certain consensus has been reached concerning 'all the things we want them to do':

> Our job is to train academic staff in how to teach. In our courses we explicitly adopt and exploit to breaking point, and beyond, the Kolb cycle model of the process of learning, because it gets people into doing all the things we want them to do and because it's a model which fairly strongly implicitly underpins the SEDA model which is our current accreditation framework.
>
> (Respondent 27)

Within the Professional Competence orientation the role of theory is subjugated firmly to the role of being the handmaiden of practice.

> And it ties – it gets the theory in its place. Practice first. I guess we're eclectic, but I think that model [Kolb's experiential learning cycle] is probably the most powerful and important one for us. Because it says things about appropriate uses of theory. Because you can use theory to test and evaluate practice. And of course you can use practice to test and evaluate theory. I'm not saying theory's always right. It provides a way in which they can make useful sense of theory. It provides a way in which they can see it as tools for thinking and doing rather than as boring old stuff to be learned, and I'd rather be getting on with my teaching thank you very much.
>
> (Respondent 27)

However, such practice-related theory, it is argued, can be a strong motivator of higher education teachers.

> It also does something incredibly important does the theory, which is that it makes – er, I know what I mean, I find it difficult to say it. Academics are largely driven by their discipline and for many of them the idea that teaching is even remotely problematic is a nonsense. I mean you know it, you profess it, they learn it or they don't, they pass the exam or they don't, what's the problem? That's a caricature I've just given but it's not entirely inaccurate as a caricature. As soon as they start discovering there's theory around here their ears prick up and they think 'Oh gosh, I didn't realise there was'. And some of the basic theory about student learning in higher education is kind of rich and powerful but not terribly demanding or punishing to learn, so most disciplines can engage in it. The scientists find it incredibly woolly and the postmodern culture people find it irretrievably modern and simplistic and so on and anybody can critique it. But the idea that there is 'theory' – models, if theory's too grand a word – turns some of them on. And I like that.
>
> (Respondent 27)

Another experienced practitioner advocates getting on with the development of practical teaching skills with only a limited use of research evidence. Contrary to the Researcher orientation, which assumed the compelling nature of research evidence in the persuasion of peers, the discourse around professional competence posits a more limited role for such evidence and often constructs an identity for academic colleagues which represents them as actually not concerned with the need for persuasive research evidence, but preferring practical advice.

> The rest of the world couldn't care a damn about what the research says. They don't want to know that, other than how can they distil some messages from that. They need it in a very focused way and in a very particular way. The fact that it informs our design doesn't necessarily have to trickle through to them, or certainly doesn't have to be transmitted on to them undiluted. Because they're not particularly fussy. We mustn't give the notion that our ideas come from Mars or were washed up on the

beach in a bottle recently, but I don't think we have to get too bogged down in it other than to say to them if you want me to explain really how all that comes about, why that is so, and what all the really very substantial literature and evidence is behind this, I'll happily do that to you, but, actually, can we just accept that that is so and just get on?

(Respondent 14)

The discourse of this orientation appears to emphasize the binary between practical teaching and research, with teaching as the positive term, and practical guidance on it as more helpful. The following developer shares this priority of 'getting on with the job'. Discussing the nature and status of educational development research, she comments:

> I don't think it needs to follow research conventions for other fields myself. I think it's very often the effective practice and reflection on it that are as useful, more useful, to anybody else than the more rigorous research.
>
> *The Interviewer: Do you undertake and publish research yourself?*
>
> Yes, but I constantly feel a bit defensive of it with academics you know, that I have to keep having to justify it a bit. I feel a bit pressured. I was included in an RAE which was a 3 in Education but I don't think I'm going to contribute to the next one. I've already published about 10 things since the last one and our Reader's sniffy about all of them for one reason or another. I think we were a 3b (were we?). But he wants to go to a 3a or 4 and I know what that means. It means more rigorous reference research stuff and I don't have the time to do it, and I don't actually have the interest in doing it. I would much rather do the stuff that helps colleagues and people in other places get on with the job.
>
> (Respondent 4)

Such an approach, of course, exposes itself to the observation, perhaps criticism, from other developers that higher education teaching then comes to be viewed more as drawing on *craft knowledge*. 'I once heard a Physics professor describe himself in a development session as an expert physicist but a DIY teacher' (Respondent 34). The physicist is presumably indicating here, as perhaps many academics would, that his approach to teaching was *instrumental* and amateur, rather than professional and scholarly. It would draw on the tacit understandings and 'practical consciousness' (Giddens 1979) of peers, rather than on a research base of expert knowledge, suffused with a set of professional values, as, no doubt, would have been the case in his practice of Physics. This is by no means to diminish the value of craft knowledge – 'knowing-how' as opposed to 'knowing-that' – the importance of which is well documented (Dewey 1922; Polanyi 1983; Wenger 1998). It does suggest, however, as in traditional apprenticeship models of learning, that although competence might be achieved to an accountable standard, the practitioner might not be able to articulate a rationale for adopted practice, which Carr argues is a mark of professional practice (Carr 1999). Taylor raises further issues about professional standards:

> How can the development of these practices be distanced from other bureaucratic impositions? That is, how can these practices, including the responses academics produce, be recognised as professional rather than instrumental?
>
> (Taylor 1999: 125)

The Professional Competence orientation is frequently challenged on the grounds of its weak research base. Taylor points out the lack of 'collective conviction' in regard to agreed pedagogic values and knowledge.

> [. . .] the actual knowledge base for their creation and review tends not to have been addressed. The instructions are instrumental. They reflect the fact that just as there is no 'professional body' of academic teachers, there is also a lack of 'collective conviction' concerning the values and knowledge which should underpin academic teaching expertise, either generally or in relation to specific disciplines. How can the knowledge base which might underpin the professionalism of academic teaching be developed in those who wish to claim this as part of their academic identity?
>
> (125–6)

The association of craft knowledge with the Competence orientation is further emphasized through the latter's frequent utilization of a wide range of popular and accessible manuals on the '*How to . .*' theme, with titles such as '*53 Interesting Things to Do in Lectures*' or '*50 Tips for Tutors*'. Such texts contain practical advice and are aimed at the novice lecturer. One of the criticisms often levelled by research-oriented developers against their fellow practitioners is that the literature of educational development can too easily adopt a reductive and too generic approach, emphasizing *technique* or 'tips' for good practice.

> I'm not convinced by the higher education research in the UK.
>
> *The Interviewer: Do you draw primarily on the psychological research or cognitive psychology?*
>
> I draw on all research that I think is relevant, and I think that you need to do that, but I'm aware that there is a lot of crap in higher education to be quite honest. People are producing books by the hundreds and I can only blame myself for not writing some of it because I look at some of it and I think 'That is nonsense. It doesn't – it might be OK in practice but that's not really what it's about.' People can use these tips and they can use them wrongly because they don't really understand what's underpinning them.
>
> (Respondent 12)

One developer notes that 'there is some kind of snobbishness' regarding this matter.

> But some of it's earned as well. Some of the stuff that educational developers do is so unscholarly as to offend the people who are scholarly. It's not that it's useless but people have different objectives in mind so that's quite interesting.
>
> (Respondent 17)

The criticism often comes from those with a Researcher orientation who emphasize the need to contextualize the use of such generic techniques.

> Do you make techniques ends in themselves? How does this impact on the student experience? What's appropriate at what stage? How is this effectively going to be instantiated, in which context, to which people?
>
> (Respondent 31)

The tips, when they're done well, it is argued, can function 'as a kind of shorthand,' but 'tips and techniques grow out of a base' (Respondent 22). Academics need to know what it is about the tips that makes them potentially useful. Merely surfacing and codifying craft knowledge appears to be insufficient in itself to provide a rationale for practice. There remain unresolved issues both of instantiation and contextualization.

> The '*53 Things*'-type stuff is OK with lecturing but you have to say something about the context. There has to be some common understanding. They get misused by people who don't know how to teach them and used by people who don't know how to learn them.
>
> (Respondent 22)

Moreover, the limits of a Competence approach may lie in its incapacity to promote enhancement of existing practice or to foster innovation. 'A danger with competence-based models' suggests Gibbs (1996b: 22), 'is that you can end up with an assurance of basic competence, but perhaps limited ability to apply skills appropriately, let alone to improve or cope with new teaching situations'.

As Gosling (1997) has pointed out, a salient characteristic of the discourse employed as part of this orientation is its strong sense of obligation towards the student body as primary stakeholders in the enterprise of higher education. This could be seen from one perspective as a hard-headed awareness of student consumerism, yet one respondent speaks of feeling that he is in the 'privileged position' of 'developing between us together a new and, I think, very important profession'. Educational development has 'a moral dimension' which 'all comes down to students' entitlement to be well taught'.

> That's the well spring of all this for me. Because they still aren't being. In many places they're being very badly taught. And I hate that. It's wrong, to use an old-fashioned word. They are entitled to be well taught. It's the only degree they'll do, probably. It's a huge personal

> commitment, and now financial commitment as well. And they deserve it. And if education matters, which I believe it does, then the country needs – I mean I could go on forever – but that's the pivot for me.
>
> *The Interviewer: It's hard to argue against that.*
>
> It *is* hard to argue. Nobody argues against it. People *practise* against it. You get no arguments on it. Well, that's not true – you get some. Academics will argue bloody anything. 'My job is to profess. My responsibility stops when my mouth closes!'
>
> (Respondent 27)

With its development focus clearly on *service* to students as (perceived) major stakeholders or beneficiaries, this discourse, interestingly, can be seen almost as countering the collegial culture, seeing it as 'self-seeking':

> I have a philosophy that is that educational development is about improving the learning experience and that the learner should be driving educational development. Yes, because I think that institutions become very self-seeking.
>
> (Respondent 5)

As was discussed earlier, the Managerialist orientation can also be represented as focusing on meeting the needs of students, but usually for the different motives either of ensuring organizational survival or as a measure, perhaps, for regulating the practice of teaching staff. The Competence orientation is often associated with an advocacy of student entitlement.

> When we were developing the oral presentation we made to Dearing on teacher accreditation, I tried to work out, what's the bottom line, where does all this come from? And it came down to a simple, very short statement. 'Students have a right to be well taught'. And I could tell that went down quite well with Sir Ron because he applauded (which is often a good sign!) and I built the whole argument off that. And that was partly about finding a soundbite that would work and get us the result we wanted from Dearing. 'Students have a right to be well taught'.
>
> (Respondent 27)

The primary focus of development work should be that of ensuring the quality of the students' experience and that 'students shouldn't be short-changed' (Respondent 21). However the phrase used by a developer above in reference to the 'Kolb cycle' (a model of experiential learning) that 'it gets people into doing all the things we want them to do' might be seen by developers who do not share this orientation as corroboration of a certain reductiveness and prescription in the approach. An Australian developer takes the following view:

> While I support the accreditation of programmes of teacher training, the very words 'teacher training', and the proposed location of

> involvement within the 'probationary period' imply limitations in this approach. It is focused on 'beginning academics', while the current availability of 'probationary positions' suggests that graduates of such training will be a very small minority within any Department. As a minority, and as novices, their presence is unlikely to have other than a very marginal impact on the academic culture, or the status of teaching within it. The word 'training' implies a focus on the development of basic skills and attitudes. The SEDA requirements are consistent with this, and require engagement with a rather traditional teaching role. Thus rather than promote doubt or change, the requirements for accreditation are likely to reinforce rather traditional and superficial attitudes to teaching. Finally, the approach offers little to those who are already working as academic teachers – those whose scholarship of teaching is likely to be the most sophisticated.
>
> (Taylor 1999: 124–5)

In fact, all SEDA accreditation schemes contain a requirement for critical reflection – an activity known on occasion to 'promote doubt or change' – and evidence of commitment to a range of professional values. However, this view underlines the notion that the Professional Competence orientation is in many respects what Barnett (1994: 138) has termed a 'competing educational code' with the research-based approach. These orientations draw on radically different discourses. The language of outcomes, standards, accreditation, credit schemes, recognition, approval, professional bodies and quality assurance derive, it might be argued, from a positivist conceptual framework. Such terminology, earlier commentators have pointed out, draws on the metaphors of technical rationality. Carr and Kemmis (1986) have argued that the curriculum, for technical rationalists, is seen in terms of a basically industrial metaphor, a *delivery* system, with the teacher-worker in the education factory reduced to a form of operative. Parker (1997: 15) takes this line of thinking further:

> Knowledge of whatever kind – is seen as a commodity to be packaged, and transmitted or sold to others. The commodity metaphor supports and is reinforced by a network of other metaphors which picture knowledge as something that can be assembled and acquired in a purely linear, additive manner.

The power of such metaphors has consequences for the way in which the teaching and learning process comes to be described.

> Knowledge becomes an atomic system of epistemic building blocks which get additively combined into larger epistemic molecules. This knowledge packaging enterprise finds expression in the modularised courses which abound today, the components of which are defined and differentiated in terms of discrete sets of *learning outcomes* or competences that the delivery system works to distribute.
>
> (15)

As we know from the discourse theory of Foucault (1980) and others, discourse is a use of language which *disposes* its users to perceive matters and relationships in specific ways. Foucault asks:

> What rules permit certain statements to be made; what rules order these statements; what rules permit us to identify some statements as true and some false; what rules allow the construction of a map, model or classificatory system?
>
> (Foucault in Philp 1985: 69)

The discourse to which colleagues must resort in order to engage in discussion of pedagogic matters for purposes of teaching quality assessment, and more recently, the accreditation of teaching in higher education, is increasingly generic. Parker (1997: 17) has argued that the discourse and practice of educational inspection as presently carried out in UK schools, colleges and universities by HMI, OFSTED, the Funding Councils and QAA, is 'grounded in a technical-rationalist framework whose values are those of the bureaucracy'. The process of quality control, he argues, is 'algorithmic', depending upon 'the use of standardized procedures and even set wordings for comment and analysis'. It is this kind of tendency that many unsympathetic academics suspect might lurk within outcomes-based frameworks, not to speak of competence statements. Such an orientation, suggests Gosling (1997: 214), is attacked on the ground of all competency approaches, that it 'reduces action to "behaviour" and emphasises the capacity of the individual to control the environment to achieve specifiable ends'. The orientation also harbours an unacknowledged value dimension in that 'individual attributes of initiative and independence are prized over the achievement of collective goals' (214).

Nonetheless, it is this orientation of educational development practice that has probably achieved the most public recognition within the higher education community of the need for academic staff to engage in systematic educational development. Because of this profile it has also proved the most contested orientation, mainly in relation to issues of a scheme of national accreditation. Early recommendations for the criteria to be used by the Institute for Learning and Teaching in Higher Education (ILTHE) were attacked publicly in the higher education press by representatives of the Russell Group of elite universities for being reductive and prescriptive, and similarly by the Association of University Teachers for separating teaching and research, and for assuming that any list of competences could adequately describe the full range of actions in which a university teacher and researcher might be engaged. As one developer in a Russell Group university put it: 'I think at the time people just saw this list of competences sort of approach – in fact any kind of finite list of things you have to do – as a form of de-skilling, dumbing down. They weren't having any of that' (Respondent 21). And another commented:

> The problem with emphasizing the achievement of outcomes all the

time is that there is an assumption of a deficit model – that our colleagues don't know anything, have never been anywhere, have never done any teaching. And nowadays that is increasingly just not so.'

(Respondent 25)

As the new Higher Education Academy (HEA) opens its doors for business, replacing the ILTHE, and gets under way with its proposed new criteria for accreditation, it will be interesting to see if this particular battle will be resumed. Moreover, in the wake of the Bologna Agreement, the notion of a common set of professional standards for university teacher training across Europe becomes a distinct possibility.

Reflective Practitioner

The arguments of Taylor, Carr and Kemmis, and Parker in the previous section point to a degree of complexity within professional practice that is not easily susceptible to a direct technical-rational treatment. Many educational developers engage in the planning of initiatives or the introduction of innovations in their organizations and clearly such measures cannot be undertaken without systematic planning. Yet however meticulously they might seek to design and implement their projects, they find them influenced by unpredictable, often unique factors. The experience of respondents suggests that the process of development tends to be altogether less systematic and logically coherent than rational accounts would indicate. It is often messy, disorganized, iterative and conflicted. It involves organizational, political and ethical issues, and, inevitably, the uncertainty, anxiety, ambivalence and doubt that Taylor sees as an integral part of the process, particularly when there is no explicit system of values to guide the planning (Taylor 1999: 143–4).

Smelser (1998: 5) points out that whilst it is factors in the external environment that generate uncertainty, the feeling of ambivalence that such uncertainty causes in individuals is a matter of *internal* ambiguity. It creates what he terms '*opposing affective orientations* toward the same person, object or symbol' [author's emphasis]. In any situation of emotional attachment, such as either teaching or educational development, ambivalence invariably arises and needs to be dealt with as a condition of the individual 'moving on'. Rational assumptions and explanations of organizational behaviour such as those that underpin a competence-based approach are not always considered sufficient by some developers to deal with these kinds of professional situations. They often turn to methods of critical incident analysis or processes of critical reflection through diarizing, logging, portfolio-building and peer support to address the ambivalent and conflicted nature of professional experience.

At the other end of the spectrum are programmes based on the notion of the reflective practitioner. Here, lecturers are helped to become

> aware of what is going on in their teaching, to reflect upon this and take deliberate steps to develop. The emphasis is not on competence but on the process of becoming more competent. Extreme versions of such philosophies concentrate largely on the theories of teaching and learning, which lecturers use in reflecting upon teaching and making teaching and course design decisions.
>
> (Gibbs 1996a: 22)

Jaques (1989), also considering the issue of conflict, suggests that the process of any project design and implementation is social as well as intellectual. Practitioners should therefore allow time for the negotiation of likely conflict areas such as values conflicts or conflicts about aims. Such conflict should be accepted as a natural part of project design, and, as the project will be a dynamic process subject to constant fluctuation and change, the communication processes within it should be given close attention. This recognition of a degree of conflict in the process of project design and implementation, and the emphasis upon communication with colleagues is also reflected in Atkins' concern with wider organizational issues.

> [New] professionals need to be able to analyse the structural, economic and political factors that affect their profession and consider wider organisational issues as well as their own performance. Too narrow a focus on the individual practitioner runs the risk of disempowerment.
>
> (Atkins et al. 1993)

One of the most influential theorists in this field has been Donald Schön of the Massachusetts Institute of Technology. Schön has been influential for his concept of the 'reflective practitioner', which, he argues, is the model for how successful professionals actually 'think in action'. In *Educating the Reflective Practitioner* (1987), he points out that:

> [. . .] as we have come to see with increasing clarity over the last twenty or so years, the problems of real-world practice do not present themselves to practitioners as well-formed structures. Indeed, they tend not to present themselves as problems at all but as messy, indeterminate situations.
>
> (4)

An earlier, prevailing view of professional knowledge, or what Schön calls an 'epistemology of practice' (Schön 1983: 20) is that of technical rationality.

> Technical rationality holds that practitioners are instrumental problem-solvers who select technical means best suited to particular purposes. Rigorous professional practitioners solve well-formed instrumental problems by applying theory and technique derived from systematic, preferably scientific knowledge.
>
> (3–4)

However, Schön argues, there are occasions when a well-formed problem does not readily present itself in a situation. The question is not so much what technical means we apply to solve a specific problem, but the framing of what the problem is in the first place. This is a more complex process.

> Civil engineers, for example, know how to build roads suited to the conditions of particular sites and specifications. They draw on their knowledge of soil conditions, materials, and construction technologies to define grades, surfaces and dimensions. When they must decide what road to build, however, or whether to build it at all, their problem is not solvable by the application of technical knowledge, not even by the sophisticated techniques of decision theory.
>
> (4)

The practitioner here is faced with a perplexing and complicated mix of relevant factors which may be political, economic, environmental, topographical or ethical. And so it is with the professional practice of educational development. Many of the problems faced in the everyday work-based situations of developers are similarly ill-formed. They arise from what Schön calls 'indeterminate zones of practice' (6). The intractable nature of problems within professional practice, Schön suggests, may stem from the fact that the issues, situations or events from which they arise are characterized by any of the following features.

Complexity

Situations are often problematic in several ways at once. The problem is not easily reducible to a clear formulation. A wide range of factors – social, financial, technical, political, organizational, moral – may be involved.

Uniqueness

A problematic professional situation often presents itself as a unique case. 'Because the unique case falls outside the categories of existing theory and technique, the practitioner cannot treat it as an instrumental problem to be solved by applying one of the rules in her store of professional knowledge. The case is not "in the book". If she is to deal with it competently she must do so by a kind of improvisation, inventing and testing in the situation strategies of her own devising' (Schön 1987: 5).

Uncertainty

A practitioner may experience uncertainty because he or she has no satisfactory model of the situation to work from. 'When a problematic situation is uncertain, technical problem solving depends on the prior construction of a well-formed problem – which is not itself a technical task' (6).

Value conflict

Some professional situations are characterized by a conflict amongst values. 'In such cases, competent practitioners must not only solve technical problems by selecting the means appropriate to clear and self-consistent ends; they must also reconcile, integrate or choose among conflicting appreciations of a situation so as to construct a coherent problem worth solving' (6).

Instability

To compound matters, problematic situations are often dynamic, changing their nature even as the practitioner attempts to formulate solutions. We often hear colleagues complaining that 'the goalposts have been moved' or that they are trying to hit 'a moving target'.

These indeterminate zones of practice are not made any less complicated by the continual flow of information and proliferating mass of knowledge with which developers are faced daily in the higher education environment. The effective practitioner, therefore, must be able both to make sense of confusing professional situations and to make decisions under conditions of uncertainty.

What is paramount in this orientation to development is reflection. We learn how to make judgements about the appropriateness of action only through the process of reflection on experience. The more experience we gain and the more we have reflected upon it, the greater the repertoire of different but related experiences and judgements we have to inform our decisions. The reflective model most commonly cited by developers of this orientation is that of Kolb's (1983) experiential learning cycle:

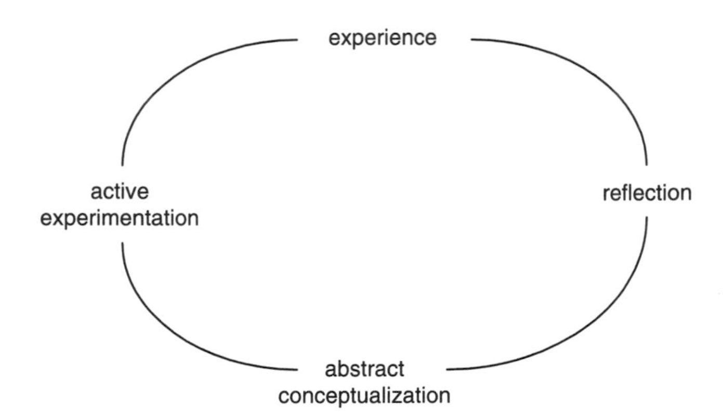

Figure 1 Kolb's experiential learning cycle

This might not be an answer but if I try to conceptualize how I develop then Kolb's cycle comes and hits me between the eyes. Because I am

> aware that I am an experiential learner. Plenty of others are I know. But quite a lot aren't. Quite a lot of people seem not to learn *primarily* from experience. Now I know that that isn't a prescription or even a healthy state of affairs. Ideally, one learns from each of the four quadrants of the cycle.
>
> (Respondent 2)

Schön's description of this process is of a 'kind of improvisation, inventing and testing in the situation strategies of [one's] own devising'. He refers to it elsewhere as 'a reflective conversation with the materials of a situation' (Schön 1987: 31). At the heart of the process is an intelligence which Schön characterizes as 'a core of artistry' (13).

> We should start not by asking how to make better use of research-based knowledge but by asking what we can learn from a careful examination of artistry, that is, the competence by which practitioners actually handle indeterminate zones of practice – however that competence may relate to technical rationality.
>
> (13)

Developers of this orientation problematize their own practice. 'When someone reflects in action,' Schön argues, 'he becomes a researcher in the practice context. He is not dependent on the categories of established theory and technique, but constructs a new theory of the unique case' (Schön 1983: 68). This process of problem setting, or problem *framing*, will inevitably be influenced by the practitioner's own personal history, by their interests, values and politics, as well as by their own role and status in their organization, and their particular specialist subject background. All these factors will affect the way in which practitioners select and name the factors within the situation to which they will attend and which they will organize.

> There are very few straightforward rules or guidelines that are of much practical help in such situations. I mean that phone there could ring right now and it could be just about anything at all. And of course we never say no. We never say 'Sorry mate, we know bugger-all about that.' We say 'Yes, of course, we'd be delighted to help you with that.' Then we put the phone down and think 'Shit! What do we do about this one? What are they after? How do we tackle this? Who knows anything about this?' In this job your learning curve is virtually vertical – all the time!
>
> (Respondent 21)

This respondent engages in critical reflection and peer consultation, where there are no firm external referents, to reach a stage of confidence in his own judgement:

> I suppose you could say the skill, the *expertise* of academic developers rests very much on their capacity to analyse the situation, make judgements about it and come to a decision concerning what will be the most appropriate action. We rarely have any firm and agreed guidelines.

We're usually in uncertain situations (every situation's more or less new, a one-off), sometimes scared stiff, and I suppose we test the *validity* of our decisions by . . . through critical reflection. You know, Schön and company, Kolb, the old reflective practice bit, and by reference to and consultation with our peers. And it's in this way, I suppose, that we become self-evaluating practitioners and learn to have confidence in our own professional judgements and values.

(Respondent 21)

The focus of development in this orientation is the individual member of staff. Developers adopting this orientation can come to feel that their practice itself is developmental for them personally.

My work in itself is profoundly developmental of me. I will discover things this afternoon about the course I've just helped to write, and put into presentation. I will discover something about the questions, hopes and fears of those who are just starting on it. And I'll discover something about the concerns of those who are helping other people through it, the mentors and so on. I will learn about my practice through my act of practice. In other words I am a reflective practitioner about my own practice. So some of my development is – my job develops me. I'm just, like, doing alternative sound-bites and headlines on it. But you get the general drift of this?

(Respondent 27)

This developer's need is to 'know how things work', to 'learn', to 'get some understanding' to 'discover'. This reflective orientation involves consultation with peers, and the 'understanding' is sought through monitoring, evaluation and triangulation.

I want a relationship with these guys. I can write courses. We can write courses. We can design courses. They're probably really quite good. I want to know how the damn things work. I want to understand what happens. And therefore I'll continue to talk to M [an academic colleague] here, and say things like, 'How's it going? What are you discovering? Give me a ring, tell me things, so I can make the next course even better. I want to learn. I want to get some papers out of this. I need to get some understanding out of this because I don't think we know much about training university teachers yet. I mean there's a lot of anecdotal stuff and a lot of practice but there's not much research. And the Centre's research is approaching that one way, and my monitoring and evaluation of what happens on the ground is approaching it another way. Because we need to triangulate all this.

(Respondent 27)

Other developers have a similar concern for evaluating their own practice:

We tried the first one, which the Dean came to, and it was uncommonly successful. We did the reflective practitioner bit. We got the feedback.

> We looked at it and then we seriously moved up stage beyond the feedback to say, 'Well the feedback was good about *that*, but we don't think that section *was* – *really* was.
>
> (Respondent 18)

And of course this orientation not only informs the individual practice of practitioners, but, reflexively, it is an approach they wish to pass on to colleagues in their development programmes, so that this can be applied within academics' own subject areas. One respondent sees 'more of a need for that on the teaching and learning side'. She has 'an interest in critical thinking' and 'how people develop critical thinking and how people make that switch, be it spontaneously or over a period of time. And that's really all to do with teaching and learning and development and so on, and I suppose it's an intrinsic interest in the subject' (Respondent 9). Others have a more formalized and explicit agenda:

> The critical reflection and research area is something personally we would be more committed to, and we do have D[member of the Unit] who has specifically responsibility for the MA, but also for what we call [name of a research group] which is a research in educational development network. And he tries to help people get published. He runs seminars of a more critical reflective kind than the more pragmatic 'How to do assessment' or 'How to lecture effectively', which we also have to do, which I suppose is more the competency sort of model. So for different purposes we use those different models.
>
> (Respondent 6)

For developers the operational approach to fostering reflective practice remains contested, and a variety of approaches appears to be in evidence.

> I think the assumption that people learn about teaching or can become critical thinkers about teaching and learning by attending courses is not a proven one and it's the subject of my research to find out how people become teachers in Higher Education. But I suppose I see our role as being one of promoting critical thinking about learning and teaching. That promotion may come about through bringing people together in seminars but I think the newsletter is going to be another way to do that. Providing forums for people to debate and discuss in supportive environments in which they can try out different things. One interesting thing which at the moment we are able to resource is providing people with the option of having somebody come along to observe one of their lectures, or a series of their lectures, and we arrange that.
>
> (Respondent 9)

However, as Gibbs (1996b: 22) reminds us, a problem with reflective practitioner models of development is that 'even basic skills can be overlooked, and you can end up with elaborate *post hoc* rationales for incompetence'. Not all developers find a comfortable accommodation between the use of competence approaches and more reflective approaches:

> I do have a tension in my own mind about how much you point out what you're doing as a reflective practitioner, and how much you hope they will pick up. Because I've seen the disadvantages of doing those things when you don't point it out. They keep asking you the question 'Well what do I do when . . .?' 'Yes, but if . . .?' and when you're actually doing it with them, and they just don't see it, and if you do point it out then it's 'Oh, common sense!' Or you're seen to be patronizing because you're actually telling them about a silly little technique that actually works, and it's obvious with hindsight to them that it works and that they could have thought of it. But they don't like it being pointed out and won't do it. And there is this gap between *knowing about* and *doing*. So going back to your earlier question about do I believe in a competence approach, well, yes, I actually do. And there's a band of competence which I think is important for all staff to be aware of at a minimum, and at least *use*. And I don't have a problem with having a mixture of an intention to require a certain competent standard and yet for it not to be all competence-based.
>
> (Respondent 16)

The tension between the two approaches expressed by this developer is discussed by Fenstermacher (1988), who questions whether Schön's ideas are intended to replace the preceding model of technical rationality or, rather, to complement it, pointing out that what Schön represents as an 'either/or' description of a situation is in reality more of a 'both/and'.

Gibbs (1996b) takes a similar view and argues that a 'balanced provision' would adopt both these approaches, 'establishing a "toolkit" of basic skills before moving on to reflect on practice'. His view is that the SEDA accreditation scheme has been able to achieve such a balanced offering 'in a way which both provides a framework for guiding and evaluating programmes, and allows considerable flexibility in underlying course philosophies'. On the basis of the testimony of respondents in this study not all developers would concur with such a view, but it remains to be seen what kind of balance will be achieved within the framework of the newly-formed Higher Education Academy (HEA) which is intended to become the main accrediting body for teachers in higher education across the UK.

Grimmett et al. (1990: 20–38) see the relation of competence and reflective practice more as a continuum of three perspectives or modes of reflection:

1) *technical* – reflection as an instrument to direct or control practice (conformity to predetermined, external standard – akin to competence)
2) *deliberative* – uses reflection to *inform* practice (considered choice among competing views of practice)
3) *dialectical* – reflection to *transform* practice

We will return to the notion of a dialectical approach in a subsequent section.

Wellington and Austin (1996) problematize the concept of reflection further, providing a sophisticated typology of five 'orientations to reflective practice': the immediate, the technical, the deliberative, the dialectic and the transpersonal (1996: 307). Their model offers interesting polarities of orientation between 'domesticating' and 'liberating' perspectives on the one hand, and between a 'systems' orientation and a 'people' orientation on the other (312). These would seem to be profitable perspectives from which to analyse orientations to educational development. A competence orientation, for example, might be more readily characterized as 'domesticating' given its concern to meet institutional and mission-directed goals, whilst a reflective approach, with its espousing of doubt and uncertainty, might be more appropriately considered a potentially emancipatory approach. These dimensions will be explored further at a later point in this analysis.

From a different standpoint, Eraut (1994) has argued that Schön takes insufficient account of the *context* of any practice. In the case of teaching, for example, the *crowdedness* of situations is often a significant factor. Moreover, he argues that in problematic situations, such as those in which developers frequently find themselves, the *time available for thinking* is one of the key determinants of the practitioner's mode of cognition.

> [. . .] professional processes like situational analysis and decision making are so strongly influenced by the time-frame and context in which they occur that they require an analysis which differentiates them according to these factors instead of assuming that some common description or theory is applicable across all contexts.
>
> (1994: 10)

He represents the pressure of available time on the reflective process in the following diagrammatic fashion.

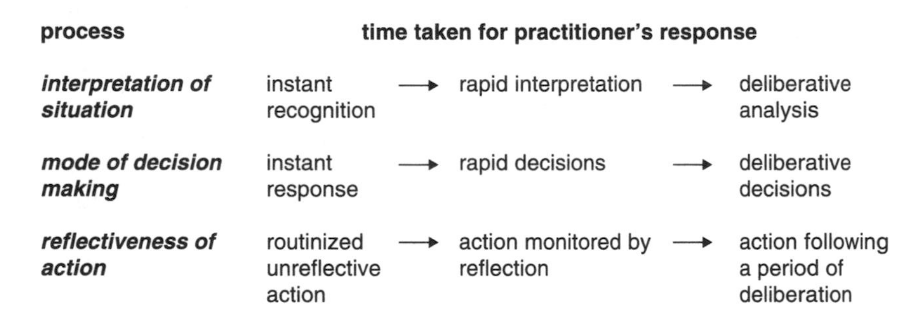

Figure 2 The effect of speed on mode cognition in three professional processes (adapted from Eraut 1994)

This concern with time pressure is reflected in the following respondent's experience. Here, emphasis is placed on the ability rapidly to 'read the situation' in development settings.

> Sometimes it's reflection-on-action and sometimes it's reflection-in-action, thinking on your feet, 'winging it' – the latter usually when you're rushed off your feet and you're not very well-prepared! Though, actually, I can think of a number of occasions when we have planned things to the *n*th degree but on the day, as an event is running, a colleague's come over to me, or I've gone to them, while the participants are busy on some task, and said 'This isn't working is it?' And there and then, 'in-action', we've rethought it, on the hoof, thinking pretty bloody rapidly, and it's usually been quite a good intervention. It's continually reading the situation isn't it? As it unfolds. Yeah. Developers need to be good at that too.
>
> (Respondent 21)

In the event, the 'sensemaking' (Weick 1995) that reflective practice requires is a demanding process for practitioners as they cope with novel situations and changes in their busy working environments. It involves a disruption of the cognitive functioning – what Taylor terms the 'autopilot' – which enables us to cope competently with routine situations, but which is usually inadequate for coping with change or uncertainty:

> As the degree of novelty increases, individuals have to pay increasing amounts of attention to that environment, and plan to act in quite deliberate ways. Cognitive functioning becomes increasingly effortful, requiring mental concentration to cope with uncertainty.
>
> (Taylor 1999: 141)

Since its appropriation by various regulatory agencies such as the QAA and the funding councils, the discourse of reflective practice has been viewed in some quarters almost as a formulaic orthodoxy of present day training programmes for new lecturers. This possibility notwithstanding, developers often report the difficulty certain colleagues experience in engaging in reflective writing. There may well be a discipline-related factor here in terms of conventions of academic writing and the differing academic identities, discourses, understandings and conceptual resources to which individual academics or disciplinary groups have access dependent on their specific academic biographies. Such identities may have a bearing on the extent to which the discourse of reflective practice appears accessible or alien to particular academics. There may well be an equity issue here meriting further enquiry.

It must be acknowledged, in concluding this section, that reflective practice is not without its critics. A number of commentators, drawing on Foucault's (1979) notion of the panopticon, see in reflective practice an operation of institutional disciplinary power. Usher and Edwards (1994: 51), for example, suggest that the imposition of external control is replaced by conformity through self-regulation.

> 'Looking into yourself' and 'finding your true self' is what humanistic psychology enables people to do and what emerges is a form of

> self-knowledge which involves self-monitoring and self-assessing, a continual self-measurement against norms apparently of one's own making [. . .] people place themselves under their own surveillance, they control themselves [. . .] by applying disciplinary techniques of confession and self-examination to themselves.

Moreover, seeing within this process characteristics of the confessional, they argue that the techniques of self-examination and confession 'do not work through oppression; people actively and almost joyously accept the "truth" about themselves' (51). In this analysis reflective practice comes to be viewed as higher education's ultimate disciplinary technique – self-regulation formalized and rendered explicit.

Smyth (1991, cited in Day 1993: 86) points out that reflection is a form of political action which is 'action-oriented and historically embedded'. It is not an internalized matter purely for the individual but, like language, is a social process, serving political interests and ideological in nature. It requires a degree of confrontation (how did I come to be like this?) and reconstruction (how might I do things differently?). In this way it becomes 'a practice which expresses our power to reconstitute social life by the way we participate in communication, decision-making and social action' (86). For this reason, Day (1993) sees reflection as 'a necessary but not sufficient condition for professional development' (83) and takes issue with Schön on this point:

> In order to move to levels of confrontation and ethical justification, reflection will need to be analytic and involve dialogue with others. Thus Schön's (1983) notion of 'reflective practice' may itself be criticised for failing to deal with the importance of the discursive, dialogical dimension of learning which can only emerge from processes of confrontation and reconstruction.
>
> (86)

Moreover, he argues, the success of a reflective approach will depend to some extent upon the culture of the organization, working better in collegial or partnership cultures 'in which power is equalised' rather than in 'adversarial interactions' (88). 'All this' he suggests, 'will not be accomplished in one meeting; nor will it be achieved without a degree of tension, even conflict!' (88). We will return to the issue of organizational culture in Section 3.

Internal Consultant

> I tend to call myself, I suppose, what I'm happiest with. I would say I'm an 'internal educational consultant', internal being *here* [the University]. When I'm outside sometimes I do external consultancies on educational things.
>
> (Respondent 12)

The focus of earlier orientations has been to the institution (Managerial), to the educational development unit itself (Political, Opportunistic), to employers or other external stakeholders (Entrepreneurial), to the discipline or community of practice (Researcher), to the individual practitioner (Romantic, Reflective Practitioner), or to the student body (Professional Competence). Certain developers see themselves operating more as internal consultants in their organizations and here the predominant operational focus is with specific departments or course teams (or groups of individuals within those departments and teams). Some units take this approach on a strategic basis, as the following respondent explains:

> There is a lot of work done and it is an increasing workload of consultancy – 'one-to-one'. There is no question in my mind that this is part of our strategy. 'One-to-one' is about one of us to a department. It is about one of us to individual members of staff. The telephone six or seven years ago rarely rang from departments asking for assistance. It now does. It rings from individual academics who want support with teaching initiatives. It rings from heads of departments who want support for teachers whose feedback has indicated that they are not performing to a level that they would like. We are asked to come in and therefore provide support consultancy to individuals. There is a lot more of this going on, and I actually think it is very healthy because it gets right down to the individual practitioner, the individual agenda, and ultimately that is the level where change takes place. So it was quite a lot of useful supported one-to-one work with departments and individuals.
>
> (Respondent 18)

Others work on a more individual basis but stress that effective internal consultancy is not a reactive process but essentially a proactive strategy of making things happen. It can be a useful means of infiltrating departments.

> Acting as a kind of consultant to departments or other groups, course teams and the like is another thing I do. But it's no use sitting in your office just waiting for the phone to ring expecting them to call you in. I mean, that does happen too, but effective consultancy usually comes about through the contacts, the networking you do. You've got to put yourself about a bit, get known, seed some interesting ideas around the place to get others interested. You have to let them know who you are, of course, and what you can do, what you can offer. Then later on they get back to you (well, sometimes!) and say 'We've been thinking about that conversation we had a while back about XYZ and we wondered if you'd be interested in helping us with it?' But you've got to make it happen. Got to drum up a bit of business. You have to be a bit *promiscuous* I suppose (*laughs*). But, strategically, that can be a really good way of getting into departments, which is important, and sometimes difficult. I mean I can think of a number of departments in this place where we've never been. Ever. And that's a pity. A lost opportunity.
>
> (Respondent 21)

Another developer emphasizes the need for credibility and for offering practical solutions.

> An educational developer has got to have good consultancy skills of being able to listen and identify the needs. But a consultant wouldn't be employed if all they do is listen. You would have to come with solutions – credible, *workable* solutions – based on experience. That may be a risk at times, but you know from working with those particular people they are prepared to take the risk.
>
> (Respondent 20)

However, this is not a question of going in telling people what to do. It is, according to the following respondent, working in a large traditional Scottish university, a much more tentative process of collaborative discussion and 'reflecting back'. The respondent takes us through his own approach. A prerequisite is being able to contextualize the issues by familiarizing himself with the department, its people, and its *modus operandi.*

> A good example is Architecture. They ring you up and they say 'Can you come in and train our tutors, who come in from practice, to be able to teach Architectural Design?' And the first thing you say is 'No, I can't do that until I see how it's – to see what you are doing. Can I come to your department? I need to really see what exactly the job is they're doing, what context they're working in. I need to be able to talk to the students. I need to be able to talk to the staff.' Then you go in there.
>
> (Respondent 12)

There is then a period of 'sensemaking' in which the consultant attempts to analyse the complexity of the learning environment and frame some understanding of it. This respondent, drawing on Lave and Wenger's (1991) concept of situated cognition, sees its 'situatedness' as important.

> Yes, it's all about situated cognition so you go in and you listen and you watch and you say very little at first. And you talk to people and you say 'Mmmh . . .' And sometimes you get a chance and you say 'Well, why don't you try that or why don't you try this?' And then some months later when you've really puzzled over this situation and tried to understand it and realized it's one of the most complex learning environments you've ever seen, where there are multiple internal representations – they're making things, they're doing things, they are working in groups, they're working individually, they're using their hands and it's creative and it's analytic – how do I understand this?
>
> (Respondent 12)

The emergent understandings are then fed back through a process of 'mirroring'. The consultant's expertise also stems from familiarity with a knowledge base of relevant research.

But you try to make something and then when you run the workshop that they've asked you to run you just feed back what's happening in their environment. You hold a mirror up and you say 'This is what is happening and this is what the research says. Is there anything there that you think you could use?' And that mirror – they see you pointing the mirror – and you're not saying (from not having seen anything) 'I think that people should be doing *this*.' They say 'Well, the students can't make any sense of site analysis.' And you say, 'Well, it's interesting you should say that. But after you did that thing on site analysis, I went round asking the students "What do you understand by site analysis?" and they seemed to be talking to me about something that seemed to mean site *description*. It wasn't really site analysis, so maybe there's a problem there in what's being communicated?'

(Respondent 12)

The Consultant developer will often incorporate a research approach, either in the form of helping establish and sustain an action research project, or, as here, in the form of evaluation research, working with students to ascertain their experience of a programme.

You have to not be judgemental. You have to kind of reflect back what's happening from their point of view and maybe that's why often a stimulus for change in this institution is an evaluation of a course. I do a lot of evaluations where I go in and I just work with the students on a kind of pyramid discussion type of procedure where I then write a report which is, say, 'Student Perceptions of Electrical Engineering'.

(Respondent 12)

He stresses, as did Respondent 20, the importance of appearing credible but not judgemental.

You discuss each point and you gauge, you ask consensus, and you've the tape recorder on as well, and you ask them if you can do that, and then you write a report. In a sense what you're doing is you're *scaffolding* their thoughts into a report. You give it back to the students. You say 'Is this OK?' And then you give it to the department. Now the department, instead of me coming in saying 'There's these problems', the *students* are saying it, and it's in their words, you know? I'm using actually *their* words. It's actually convincing because I'm using data. I'm using actually three levels of data and the individual responses of all the students which I can collate. I've got the group responses, how many people in a group raised this, then I've got the overall framework that they agreed. It can be a powerful thing if the department uses it. Or it can be something that they just decide to bury somewhere! (*laughs*).

The Interviewer: It's difficult to ignore that kind of thing?

Yes. So I mean maybe that establishes your credibility a bit because you've produced something that's useful to them. You're not being judgemental.

(Respondent 12)

However, the consultancy approach raises the issue, within organizations, of what departments *want*, and what, in others' view, they *need*. Some developers, often working in strongly collegial cultures, do not see their role as being in any way directive. As Gosling (1997) has pointed out, the model of consultant-as-expert can easily be trapped into a discourse of 'quality' which may beg many (unexamined) questions. 'We can't afford to be considered in any possible way as the police', says one developer in an ancient university. Even the notion of 'development' is seen as too intentional. 'I don't think I would use the term development. I see myself more as being here to offer support' (Respondent 25). This orientation can also represent the consultant as having some Platonic notion of truth as to what form development should take. But as Webb (1996b) has argued, the notion of development is itself problematic, suggesting that developers may harbour unexamined assumptions about the direction, purpose and goal of development. He points out the influence of 'embryo metaphors' of development as 'the idea of development as directed towards a given end and passing through a number of predetermined stages' (Webb 1996a: 64). In a number of areas concerning teaching and learning, and cognitive and moral development (such as Piaget's), educational stage theories, he points out, 'pick up the embryo metaphor of development and claim to describe progress from the simple to the complex'. Moreover, he argues:

> Stage theories do not give us a universal view of human nature, learning or morality, but instead they give us a normative view from the perspective of the author. With monotonous regularity, the highest point reached in each stage theory accords with the author's self-perception and cultural experience. The highest point of learning is usually to demonstrate intellectual control over the material world, obtained by processes synonymous with those of western science. The end point is, of necessity, the stereotyped image of the culture-free, presumably white, middle class, western, male scientist/researcher: the mirror image of the author.
>
> (65)

The main line of Webb's argument is that we need to break the connection of the idea of development from existing related modernist notions of nature, evolution, growth and progress as this link tends to 'suppress the *contestable nature of development* and make it seem inevitable and good' (64) [author's emphasis]. A developer from a large traditional university in Scotland shares Respondent 25's unease. 'Development I don't like as a term,' he says 'because – especially "staff developer" – as if *we* develop other people. I really think people don't want that. It's going into areas that we are not necessarily entitled to' (Respondent 12). A respondent from an older English university also recognizes this problem in her work:

> Development implies progress and that people need to be developed and that what we have to offer is necessarily better than what they're already doing. That's what's really offensive about it! But what's the alternative? I mean, it implies progress, which is the positive bit, but it's the assumption that you know what that progress is. Those are the connotations that I think people attach to the terms. Because there is so much diversity here. I think coming in with a model of what you think people should be doing is fatal.
>
> (Respondent 9)

However, the same respondent's unit does not consider the consultancy approach sufficiently systematic, and looks for more powerful and formalized drivers of change.

> We respond to invitations from faculties, departments and colleges to do specific things for them. We haven't been very systematic about it – we've acted like a consultancy and responded to needs and tried to differentiate between wants and needs and those sorts of invitations, but we would like to be much more systematic about it and tie it in with TQAs [Teaching Quality Assessments] and that sort of thing.
>
> (Respondent 9)

Modeller-Broker

Whilst some developers, as we have seen, are hesitant to be seen as overly directive in their relations with colleagues, others feel it is appropriate, indeed helpful, to direct colleagues to exemplars of effective teaching and learning.

> Doing work with particular people who are interested, you know, departments who are interested, and just trying to drive that forward because they've become exemplars that you can attract other people to. Doing these sorts of things – that's a deliberate strategy.
>
> (Respondent 14)

We recall our predatory Opportunist mentioned earlier, alighting 'raven-like' on shiny substances, but we note, too, that what was seized upon was then modelled for the benefit of others:

> I think it's like most things in educational development. You alight on some shiny substance, raven-like, and if it's really nice you kind of fly off with it *and show it to as many people as you think might be interested or something.*
>
> (Respondent 2) [author's emphasis]

This approach, of course, can also be undertaken indirectly, to reach a wider section of the higher education community, through publication or electronic delivery. The ASSHE Project established an electronic database of some 300 case studies of changing assessment practice in Scottish higher education, and distributed a print-based *ASSHE Inventory* (Hounsell et al. 1996) of some hundred examples, with contact addresses of the practitioners concerned. The MARBLE Project, similarly, provided an online set of exemplars of Web-based teaching and learning materials in ten different discipline areas (Price et al. 1997). Many educational development units, where funding permits, also house collections of similar practice-related material in their resource centres. Organizations such as SEDA in the UK, HERDSA in Australasia and STLHE in Canada have long provided this form of brokerage service through publications, seminars and conferences. More recently the Institute for Learning and Teaching in Higher Education (ILTHE), the Fund for the Development of Teaching and Learning (FDTL) and the Learning and Teaching Support Network (LTSN), through its national network of Subject Centres, have fulfilled this role at national level. No doubt the newly established Higher Education Academy (HEA) will continue this tradition.

As well as exploiting the use of exemplars, developers of this orientation often model their own practice directly to colleagues. The emphasis is on active involvement, rolling up the educational sleeves and getting the developmental hands dirty. 'Doing as I do', rather than 'doing as I say'.

> I think we actually are what good old Mike O'Neill [an educational developer formerly of Nottingham Trent University and well regarded within the educational development community, who died tragically in a car accident] would call the 'brown knees brigade'. That is, we put our shorts on and we get out there and we go in and we do things. That's obviously limited by how few we are, and what we can do, but we do actually go in and support and encourage and work with people. And I think it's true to say – and I don't think this is vanity – that our reputation is such that people trust us. So we can press for change on that level.
>
> (Respondent 3)

For many developers, most of whom, of course, have been mainstream teachers earlier in their careers, this is an attractive way of working:

> Actually I adore doing it. I love getting into a workshop environment with people and helping them to think about how they might develop their practice. So whatever the topic is, I love working with people in that sort of way. I like the individual consultations as well but not as much, I have to say, as working in groups.
>
> (Respondent 17)

Modelling can also be undertaken in a self-consciously *covert* fashion. A developer working in a strongly research-oriented ancient university, knowing that certain research-minded colleagues would be unlikely to attend educational development sessions on teaching and learning issues, uses events which are explicitly addressing research themes as a vehicle for modelling good *teaching* practice.

> I play the covert game in exactly the opposite way round! So, for example, we run a number of research-based training courses and are trying to extend that and I'm quite happy to do them because I can then use what I would call good practice models of teaching and delivery in those and hope that the message gets through to those that come along to those events in preference to some of the teaching events. But you use the *teaching model.*
>
> *The Interviewer: The Trojan horse!*
>
> D. [another developer] has used that phrase before and I like it and it's absolutely right!
>
> (Respondent 16)

This activist, modelling orientation places heavy emphasis on the need to be seen as a *bona-fide* teacher or academic with considerable practical experience. There is a perceived need to have credibility in the eyes of academic colleagues, to be able to 'hack it', to be seen as 'reliable'.

> I think I'm in a very special position. I've been here since 1980 and I am known across the University as somebody who does teach, and has taught. And when I worked in the Communication Unit I taught into – actually probably about 40 per cent of the University there was somewhere where I had taught. This means any grouping I go to in the University – oh, and I also was involved in the University induction – so anybody who joined this University for about a five-year period was inducted by me. Right? Which means that – you will have noticed this as we walked round the University – I can't walk anywhere without talking to people. Now once you've got that kind of thing and you've got a reputation – I think I have a reputation – of helpfulness, and hard work and, you know, being good fun, but also a bit of astuteness and advice, then people will take things from you that they wouldn't take from anywhere else.
>
> (Respondent 3)

Such intervention requires the developer to be in possession of appropriate attitudes, knowledge and interpersonal skills.

> And you've actually got to be seen to be a grafter but you've also got to be seen to be somebody who takes the job seriously and is aware, and is humane.
>
> (Respondent 3)

This kind of orientation is associated with a discourse of educational development as a form of *brokerage.* Putting those who might benefit in touch with those who have valuable practice to offer. But effective brokerage, as the following respondent emphasizes, is dependent on good *collaboration.*

I led an initiative in the University which was about teaching large groups, which I deliberately set up as a collaborative model. And I regarded what we were doing in EDS as being a brokerage. And what I did was I tried to run and manage events. We had people who were put in touch with each other and actually I could step back from it to some extent. And for example we produced a collaborative publication which was 'Here are ten things that people across the University think you can do when classes get bigger'. And it was entirely collaborative. Now obviously I led and managed it, but I was proud of that because I have a belief that you can't change the way people behave in teaching and learning if you're the only driver. You've got to be working with people. And if you don't work with people they won't do what you want to do.

(Respondent 3)

A belief in the efficacy of modelling and brokerage is seen by some experienced practitioners as ultimately a more effective operational approach than the patient development and implementation of policy.

I think probably in my first couple of years here I was a bit too confident about the value of policies and guidelines and putting them through committees and then somehow thinking that would influence people. I've become much more sceptical about those although that's not to say occasionally we don't still do that. I mean our student feedback policy was an example; we did that last year. But I think we work much more effectively by working with departments we know are active, then try to get some examples out to other people. They see that it works and then we try to bring them on board.

(Respondent 6)

The use of one's own practice as exemplar does of course bring a sense of obligation to ensure that one's current practice remains sufficiently professional and of an appropriate standard. This inevitably raises the issue of what it is that qualifies the educational developer to assume the role of development with his or her colleagues, and of the possible need for an effective scheme of accreditation.

It would be bloody hypocritical of us to be telling teachers they ought to become professionals if we carry on as bumbling amateurs in the worst sense of that term ourselves. We have to practise what we preach. We have to model good behaviour. That's where the SEDA Fellowships came from historically. There was a moment at which we had been busy rushing around recognising courses and accrediting teachers. I don't know who it was, but it cropped up in a meeting. Somebody said, 'Hang on a minute, who the hell are we?' and that's where the [SEDA] Fellowship came from.

(Respondent 27)

Interpretive-Hermeneutic

A radically different orientation of educational development practice is that associated with the philosophical tradition of hermeneutics. The hermeneutical tradition of 'understanding' (*Verstehen*) can be characterized, in its simplest form, as 'a conversational kind of process in which the interpreter learns by adjusting his or her perspective. It necessitates entry to the inner world of the thing or person to be understood – the "other" ' (Webb 1996a: 66).

Hermeneutics is the branch of knowledge concerned with attempts to interpret human activities, to reach an *understanding* of them. Its application to educational development has been most closely associated with the work of Graham Webb (Webb 1993, 1996a, 1996b). He takes issue with the 'bipolar', 'hierarchical, linear and causal' nature of much educational theorizing. He cites such hierarchical knowledge constructions as Bloom's taxonomy, or procedural linearities within staff development, such as teaching observation →diagnosis →formulation of new approach. The insights gained from the moving back and forth between part and whole that are characteristic of the hermeneutical circle allow 'a somewhat different view'.

> As learners we may be both one thing and another, constantly moving between positions. In order to gain a global understanding of a concept, we may have to reduce it to its elements, label it, take it apart, and analyse it. As we do this we learn more about the element, but also gain a new perspective on the whole concept. Alternatively we might make a single intuitive leap to a grasp of the concept as a whole, perhaps through the application of a metaphor or analogy from elsewhere. We are then better able to locate and appreciate a particular element within the overall concept
>
> (Webb 1996a: 66).

It does not matter, suggests Webb, when or where one enters a 'circle of understanding'. What is paramount is 'the subtlety of the relationship and the constant shifting of position between part and whole' (66). This kind of conceptual and emotional 'shifting' is a recurrent feature within the relationships in which educational developers engage. It is a feature of the way they translate theory into practice, and vice-versa, and of the dialogues which they enter with colleagues.

> [. . .] layers of understanding are developed which allow the detail of encounters and utterances to be interpreted with greater empathic understanding and care. The staff developer constantly interprets and re-interprets the particular and the whole. This essential insight of the hermeneutical perspective has been 'reinvented' time and again in the language, models and diagrams of educational and learning theory.
>
> (66)

Webb considers that there is no single method to follow in this approach, no applicable rules, and he warns, 'after so many years it can be disconcerting to think that one is starting from scratch, yet again.' Yet, he argues, if educational development activities are to be ' "life" based and not formulaic' then this is the necessary order of things. Educational development, within an interpretive or hermeneutic orientation is 'a dialogical activity: it is staff development by conversation'. Educational development relationships, like teaching-learning relationships, 'are conversational, and imply an authentic openness to the "other" ' (68). Webb also strongly emphasizes educational development's concern with people. 'My own experience has been that the feelings, emotions, humanity and "being" of the people involved play an important part in staff development encounters.' Staff development relationships provoke a need for those involved to understand each other better and for both parties 'to change and adjust their views' (65). This approach is reflected in the experience of certain respondents in this study.

> For me the key issue is about how educators come to judgements. The key function is the socio-cultural process by which they come to, or fail to come to, working agreements on judgements. This is not a matter of simply 'applying' pre-defined criteria and 'scientific' procedures. We need to try and understand what *shared* judgemental processes might involve – positively involve – in academic life.
>
> (Respondent 21)

This respondent argues that there needs to be 'a reconceptualization of academic practices'.

> I mean look at assessment practices. We can all troop out marking schemes and lists of grade-related criteria, credit ratings, all that stuff managers like. But we all know, as well, that, when implemented, these things are much more qualitatively derived. We need to know more about the ways in which qualitative criteria are articulated and used within communities of practice. I think we get a better understanding of these things through *intelligent conversations* here and there between interested and well-disposed colleagues. I think good educational development is more a *mutually developmental* process.
>
> (Respondent 21)

John Reynolds, in a personal communication with the author, makes a similar point that 'Multiple criteria can never be mechanically "applied" in complex real world situations' arguing that in such situations 'the interpretive and / or negotiated nature of their use is crucial, which implies intersubjectivity and shared values'. A developer in a large traditional English university also draws attention to the value of the conversational mode.

> What I like about it [working in educational development] is the permanent conversation. I suppose it's just like one long conversation with all sorts of different people. Yesterday I talked with a Professor of Crystallography. I talked with the Professor of Statistics. I talked with a young

> American woman who was an Applied Linguist and I talked with a Psychology woman who has just got a grant for studying gay fathers and it is marvellous, and I get paid for it!
>
> (Respondent 8)

These experiences are much in keeping with Webb's own involvement in educational development relationships 'which have changed and educated both parties'.

> We, the people involved, have come to a better understanding of a particular problem, mainly through a better understanding of each other. We have learned where we disagree and for what reasons. But we have also developed a unique common understanding of the problem in which persistent themes from our own lives are played out in unique situations.
>
> (68)

Webb cites Schleiermacher as the founder of a modern understanding of hermeneutics in his relation of philology to psychological understanding and his emphasis on the need for *empathy* between interpreter and author. In this respect, and in its emphasis on a holistic understanding of the interpreter, this orientation has much in common with the Romantic orientation considered earlier. The valorization of the teacher 'as a human being' also recalls Rogerian emphasis on the need for the facilitator's 'authenticity'.

> I suspect that the essence of good teaching lies in this laying bare of one's being and humanity, where content material and teaching methods are enmeshed with a person's experience of life. For good teachers, the content and method is the person, and they illuminate and enlarge the world and its possibilities in each of their students.
>
> (68)

Webb, a philosopher, considers that much modern 'qualitative' research has lost 'the human understanding origins of the tradition and become reduced to a "technical", "bracketed" or "objective" method for the management and control of human subjectivity' (69). In its emphasis also on critical reflection, self-evaluation and reconceptualization, it also has certain characteristics of the Reflective Practitioner orientation. Indeed, Webb comments that 'I would interpret both Schön and Rogers as branches on the trunk of hermeneutics' (68). However, the Interpretive-Hermeneutic orientation differs in its emphasis on what Respondent 21 termed 'a mutually developmental process'. This involves 'being more open to the experiences of others, and to re-evaluating and re-interpreting our own experiences' (66). This means reconceptualization on both sides, for developer and developed, though these terms would be anathema for Webb. In an earlier work he pointed out the challenge that a hermeneutic approach raises for educational developers:

> If you are a staff developer, try thinking about your dealings with the people you 'develop'. How do you attempt to privilege your own view of the world? What developmental notion are you pushing and is the high point of development someone just like yourself? What stages do you see people going through to become like you and how do you go about creating the recapitulation of your own progression in others? Then think that your message is wrong.
>
> (Webb 1993: 104)

This notion of the developer as 'pusher' is a disturbing one and a challenging one for the consultant-as-expert, and indeed all orientations of development. The open-endedness of this orientation, its emphasis on mutual exploration, dialogue and critique fits a collegial culture but is clearly antithetical to a managerial orientation. It also is wary of the Political orientation in its recognition of the vulnerability of the hermeneutic approach to abuse, to 'the possibility for mischief, in the hands of a staff developer with manipulative, exploitative or abusive intent' (Webb 1996a: 67). This approach also, in an anti-foundational stance much akin to that of poststructuralist critique, distances itself from a Researcher orientation in that 'not only are the foundations upon which staff development is based somewhat limited, but the very desire to secure a foundational position may be misconceived'.

> Richard Rorty (1979) has warned against 'systematic' philosophy and its attempts to provide secure foundations. He prefers to speak of philosophy as 'edifying'. By this he means that the conversation of philosophy should be an open-ended and enlightening one, rather than one possessed by the search for closure and foundational explanation.
>
> (64)

It follows from this that in the Interpretive-Hermeneutic orientation educational development has to be *contestable.*

> The embryo metaphor of development as described in evolutionary recapitulation can be seen at work in much of our ordinary thinking about the nature of education and educational development. Use of the word 'development' thus brings with it much that we could do without. In some ways it is a cursed word, and one we could be well rid of.
>
> (65)

The dialogic nature of interaction which Webb advocates is reported by a number of developers as a form of dialectic, as this respondent explains:

> So I'd say part of my conceptualisation of how I learn is phenomenological. That is, I see a direct link for me, and for some other people I know, between our experiences in the world and our sense of our own skills, qualities. It's as if a range of possible futures is developed in that dialogue almost – what's the Marxist term?

The Interviewer: Dialectic?

> Thank you! Dialectic – between what happens to you and what you learn about yourself in the process. The result of which is that although I describe what I do as largely pragmatic there's always been a kind of self-investment in it. I've not often found myself doing things I didn't want to do, or only doing them half-heartedly.
>
> (Respondent 2)

The following respondent also typifies this orientation and presents an interesting case study. He emphasizes dialectic:

> I'm not saying that X [Head of Unit] has great qualities; he's a great politician but I don't think he understands education deeply, deeply in the sense of *really*. Because to understand it deeply you have to be at the interface of theory and practice. It's not about reading the theory. What happens when you work in my job is you look at what's happening in practice and you look at the theory that people are writing, and you say, 'Well that's nonsense, it just doesn't work'. There's always a dialogue between theory and practice. There is a dialectic. Maybe some people will say you can't have practice without theory and that's probably true as well.
>
> (Respondent 12)

and dialogue:

> Its all about creating dialogue. I mean I like that word because I think all of the whole process is about creating a dialogue with staff around some of these issues but it does help if you can talk knowledgeably and you have examples and experience helps.
>
> (Respondent 12)

He is also 'open to the experiences of others':

> When you go in you have to build on where people are. You can't go in and say 'Throw out this assessment system, it's complete nonsense and use this one' because you have to start from where people are, and maybe present them [. . .] and try and recognise what it is they want to solve. But at the same time I think you're widening that a little bit by saying 'Now here's a thing you could do to solve that immediate problem'. You know, after you've worked with them a bit you might kind of present the package back to them and say 'You could solve the immediate problem just by doing that. That might have the most effect for the least effort, but maybe in the long term you might consider this, and in the even longer term you might want to consider this'.
>
> (Respondent 12)

He is also wary of managerialist imperatives, and hierarchical interventions:

The Interviewer: Does this way of working, creating dialogue, create a tension with, say, managerialist demands e.g. 'Investors in People'?

> To tell you the truth when IiP came on the agenda and it came up in our staff meeting and, you know, the issue was that we would facilitate the process in the department, I said that I didn't really want to be involved in that. I said I didn't really see that as my role and I might be perceived in ways I didn't want to be perceived in. I was quite resistant about it but I agreed, under a sort of bit of pressure, to go with it for the kind of pilots, a few departments.
>
> (Respondent 12)

But is also, in sound hermeneutic fashion, open to 're-evaluating and re-interpreting' his own experience:

> I was never really completely behind it. I mean I didn't like the imposition of the model. But I was a bit surprised actually that the departments were more receptive to it than I thought they would be, so it kind of softened my attitude a little bit about it.
>
> (Respondent 12)

There remain a number of problems with any interpretive orientation that is based on dialogue or discussion. It assumes, for its perfect operation, what Habermas (1970) has termed 'an ideal speech situation'. However, the power distribution in educational settings is rarely equal, particularly in hierarchical and managerial cultures. 'The staff developer and lecturer, the lecturer and students, are not equally empowered or equally invited into the discourse of learning, teaching and staff development' (Webb 1996a: 68). Constraints on conversationalists' capacity or opportunity to speak openly as a result of factors related to class, gender and ethnicity and to social and cultural identity are well documented. Traditional hermeneutics and humanistic psychology, suggests Webb, are inadequate to tackle these issues. Insights are required from the domain of critical hermeneutics and poststructuralist critique.

In terms of institutional implications the strength of this orientation, like the Romantic orientation, lies more in terms of its impact at local level than any wider institutional presence. In terms of its operational aspects it requires particular interpersonal skills and a high degree of communicative competence. It is essentially 'unscripted', though not unplanned, and relies on intuitive understandings and 'thinking on one's feet'. The following respondent, an experienced practitioner, using a chess analogy, interprets development positively, though as a 'strange' process. He sees the skills required in this conversational process, and in the use of dialogue and talk, as being to 'unblock', to 'open up spaces' and use resources to the maximum.

> The role certainly does involve developing people, really, but development is strange. Do you play chess? You know that 'development' in chess involves arranging your pieces so that the big pieces can use their resources to the maximum. So your bishop isn't blocked on this diagonal. So you open things up really. So I see development as 'opening up' so that people's potential could be fully realised. You haven't got this

powerful queen . . . you don't want to move really. Open spaces really. Of course the point is when you've opened it up the queen can go straight, left, all sorts of places. It just doesn't open up one single channel which is pre-determined as the queen's route. It means that the queen is able then to go in five different directions, backwards even. It's an unblocking. Yes, well not a bad analogy to . . . A lot of people are actually just blocked really, and for various reasons, and if you can open it up, open the spaces . . . It's quite a bit of individual . . . I mean, I do think it's all very eclectic and *ad hoc* I suppose. But I see quite a few individuals who just come here and they sit and they say . . .

The Interviewer: They approach you do they?

Yes. Not masses, and I'm surprised sometimes. Given that, I see that as a terrific resource really. Going to someone who hasn't got an axe to grind. But more and more people do come, and say 'I just want to talk about . . .' or 'Maybe I should just go for this research grant?'

(Respondent 8)

But the Interpretive-Hermeneutic orientation, like the others, is not without its problematic aspects. The notion of 'conversation', for example, on which Webb places so much emphasis, is complex. Jenlink and Carr (1996) distinguish between 'dialectic', 'discussion' and 'dialogic' forms of conversation as different means of promoting change. 'Dialectic', in their definition, tends to take the form of disciplinary debate about competing truth claims, and suggests a form of conversation likely to characterize Researcher orientations or Discipline-Specific orientations (see below). This form would seem too adversarial to meet Webb's criteria for hermeneutic intersubjectivity:

We believe our view of biculturalism, multiculturalism, liberalism, feminism, emancipation, class politics or post-structuralism is right and important for educational practices. We attempt to defeat alternative views by the force and rhetorical skill of our argument. Often we want to win rather than understand.

(Webb 1996a: 67–8)

'Discussion' is primarily negotiative and involves advocacy of personal values, beliefs and assumptions. It can foster consensus in educational relations where participants hold similar views but equally can emphasize divergence of views where this is not the case. It is perhaps most characteristic of the Political-Strategic orientation of educational development. 'Dialogic' conversation would seem best to capture the sense of collective conviction valorized by Webb. Taylor describes dialogic conversation as 'a community-building form of conversation, creating a conscious collective mindfulness – a collective commitment. It recognises the importance of multiple perspectives and opinions in ways that require the suspension of personal preferences and avoidance of judgements.' He relates the notion to Brookfield's (1996) use of the term 'critical conversation', and Nixon's (1996) vision of a 'learning profession'.

Some developers also are concerned that a wholehearted adoption of this approach to their work might lead to a denial of their expertise, which they see as ultimately unhelpful to their clients.

> It had been relatively unproblematic for me until I read Graham Webb's two papers in IJAD. I can't claim to have read the book yet, but I've certainly read the Reader's Digest version! *(laughs)* No, sorry Graham, I read the condensed version of it! He has reservations about the idea of development as doing things to people.
>
> *The Interviewer: A hegemonic idea?*
>
> 'We are the experts'. I think he's helped me to shift my view, a bit. I see my role now, as a developer, . . . what did I say development was before? . . . helping people, changing people? I see it more now as working *with* people, to effect change. I think it's possible to overdo the humility here. I have expertise as an educational developer and indeed as a staff developer. I'm quite good at it, as with any luck I'll prove at [name of conference]. And I run a good workshop and I'm a good consultant, and I'm very good at helping people to clarify difficulties in their area of work. I'm very good at suggesting additional new ways forward. I'm very good at not suggesting too many and drowning them. And I'm very good at helping them evaluate what progress they've made and what else might help. It's not quite semantic to say that's *working with* rather than *doing to.* I think there is a real distinction and a real issue here. But the danger with objecting to development as containing any element of doing things *to* people is that you can end up denying your own expertise if you're not careful.
>
> (Respondent 27)

This developer points out that if a colleague comes to him with an educational problem then 'I don't do them a lot of good just by sympathizing'. This might be a starting point. 'But they come to me presumably because they think I can help.' If this help is not seen to be forthcoming then 'I'm going to let them down'.

> The crucial thing is that the help I give is empowering – that I teach them to fish rather than just bunging them a sardine – so that they can solve the next one themselves. Or solve the next one themselves with less help from me than they had this time. Or if I'm really cooking, solve it themselves, come back and tell me what wonderful things they've done and help their mates to solve problems. It's not terribly coherent but, I mean, you understand?
>
> (Respondent 27)

It is interesting to attempt to locate these differing orientations within a broad social scientific framework of practice. Van Maanen (1977), drawing on Habermas (1970), outlines three fundamental conceptions of social science which underlie three distinct notions of the practical – logical-positivist, hermeneutic-phenomenological and critical-dialectical. The first of these is concerned with 'techniques, control, and with means-end criteria of efficiency and effectiveness' (209). This could be seen as underpinning the 'domesticating' tendency of Wellington and Austin (1996), mentioned earlier and accommodating orientations such as the Managerialist and Professional Competence. The hermeneutical-phenomenological tradition of social science puts much more emphasis on qualitative methodologies and is concerned less with efficiency than with 'validity, understanding and communication' (Wellington and Austin 1996: 308). This accords much more directly with the Interpretive-Hermeneutic orientation under discussion, but it is worth noting that Van Maanen's third conception of social science, the critical-dialectic, goes further in the direction of emancipation. It advocates a praxis of liberation and prioritizes questions of 'worthwhile educational ends, in self-determination, community and on the basis of justice, equality and freedom' (Van Maanen 1977: 227). Certain educational developers of an Interpretive-Hermeneutic orientation might also lean towards such a praxis of emancipation, as might certain developers of an Educational Researcher orientation.

Provocateur (Discipline-specific)

Squires (1987: 177) has argued that academics are almost always concerned with the content of what they teach, 'even if they display less concern with how they teach it and to whom, and in what circumstances, than one might wish'. The subject, or the field, of these academics is, Squires adds, 'in many ways their identity, even their life'. The final orientation to emerge from the research data is a somewhat different and more recent category, and relates to practitioners working within specific subjects or disciplines to develop practices of teaching and learning related to that discipline. These may be mainstream subject specialist lecturers who have a particular interest in the pedagogic dimension of their specialism:

> It's something that I argue very strongly that SEDA is not an organisation for staff and educational developers only, but good teachers are educational developers and we have to support them in that.
>
> (Respondent 20)

They might be mainstream educational developers who retain an interest in their former specialism:

> I've been an educational developer for fifteen years now but I'm still interested in the teaching dimension of my subject Geography. My

> Educational Development colleagues can't understand why I still get excited about things such as field trips!
>
> (Respondent 24)

Or they may be developers who have a specific managerial remit to foster discipline-specific development either within departments or at an institutional level. For example, this head of unit has a brief:

> to run a task force and I have 26 half-time seconded people. They're seconded for two or three years so they're a big substantial project. They are change agents inside the subject area. They are the spokes. I manage that project. My job really is to make more out of that than just a series of projects. They've all got individual projects which are subject-based. I'm increasingly trying to push them towards staff development inside the subject area and working together on thematic issues. They are quite a powerful group.
>
> (Respondent 17)

These 'change agents inside the subject area' operate in the manner of *agents provocateurs* within their disciplinary community of practice. This might be within a specific institution, or they may operate at a national level in large government-funded projects, or national subject centres such as those of the LTSN:

> I think what [name of national project] is about is helping to identify the problems within a subject. We help people to say 'These are the difficulties inherent in teaching Sociology. How can we use some of the identified good practice within Sociology or take ideas from elsewhere?'
>
> (Respondent 13)

Webb (1996b) has pointed out that the prevailing discourse of educational development 'especially values generalisable theory rather than context specific (subject orientated theory)'. This, he suggests, is because 'general theory empowers and better serves the interests of educational researchers and developers whereas context specific theory empowers and serves the interests of subject specialists.' Rowland (2000), long a scourge of generic theories of teaching devoid of any disciplinary context, and of teaching 'experts' whose expertise, in his opinion, lacks any coherent subject matter, advocates a discipline-based approach, but one which emphasizes social context, frameworks of values and critical scrutiny. The approach he takes in his own course might be seen to characterize the Provocateur orientation:

> On the Masters course [. . .] there have been a number of teachers who, having been introduced to a literature that raises questions about the philosophical underpinnings of their subject, have found that this radically alters the way they orient themselves to their discipline and the manner in which they teach it. The word 'philosophy' comes from the Greek meaning 'a love of wisdom'. Understood in this way, an under-

> standing of the philosophical basis of a subject should be an essential part of any higher education practice, and certainly of any enquiry into university teaching. It is a discipline that helps us to open up to critical scrutiny the assumptions and values that underlie the subject and inform the ways it is taught.
>
> (2000: 114)

Gibbs (1996b) has argued for some time now the need for educational developers to recognize the need to work more closely with departments. Though the greater part of educational development activity is still organized and delivered centrally, 'by centrally funded and managed units and staff', and though 'it is often generic rather than discipline-specific and targeted on individuals rather than on departments', nonetheless, he points out to, indeed warns, his fellow developers, that universities are organized first and foremost through their departments, which are the natural 'home' for most academics (1996b: 27). Many universities, moreover, 'give departments and disciplines considerable independence'. This situation presents developers with a potential threat and an opportunity (27).

> Recent organisational change in universities often corresponds to current management practice outside higher education by devolving responsibilities to smaller organisational units. In the USA burgeoning administration is beginning to be cut back. In the UK the 'unit of assessment' of most internal and external reviews of quality is the department, not the university. Many universities now devolve responsibility for the quality of courses, for appointment decisions, for promotions and even for staff and educational development, to departments. In Australia there is also more emphasis on department-focused development in universities such as the Queensland University of Technology. The new challenge to centrally located and funded educational development agencies is how to support educational development within academic departments. Departments are generally weak at educational development, so this organisational change offers considerable opportunities to educational developers who are prepared to change their mode of operation.
>
> (27)

Jenkins (1996), similarly, points out that the 'primary allegiance' of most staff is to their discipline. 'In my experience' he reflects, 'educational developers often fail to recognise and value staff's focus on their discipline – or see it as an obstacle to improving the quality of their teaching' (50). The central import of Jenkins' article is to advise developers that 'to have a significant impact on the broad mass of staff, educational developers should work with these discipline-based concerns' (50). He recommends a strategy that recognizes and values staff's disciplinary concerns, recognizes particular concerns of the disciplines, trusts discipline-based staff to 'develop wider concerns', helps them locate 'relevant discipline-based pedagogic literature, organisations and contacts', helps them research the teaching and learning of their discipline and helps them produce discipline-based publications and organizations (50). He also stresses the importance of helping academic colleagues to build careers in the teaching of their discipline, and warns that this transformation will be a long and difficult process.

Recent developments at national level in UK higher education have attempted to translate such views into tangible realities. The Fund for the Development of Teaching and Learning (FDTL) was established by HEFCE and DENI with £50 million pounds of support to promote and disseminate projects based on aspects of good practice recognized within specific disciplinary areas during the TQA exercise. Project funding was made available to departments gaining excellence ratings in the TQA. On 14 September 1999 the Institute for Learning and Teaching (ILTHE) published its criteria for the accreditation of courses. Like its predecessor, the Report of the Booth Committee, which emphasized 'the importance of recognising subject specific teaching contexts' (Booth 1998: 5–6), these guidelines state that:

> The programme must ensure that participants obtain sufficient knowledge of generic pedagogical issues to enable them to develop teaching and assessment strategies that are appropriate for the specific goals of the institution and the students with whom they work. The programme should also support participants *to help them engage with discipline-specific issues either within the programme or through associated work-based activities.*
>
> (ILTHE 1999: 2) [author's emphasis]

The criteria for Core Knowledge in such programmes require that 'Members of the ILTHE will be expected to have knowledge and understanding of' amongst other requirements 'the *subject material* that they will be teaching' and 'models of how students learn, *both generically and in their subject*' (7) [My italics]. More recently the Learning and Teaching Support Network (LTSN) was brought into being (modelled largely on the former CTI Centres) as 24 newly constituted national Subject Centres, designed to act as focal points for pedagogic development and the scholarship of teaching and learning.

These national drives towards discipline-specific development are described as 'more "needs-pulled" rather than "good idea-pushed" ' (Respondent 13). A developer involved in the management of one such large national project describes the new kind of practitioner becoming involved in discipline-specific development:

> They are enthusiastic teachers who run the projects but that doesn't necessarily mean that the whole culture of that department is interested in educational development. It certainly doesn't mean the subject is. So they've got quite a big job to do. They are like educational developers [. . .]

The Interviewer: Would you class them as educational developers?

I do; they wouldn't all yet. But some of them for example are going to do Associate Fellowships of SEDA because they are hoping to move into educational development, perhaps even with the label. The others of them *I* describe as educational developers but they wouldn't necessarily put their hand up for that label yet.

The Interviewer: This is potentially a big pool isn't it? Do you see this really as an expansion of the community of practice?

Well it could be. If we are successful and if we can help them to see how they could do that, they could be some of the next generation of educational developers.

(Respondent 13)

This developer is committed to the notion of discipline-specific development, but is also conscious of the need to avoid 'ghettoization':

We believe that it's really important that development is owned within the disciplines. And that's been a really important strand of [name of project]. However we also know that if you just, as it were, 'ghettoized' it, we'd lose a lot of the benefit. So we have a difficult balance between saying to the Music projects 'Yes, this is a *Music* project; it's about learning in Music' and 'Hang on a minute, a lot of those things you do with one-to-one instrumental teaching might be very similar to the stuff that people do in Art and Design by doing one-to-one studio work.' It's not making them all go generic because what would happen then is we would lose that ownership that people need. So it's not *invention* but it's innovation – taking ideas and adapting them and working with them in your own sector.

The Interviewer: Right. But transfer is . . . ?

Transfer, I think, is the name of the game. Right from day one start working with the transfer partner so that you will actually help them to invent their own version of it that will work for them.

(Respondent 13)

She describes why, in her opinion discipline-specific development might offer a more comfortable relationship with academic colleagues than conventional educational development:

The Interviewer: These people are in disciplines aren't they and that is their primary cultural identity at the moment isn't it? They are not developers, they are musicians or they're sociologists or whatever. You're an 'outsider' in that sense presumably, in terms of the discipline?

Well I think it's quite good because I don't *challenge* or take away from them their expertise in, say, Music, and very much I support and monitor. I can support because I can say well other disciplines have found this or broadly educational developers would ask these sorts of questions. But I'm not challenging the fact that they're the experts and they've been told they're excellent in Music. And in some senses it's an easier relationship than the equivalent one in an institution where the educational development unit is often seen as 'taking funds away from', or 'being in opposition to' the Music department. People seem much more comfortable, because anyway it's money that was *found*. So I don't think we sit in such opposition to the project. It comes to the crunch over our monitoring. Because if we recommend that the funding be withdrawn, we do have a real stick there, and people know it.

(Respondent 13)

She explains the philosophy of supporting academic colleagues in discipline-specific development. The notion is 'that through their *own* development they will become clearer about what work in this area needs, and then they may need to redefine *their* aims, so I would see that as all part of development' (Respondent 13). However, she regrets that the theoretical research literature needed to underpin discipline-specific development is not yet sufficiently established.

The Interviewer: What kinds of theoretical literature underpins your practices?

The first thing to say is there isn't enough of what I need. Or I can't find it. Because what I need is very specific. What I need is actually what I want the people I'm working with to write. And that is stuff about doing educational development in their disciplines. And there isn't a lot of that. Sometimes somebody will be ready to read something more theoretical about the stuff that they are practically doing on the ground but they don't know that there is a research background to it. And sometimes the literature I have to send them to read for them to try to make sense of their practice is too big a step away from where they are. It's written from a researcher's point of view. And what I want is for these people to add to the literature.

The Interviewer: Or to translate that other literature into their disciplinary context? And that's not there yet?

Not in sufficient scale. And that's where, you see, if we could get a change in the RAE this generation of people could begin to create that literature, because they're capable of it, they want to do it . . .

The Interviewer: But the system's pulling them the other way?

Yeah.

A Head of Centre also advises caution in the extent to which developers delve into the educational development research evidence when adopting a discipline-specific approach:

> As a Geographer I would talk the language of Geography, and I would expect – you know, I would just talk the language of Geography. But as an educational developer or as a faculty developer or an organisational developer I will get nowhere if I try to get other academics on board talking the language of educational development, faculty development or organisational development. They consider that I'm erecting a jargon that is unnecessary and if they come from certain sorts of disciplines we even get into all sorts of stuff about being pseudo-scientific.
>
> (Respondent 14)

This same developer, though accepting the need for a Discipline-Specific orientation, recognizes that it needs sensitive handling and 'clever wrapping':

> We're trying at the moment to see if we can possibly move what we do up from individuals to departments, departments to faculties, in that type of way.
>
> *The Interviewer: Upscaling?*
>
> The more we can do that, the better. It has to be so because you have a wider impact. But you still have to recognise the divided tradition that prevails in academia. And you have to certainly be incredibly sensitive to that. You can't just say because Physics and Chemistry are in the same Faculty, what you do for Physics, Chemistry will just say, 'Yeah! Absolutely! It's completely appropriate for us.' It may actually be, but you've got to wrap it a lot more cleverly than that, or else probably you're going to run into trouble.
>
> (Respondent 14)

However, not all developers are convinced by the notion of discipline-specific development. One respondent remains wary of the risk of 'idiosyncrasy':

> I can see the tension and the dilemma about taking the work as close to the disciplinary foundation as possible. At the end of the day I don't think anyone can object to the logic of that but I think what is crucial is how you do it. And I think recently there has been quite a lot of talk outside this institution about the inadequacy of central departments and that the stuff should be devolved down and so on. Now I fundamentally and totally disagree with that (*laughs*). Absolutely! You *cannot* have a profession based on idiosyncrasy which is what I think the real danger is. I think if you pass material out, at the end of the day the people who at the department level might know about 'teaching in Physics' might actually know more about 'teaching in Physics in Department X' than about good principles of teaching physics necessarily.
>
> (Respondent 18)

He also warns against lack of commitment and fears that a certain 'building on sand' might ensue:

> And I think there is a real sort of building on sand here. Frankly, as the literature grows and the insight's deeper I don't see disciplinary colleagues giving this, over time, a high priority. In other words, I think there is something like a web of forces here which if we are not careful will result in . . . Under the plausible argument that being close to the disciplinary foundation is important – and I agree with that – we could give away an awful lot, and I don't think it's very sensible. I know too many idiosyncratic teachers and I know how difficult it is for B. [name of colleague] to keep people tied into commitment to staff development activities. I don't think they have a high priority on that, on their own threshold either, so I would be concerned about that.
>
> (Respondent 18)

However, he is much more sanguine at the prospect of ownership and responsibility passing, not to the Department, but to 'the hands of the individual disciplinary practitioner'. Like Respondent 13, he sees this as a potentially more comfortable transaction, a 'different dichotomy':

> I think those are the risks but there are also some very positive things on the other side and one of the positive things might well be one of the things that might actually bring a new shape to the overall map. It's that in the past I felt that in the good ship staff development *we* had to fuel, we had to row, we had to put the coal in the bunker and we had to steer it. Well I think that's now going to come from accreditation and the ILTHE. I think therefore, if you imagine portfolio work, the real disciplinary reflective practitioner element is going to be much more located in the hands of the individual disciplinary practitioner. I think that actually might just help us to see that, well, these people will be rowing their own small boats anyway. You know what I mean? They have got to get that [ILTHE accreditation]. I think that, in other words the shape of the map is changing very very quickly, and strongly. Ownership will be much more easily located in the individual practitioner and I think that in a way there is a paradox also in that. Because it might take away, it actually might remove this tension between . . . and I am not sure that I have read it rightly. Does the department do it or does the centre do it? I think it is going to become a different dichotomy. It's the centre on the one hand but it's not necessarily the department on the other hand; it is the individual departmental practitioner, where the nub of this is going to lie.
>
> (Respondent 18)

He views this as the emerging dispensation and considers that it will provide a strong and positive motivational impulse.

> I know that Graham Gibbs' argument has been it is time to pass it down to the Department of Physics. Well I don't think that was ever very sensible

> because I've never felt that in a management unit that would ever happen – put a high priority on teaching and learning. But I *do* think there can be a passage down from the centre to the individual physics lecturer in physics and that is exactly what is going to happen. And for me, I just wish I was twenty years younger because that has always been my perspective on working. I never felt it was me working the head of department to get his recalcitrant staff to staff it. But with the ILTHE and the opportunity of an individual member, I mean you can't have a stronger motivational impulse, and a professional ladder to climb. Much more positive. And then you get the best of all worlds because that is rooted in disciplinary practice. It is rooted in evolving disciplinary practice. I still think by definition over the next twenty years it is likely to be the next generation of teachers where the most helpful work is done and I think that is just wonderful, it is a great position to be in where ten years ago we couldn't even envisage it. I think it is very good.
>
> (Respondent 18)

He does however point to an interesting distinction between programmes of development that are 'focused on collectives' or *functional* models and those that have an 'individualistic' focus. A functional model takes a role, such as 'course organiser' as the locus of development, as opposed to the individual practitioner.

> You target 'Directors of Studies' as an activity; you target 'Course Organisation' as an activity. You target 'Demonstrating' as an activity. And hinging things that way has meant that we have set up an institutional set of structures which have focused on *collectives*. What the whole ILTHE approach offers is *individualistic* disciplinary focus which is actually different. Now it doesn't mean that they have to be in conflict but if we are to articulate the two approaches then we need to be very, very clear that we are operating on a frame that isn't necessarily going to be the one that the individual staff member is totally motivated by.
>
> (Respondent 18)

He contemplates the likely import of such a shift for his own programme, which is currently predicated on a functionalist model.

> This has got real implications for the way we design our programmes over the next three to five years because, yes, you can use 'Course Organisation' work for portfolio work. Yes you can. But . . . we have to be very clear what model we are looking at. Are we looking at the model of the individual disciplinary practitioner . . . or are we looking at the model with the functional groupings? Which way are we going to map this? Maybe you *can* do both. What I am saying is it would be sad if by default we gave away the strengths of the present [function-based] system. On the other hand you don't want to go against the grain. I think actually it is quite a tricky thing, but it is an important one.
>
> (Respondent 18)

Other developers see discipline-specific development as a means of achieving wider penetration. 'I think it's a good idea to do it with departments as much as possible', says a developer in a new English university. 'You get to more of the people rather than just the earlier adopters or enthusiasts, and you can actually then tailor what you say to them to suit their discipline' (Respondent 4). Another sees it as important to accommodate powerful cultures and traditions, 'to try and work where people are coming from, to recognize that they've got their background, they've got their traditions and their subjects'.

> Different subjects will have different traditions and in different universities. I'm finding that particularly working with [name of project] and running workshops in other universities. Yes, I go into a number of old universities and to support projects and the culture is totally, well, from a different planet!
>
> (Respondent 20)

A developer in an ancient university sees secondment as a potentially useful strategy for engaging academic colleagues in discipline-specific development.

> I am involved in [educational] research, S. [name of colleague] is involved in research, but I also think we should foster it as we were talking earlier, to disciplines at a certain level. I think we could use more secondment. I know you've used that model and it hasn't worked too well but I'd quite like us to have more secondments. Not just the chair of ASDC [Academic Staff Development Committee], as S. is, but maybe smaller secondments of ten and twenty percent, and maybe we'll need to do a larger number of those and among those, maybe only two or three people will have an abiding interest in the subject of teaching as it relates to their discipline. Nevertheless I think it's a way of doing it.
>
> (Respondent 9)

A case is still made, however, within a discipline-specific culture, to retain a generic central function.

> *The Interviewer: Is educational development your profession – why is it a profession?*
>
> I think it should be a profession. Everyone can't specialise in everything. Someone has to do the research in pedagogy. Whilst I think discipline-specific stuff is valuable, if we lose the generic approach we lose something very valuable. If we're trying to achieve ownership within the faculties of their own initiatives and their own development, curriculum and teaching development, then our aim should be to do ourselves out of a job. But actually, there would still be a need for a centre for higher education research of some sort, even if we ceased to do the consultancy/advice work.
>
> (Respondent 9)

Finally, an alternative way forward might be that which Ference Marton has outlined – a tentative vision of a new discipline of knowledge-formation, in which academics in disciplines in all branches of learning take responsibility for the understanding and development of learning processes within their own disciplinary field (Marton 1999).

Variation

What we should keep in mind, however, is the essentially permeable nature of any categories within a typology of educational development. As was stated at the outset of this section the differing orientations we have considered can be viewed as variations on educational development practice. It is likely that most developers would be eclectic in their adoption of different orientations as they traverse the differing academic and cultural terrain of their institutions. Though it would probably be unusual for any individual developer to display characteristics of all the orientations mentioned here, it is interesting to consider how the various orientations may co-exist across the team of an Educational Development Unit as individual personnel take on specific functions. In the following account, for example, we can detect Competence, Romantic, Researcher and Enterprise orientations in the different roles described:

> We're quite clearly divided – not divided, not the right word – I think we each have quite clear functions, which is sometimes a problem when we meet together. When one person is speaking everyone else loses interest! (*laughs*) Because they've all got very specific roles. So we've got the whole supporting writing and oral language skills, which is one guy. We've got the Academic Adviser for black students, and very much involved in all the issues around multiculturalism and equal opportunities for black students. For disability we've got quite a strong Disability Unit here, and Dyslexia, and they've got very special concerns. A as I say, looks after the research side of things, tries to develop research into educational development. B is the Co-ordinator. But also another big job we've taken on which C takes all the credit for, we now run Work-based Learning for the University. And this is something that derived from his Enterprise days. It was a particular thing that he wanted to do.
> (Respondent 6)

Another developer working at a national level, describes the variety of roles she finds herself having to take as she goes about her practice:

> We also do workshops and group things and produce briefings and newsletters. I'll come to meetings and do a bit of input. I quite often have to go and talk to Pro-Vice-Chancellors and say 'This project's doing really well, can you give them a bit of a boost?' I do some problem-solving and unblocking. Sometimes because I've got the Funding Council

label on my head, if I pick up the phone to the PVC it happens and then I'm sometimes the expert in terms of educational development so if somebody's arranging a conference they would expect to get some expertise from me. Now that could be me working one-to-one on *their* conference. It could be me writing a briefing on how to run a conference. It could be me running a workshop on how to run conferences.

(Respondent 13)

Such diversity seems to be of the essence of educational development. As one practitioner points out, the complexity of the field inevitably implies variety of practice:

Personally I do not think that is problematic. I would think it personally unhealthy if there was a singular view, in any case, of what is by definition bound to be a diverse, multi-stranded, varied field. I mean there is no way that it can only be done one way. And therefore there must be differences of view that will exist in terms of that.

(Respondent 14)

As the following respondent explains, the source of the work's complexity is also the source of its fascination. But the specific mix of orientations adopted by any single practitioner is inextricably linked not just with organizational context but with personal values, beliefs and professional and academic identity.

I'm eclectic as to method. I'm quite clear about that. It almost comes back to my personal values about why I'm in educational development. And that's about a strong personal belief that people are wonderful resources but they're often constrained and aren't able to . . . so it's partly a personal belief about fulfilment, but a belief that people can be much more effective. I mean that's the 'staff developer' bit of me. But educational development isn't just about training for skills it's about unlocking people to be able to achieve what they want to. But there's also the political thing which is I believe in widening participation and in higher education for all and if I believe in that I'm also aware of my responsibilities to make the system *work* at that. So I am genuinely drawn to educational development for all those reasons. I think they all influence the way I work, and more so in being a national co-ordinator than in anything else I've done I have to work on all those standards at once. I *can't* leave the political; I *can't*, you know, just see myself as a developer of people. I have to do all of them.

(Respondent 13)

The same developer speaks of the skills required when developers work at a national level.

Well it is more of the political skills. More of the interpersonal skills and more of the understanding. Because you have to very quickly learn the politics of the institution you're going into, of the subjects that you're working with, and of the particular project team that you didn't create, somebody else did. But you have to be able to read all those agendas, as well as the stuff that's on paper, which is this project is to do *this* for these things for *that.* That *that's* the remit. But if somebody can't work with the national agendas, the institutional agendas, the subject's agenda and then the team's agenda they can't [. . .]

The Interviewer: They'll rub them up the wrong way?

Yes. And that's why I think it's a fascinating job. But I think it's quite a complex job.

(Respondent 13)

2

Stances on Change

One significantly defining attribute of educational development practice is the practitioner's stance in regard to change. Though developers seem to be a fragmented tribe, dwelling in many neighbourhoods of a divided village, one feature which the great majority would appear to have in common is an identification with the notion of change. As noted earlier, some developers are uncomfortable with being seen in any way to predetermine the direction of development. Yet all recognize that a process of change must be negotiated in some fashion, some form of engagement entered into and supported, if the developer's role is not to be superfluous. Such engagement may well lead both parties into a state of what Meyer and Land (2004) have termed 'liminality', a transformative state that engages existing certainties and renders them problematic, and fluid. In this way change through educational development might be seen as a form of 'troublesome knowledge' (Meyer and Land 2003) that can be unsettling, entailing a sense of loss, a stripping away of an older professional or academic identity and the reconstitution of a new one.

> the transformation can be protracted, over considerable periods of time, and involve *oscillation* between states, often with temporary regression to earlier status. [. . .] It would appear too that within liminal states the new status [. . .] is anticipated simultaneously both with desire and apprehension. It would appear however, that once the state of liminality is entered, though there may be temporary regression, there can be no ultimate full return to the pre-liminal state.
>
> (Meyer and Land 2004: in press)

Liminality may become a suspended state, however, in which understanding, or the performances of understanding, can approximate to a kind of mimicry. Cousin (2004), for example, in discussing the dynamic between pedagogy and technology, argues that the invoking of an earlier pedagogic regime within a new technological environment is often an attempt to give academics reassurances of stability and continuity.

> A further indication of the ontological dimension to our *being-with* technology is that the declining use of any media which have played a part in our identity formation is understandably experienced as loss. For some this loss prompts a Luddite yearning for the apparent safety of the past. Consciously or not, are higher education e-learning strategies plugging into this yearning? Does the insistence that pedagogy is running the show calm fears that headstrong learning technologists might dethrone the thoughtful, bibliophilic academic? Another possible way of reassuring academic colleagues that the past is intact lies in the reference to technology as an 'enhancement tool'. Here the attempt is to avert any possible protest about C&IT usage with the compliment that it will only make better what is already good. It won't alter the status quo; it will simply dress it in finer clothes [. . .]
>
> (Cousin 2004: in press)

As Cousin argues, however, this is a false promise, which 'creates an unexamined friction between past and future and, in consequence, inhibits a debate about the losses and the hopes held out by learning technology'. The seeming continuity of the earlier pedagogical system, of course, also promises to retain the original power relations contained within it, leading perhaps to the phenomenon of 'change without change'. In this way, as Elton has remarked (perhaps not entirely in jest), the pedagogy of higher education has changed little since the teaching, learning and assessment regime that would have been familiar to Abelard. Elton argues elsewhere that for the educational developer both iconoclasm and innovation have to be seen as 'parts of a common strategy' (Elton 1998a: 2). He sees the developer's negotiation of change within a culture as considerably more difficult than that faced by the original religious iconoclasts as the latter, through their destructive actions, had destroyed the original images of the preceding culture, and were replacing an earlier practice with new worship, involving no new icons. For these change agents 'the effect was immediate and the power was all with the iconoclasts':

> The task of educational innovators is very different. They want to achieve over a considerable period of time significant change in a well established system in which most of the power continues to reside with the forces of tradition. Perhaps educational innovators should follow Jesus rather than Cromwell: 'Be ye therefore wise as serpents, and harmless as doves' (St Matthew x.16), possibly with an added touch of Machiavelli. And this is where an understanding of change processes comes in.
>
> (Elton 1998a: 2–3)

Educational developers, unlike, perhaps, other professional groups within higher education, have no vested interest in maintaining the status quo. As we have seen in the analysis of other complex concepts, such as orientation to educational development and, in the section that follows, understandings of organizational culture, attempts at definition inevitably lead to understandings that are multi-faceted, inter-related, overlapping and dynamic. It is not surprising therefore to find that developers' stances on change are equally variegated and complex. This section will attempt to assess the relative explanatory power of different change theories for developers. The uses of discourse and power in environments of educational change, of course, provide keys to the ways in which the subjectivity of educational developers might be constructed, and reconstructed.

'And who are you, anyway?' – change and perceived resistance

One particular way in which the identity of developers might be constructed is through polarization with a resisting 'other'. This is not to deny that academics, like many professionals, when faced with change to established practice might exhibit tendencies of a 'defended subject'. Consider, for example, the following lecturer's account of attending an educational development induction workshop.

> We've all taught before, of course. Most of us have been doing this work as part of making ends meet for some considerable time. And then you come along to tell us, with apparently no sense of irony, how to 'get started.' And who are you anyway? You have an academic title. You tell me something of your background. You say that you are, or were, an '. . . ologist', of sorts. But in telling us who you were you tell us nothing of who you are now. You have moved into this area because it is important. You are here because most of the time we academics do this important work badly. We bristle. We recognise our colleagues, if not ourselves. A string of new acronyms follows – ILTHE, NLP, LTSN, QAA . . . and our eyes glaze over.
>
> (Ashworth et al. in press)

However, particular attention needs to be given within the development community to the notion of 'resistance' to change, which has long been a matter of concern to education developers involved in policy implementation. How, and by whom, does 'resistance' come to be identified, located and represented? And how are strategies devised to 'overcome' such perceived resistance? Issues of how change and resistance come to be represented need to be problematized in terms of these discursive understandings. There is an accompanying need to deconstruct (in the loose sense) notions of resistance, in the hope of reframing such problematic situations in ways that may allow more movement or productive collaboration with colleagues. This is a point emphasized by Taylor (1999: 8):

> Loss is seldom mentioned by those who comment on the issue of change. Resistance is, and it is to be overcome. Anxiety is, but less frequently, and it invites reassurance. Uncertainty is also discussed, and

> here the usual response involves calls for vision and leadership – calls that may deny any experience of loss. Actions of resistance, expressions of uncertainty, questioning of visions of certainty – all these tend to be seen as obstructionist by those who write about change in higher education, and, in my experience, those who see themselves, or are employed as, agents for the achievement of that change. For example, staff who promote the use of the new technologies tend to be dismissive of those who exhibit such behaviour. The literature tends to provide mutually exclusive discourses – a binary formulation of pro- or anti- any focus for change.

This capacity of developers to construct an identity of 'otherness' for certain colleagues, characterizing them as resisters or obstructers, is a non-trivial issue. The strategies that both developers and academics adopt to cope with the complexity of change and uncertainty in higher education include 'assumption-based reasoning, weighing pros and cons of alternative action, or simply suppressing uncertainty (through tactics like denial or rationalisation)' (142). Decision-making in these contexts, suggests Taylor, becomes 'a reasoned but non-rational process' (142). There is an affective dimension here, in that 'cognitive functioning is not "cold" ' and this framework of beliefs and understanding is less open to change than rational ideas. Such disjunction in cognitive functioning disrupts what Taylor calls 'autopilots', the routine or habituated coping strategies which academics routinely use to cope with their working environments. This may well explain the developmental 'plateau' that many developers identify in more experienced, mid-career colleagues and which is often interpreted as resistance to change or indifference.

> Autopilots tend to be governed by purposeful beliefs, rather than the totality of our knowledge. The meaning of events includes their perceived emotional consequences – good, bad or indifferent. Thus, restructuring involves more than rational processes.
>
> (140)

The sources of such perceived indifference might well be explicable in terms of the resilient recurrent practices which Bourdieu (1977: 78) has termed 'habitus'. Hayles (1999) refers to such habituated responses as 'regulated improvisations', and sees them as 'durably installed'. Alternatively, such practices might constitute behaviours that are installed within the activity systems described by Engestrom (1991), and may be linked through such activities to strong cultural or professional identities.

It is tempting to speculate too that the characterization of the resisting 'other' is a necessary part of the identity construction and identity maintenance of developers who wish, for the benefit of their own longer-term professional career trajectories, to associate themselves with discursive stances on change. Alvesson (2002: 184), discussing managers who wish to be seen as change agents in organizations, draws attention to the problem of 'fashionability and the symbolism of appearing dynamic and change-oriented'. He cites Giesen and Schmid (1989: 80–81), who suggest that:

> The institutional premium is on new ideas, new perspectives, new definitions of catastrophe, new promises of salvation. Attention and consideration are not given to the glance backward at continuity-preserving traditions or to the contemplation of unifying dogmas, but to the hectic production of cultural goods.

Jackall (1988) goes further and points up the issue of self-interest in this affiliation with novelty at the expense of seeing things through, and fully implementing an earlier development:

> A choice between securing one's own success by jumping on and off the bandwagon of the moment, or sacrificing oneself for the long-run good of a corporation by diverting resources and really seeing a program through is, for most managers, no choice at all. Ambitious managers see self-sacrificing loyalty to a company as foolhardy.
>
> (1988: 143, cited in Alvesson 2002: 184)

Whether comparisons with educational developers in this respect would be fair is open to debate. As with many areas of practice there is most probably, amongst developers, considerable variation in terms of this self-alignment with the new. It might be that we would find another instance of the polarization between what Gouldner (1979) has termed 'cosmopolitans' and 'locals' within the community of practice. Cosmopolitans tend to be the more entrepreneurial academics whose status (often derived from publishing or a reputation outside the institution) allows them a privileged role within the organization, whilst the less privileged, more managed and put upon 'locals' mind the academic shop and keep things running efficiently. In regard to developers and change we might characterize the cosmopolitans as identifying more with quick fixes, with fashionably novel practice and the raising of its profile, whilst the locals exhibit the 'stamina', 'skills, persistence and enthusiasm' needed to effect the more problematic goal of longer-term cultural change. Alvesson (2002: 185), discussing managers who push through new ideas and then move on in the pursuit of reputation and career without seeing the changes through, identifies what he sees as 'a fascinating paradox: the great value placed on novelty and change undermines the chances of actually accomplishing significant change'.

Notwithstanding these provisos we need to consider how best to analyse change in terms of how it is framed and re-framed (that is, re-presented) by both academics and developers. We might do this by considering the different 'stances' on change that seem to be adopted, or which seem to inform the differing orientations to educational development practice that we considered earlier. These stances are predicated on accompanying discourses and frameworks of beliefs and understandings. They are realized through the practice of developers. The ways in which meaning is managed, made sense of or resisted in the light of these discourses is considered below in terms of developers' own practice and experience and this is linked back to the orientations of developers discussed in Section 1. The issue of whether change *can* actually be managed will be discussed and due recognition given to the point made by Trowler, Saunders and Knight (2003) that in all these stances we should remain aware that change begets change and complicates its own process.

Diffusion stances

The classical tradition of research into change and innovation views the development of innovations as a process of *diffusion*. The work of Rogers (1967) is representative of this approach. Diffusion is seen as occurring between individuals, even though the innovations take place in a geographical and social field, which has a bearing on the nature of the diffusion.

> Diffusion is seen as dependent on geographical communications, on information through social contacts, and individual acceptance occurs through imitation or through some process of intellectual conviction. Research of this kind is rooted in ethnological research on innovation diffusion in ancient times and within primitive cultures. It was carried over to research on the diffusion of industrial products in modern societies.
>
> (Berg and Östergren 1979: 262)

Another perspective on diffusion is Havelock's (1973) 'stepping stones' strategy. The following respondent self-consciously models his practice of innovation on this view, and provides a simple account of its operation:

> I don't think I'd look at it that way. I don't know if you've come across the 'stepping stones' strategy for introducing change? It's by a guy called Havelock, and he's an American author. He wrote something like *A Change Agent's Guide to Innovation in Education*, some years back now. It was quite a simple idea, and it's something that almost instinctively one tends to do. Do you want to bring about a change? First of all you contact the people you know are already on board with it, and you work with them in order to approach the people that you think are potential converts.
>
> (Respondent 2)

Respondent 14 describes 'Doing work with particular people who are interested. You know, departments who are interested, and just trying to drive that forward because they've become exemplars that you can attract other people to. And doing these sorts of things – that's a deliberate strategy.' Respondent 18 reflects that 'I suppose it is a kind of accumulative osmosis'. Respondent 7, similarly, trusts to 'good contacts' and 'personal contact':

> I know how I operate, and it's that I believe the only way that we can be successful is by personal contact. Which means that you work with people who want to work with you. You hope that they will tell other people and in that way that it will spread. And that takes a number of years. And we've made a substantial number of good contacts this way. The alternative is that we announce what we are capable of doing. What we have done and so on and spread it through the Web, through newsletters and so on, and our Director is more inclined towards that. I don't believe people take sufficient interest to actually do anything to change as a result of reading something. So I very much believe that the personal contact is in fact the only way that we can make progress.
>
> (Respondent 7)

The ACORN approach (Hawkins and Winter 1997), which was developed from the experience of the 66 UK higher education institutions that were engaged in EHE projects, is also a diffusion stance, a prescriptive view which places much greater emphasis on the proactive and strategic characteristics of the change agent. The acronym stands for Action, Communication, Ownership, Reflection and Nurture, and the model stresses the characteristics of the successful change agent. These are listed as:

1. has a sense of purpose
2. has the capability to act
3. sells success
4. is strategically connected
5. is critically reflective
6. builds supportive structures
7. is opportunistic

We can see a similar notion reflected in the approach of the following respondent.

> I think it helps to do things like identifying champions or nurturing champions, thinking about incremental change and embedding that, bringing others along. I think about involving key influences. Sometimes, you know, the 'not-invented-here', the champion-from-outwith-the-institution person. I think that there's a range of tactics you might want to think about depending on the given change and what would be the most effective way to manage that and the strategic change environment.
>
> (Respondent 10)

Respondent 6, operating on a similar basis, says 'I think we work much more effectively by working with departments we know are active, then try to get some examples out to other people. They see that it works and then we try to bring them on board.' The diffusion approach would be a strategy particularly favoured by developers of a Modeller-Broker or Entrepreneurial orientation. It also would seem to be a major strategy deployed by developers of a Discipline-specific orientation, particularly those working within LTSN Subject Centres or FDTL projects.

Systemic stances

An early and influential contributor to theories of organizational change was Lewin (1952), who posited the notion of a *force field* operating in a social system, and emphasized the need when contemplating organizational change to consider not just the forces at the point of change, that is the destabilizing forces for change, but as far as is possible all the forces operating in the system.

> [. . .] the system had been stable before the change, and any stable system which is disturbed in the first place tries to return to its former stability. The result is that the forces which previously ensured the stability of the system will now act so as to re-establish that stability, i.e. they will oppose the change.
>
> (Elton 1998b: 1)

As the reactive (stabilizing) forces oppose the original force for change this can mean that the pressure for change produces unintended effects quite dissimilar from those envisaged.

> Social systems frequently respond to change by creating secondary effects which may act so as to reduce or even negate the effectiveness of the primary effect. Even worse, the primary effects may act in the opposite way to that intended.
>
> (1)

This tendency was noted by Tutt (1985) and has come to be known as Tutt's law or the 'law of unintended consequences'. Tutt states that 'Social systems frequently respond to change in the opposite way to that intended by those who initiated the change' (1985: 34). The important implication of Lewin's and Tutt's theories for educational developers is that there is, as Elton has pointed out, a continuously changing balance between the forces which support the change and those which are perceived as resisting it. Educational developers need to concentrate as much on the barriers to innovation as on the forces supporting it.

> As the drivers of change invariably have more control over the supporting than over the opposing forces, they tend to increase the former with the inevitable consequence of the latter also increasing, which is usually a recipe for disaster. The alternative strategy, which involves the drivers of change attempting to reduce the opposing forces, over which they generally have little or no control, may be a difficult one to pursue, but it is the only one which is likely to lead to success. It certainly requires patience and time [. . .]
>
> (Elton 1998b: 2)

We recall that one respondent, with a Discipline-specific orientation, seemed to characterize Lewin's notion of force field analysis when she spoke of performing an 'unblocking' role to release space for potential innovatory practice:

> I do some problem-solving and unblocking. Sometimes because I've got the Funding Council label on my head, if I pick up the phone to the PVC it happens.
>
> (Respondent 13)

Another exemplifies the stance explicitly when he says:

> I think a lot of it is about identifying what barriers there are around in the system that're getting in the way of changes – positive changes – that need to be happening. And that's not always easy because there are so many conflicting forces pushing things this way and that. But it's often more effective to try and remove barriers if you can identify and locate them than just banging on trying to change things and hitting a brick wall all the time. It's that notion of a force field with change forces and resistance forces all held in check, in a balance, an equilibrium, and if you move away certain of the resisting forces then you don't have to keep driving the change. It will just flow, it will free things up. De-constipate it! (*laughs*)
>
> (Respondent 21)

So the innovation process, according to Lewin's theory, is a *political* process, taking place in a field of mutually opposing forces around an equilibrium, and has to be appreciated in the light of the state of the field as a whole. The main phases of the innovation process are *unfreezing, moving* and *refreezing*. 'Unfreezing', explain Berg and Östergren (1979: 267), 'signifies that the possibility for change is created. Moving denotes a continuous disequilibrium, caused by the dominance of the driving forces over the restraining forces. Refreezing means that balance is created around a new equilibrium.' This perspective has obvious implications for the *modus operandi* of developers of a Political-Strategic orientation, though, as we will see below, not all developers feel that in an age of increasing complexity equilibrium, or stability, can ever be fully regained. Perhaps the most that can be hoped for is what Bonamy et al. (2001) have termed 'provisional stabilities'.

A key question for developers is the extent to which change can actually be managed in complex organizations. Elton (1998b) points out that organizational change has to be considered strategically as a *systemic* phenomenon, but also that *as* systems, higher education institutions tend to be very different from each other. The following respondent endorses this view of tackling organizational change systemically:

> You've got to be capable of systems thinking and of working in the political domain. I think one of the things that educational developers have to get good at is *creating the context in which change is possible*, and you

need these qualities to be able to do that. I think educational developers should pay more attention to creating the context of change rather than just 'getting on with the change'.

(Respondent 28)

An alternative view has developed which considers change not merely *within* a system but also *of* a social system (Berg and Östergren 1979: 262). In this approach 'there is a greater emphasis on the behaviour of groups and organizations and on interaction within and between groups.' The approach can be described as 'a combination of a systems approach and a contingency approach' (262). Danforth Ross distinguishes between *paradigmatic* and *extraparadigmatic* innovation systems (cited in Berg and Östergren 1979: 262). Berg and Östergren's model is of the latter type, though they prefer to distinguish between *system-consistent* and *system-divergent* innovations.

Our terminology is designed to emphasise that the innovation process is either consistent with or divergent from the main characteristics of the system. In the former case the process is one of dissemination, and in the latter of a political battle.

(262)

Berg and Östergren reject the efficacy of power-coercive strategies in educational settings because 'to produce new knowledge or transmit it to students is itself a creative activity at the heart of the system and closely depending on its main properties. Such innovations cannot be inserted from outside: they have to be created anew within the system, by those who are members of it' (262). The question is, if, as we have seen, any system has a tendency to resist change, how can systemic change ever occur?

How can we understand that system-divergent innovations do occur? The answer is that few systems are completely homogeneous. There may be – and this is a precondition for change – lack of concordance, for instance in membership interests or ideology. This lack of conformity gives rise to 'cracks' or conflicts in the system, and these in turn constitute a further precondition for change. Change also presupposes that the system is open, i.e. that it has contacts with its environment. One could put it that such contacts allow impulses from the outside to flow into the 'cracks' in the system and to break the system by creating a potential for moving.

(264–5)

This too is a perspective favoured by developers of an Opportunistic or Entrepreneurial orientation. Respondent 21, discussing working within an 'ambiguity' culture, comments that 'There are opportunities. *Gaps open up.* People's eye goes off the ball and things can happen.' Respondent 10, similarly, reports that 'Other changes happen because there's various influences on a system.' We recall from Section 1 also the developer who used a chess analogy to describe development as 'opening up':

> So you open things up really. So I see development as 'opening up' so that people's potential could be fully realised. You haven't got this powerful queen . . . you don't want to move really. Open spaces really. Of course the point is when you've opened it up the queen can go straight, left all sorts of places. It just doesn't open up one single channel which is pre-determined as the queen's route. It means that the queen is able then to go in five different directions, backwards even. It's an unblocking. Yes, well not a bad analogy to . . . A lot of people are actually just blocked really, and for various reasons, and if you can open it up, open the spaces.
>
> (Respondent 8)

Rationality stances

Another respondent also mentions a 'balance of forces' within an organizational perspective, but at the same time this developer introduces the notion of *rationality* as a mechanism for change in higher education. He speaks of colleagues 'coming on board' because 'they will see the logic' of 'a compelling idea'.

> A lot of the job is really about changing attitudes and conceptions and in that sense we are being proactive. I think we should be focussing on changing attitudes, the attitude that students are at fault when they don't learn. We have to switch to organisational development, balance of forces and, I think, the power of ideas as a change mechanism. I think that that's the thing that is critical to the development process – that academics will respond to the power of ideas. Sometimes their attitudes will make them not respond but if you can really marshal together a compelling idea then people will find it hard to (and some of them may still resist it) but people will come on board because they will see the logic of it. I mean they haven't spent their whole life trying to understand these things – so as long as they've got a modicum of the attitudes.
>
> (Respondent 12)

Respondent 12's view is in keeping with influential perspectives originally proposed by Benne and Chin (1969). They suggested three 'general strategies for effecting changes in human systems' which were an empirical-rational strategy predicated on reason, a normative re-educative strategy based on motivation, learning and positive affective factors, and a power-coercive strategy utilizing power relations. In the empirical-rational strategy the underlying assumption is that people are reasonable and, given sufficient understanding of a situation, will act in a rational fashion. Hence the primary task of the innovator is to demonstrate through the best known method the validity of a certain change in terms of increased benefit. This can be seen to accord well with Educational Researcher and Consultant orientations to educational development. Of course the success of this approach depends on the extent to which colleagues *will* respond rationally.

Motivational stances

Whereas Respondent 12's perspective was very much in line with the empirical-rational perspective the following respondent can be seen to be working within a 'normative-re-educative' framework (Benne and Chin 1969) in which the motivation and conviction of colleagues is seen as crucial to organizational change.

> I don't feel those sort of [managerial] pressures. Well, they're probably there but I don't feel them. No, fortunately, either you are working with people who want to bring about the changes themselves, for whatever reasons – there are not many ostriches we have to work with. I know we ought to reach them but my feeling is, given that there's two of us in the Unit, and life is short, it's better to help the people who want the change, than to go in with a rigid preconception of what and where they should be going. It doesn't work.
>
> (Respondent 1)

This respondent, with a background in Nursing, introduces a biological distinction between growth and development, but points out that, as an educational developer she can only establish a *context* in which development can occur:

> Growth is an increase in size. Development is a change in function. Ah! That is actually true, biologically speaking. Change in function.
>
> *The Interviewer: Would that apply to higher education?*
>
> Yes course it would. As well as the growth of the present methods we use. But I can't do that. I can provide opportunities for that to occur. But it's the individual who [. . .] I can provide opportunities for people to develop. They can only develop themselves. You can't change someone. They can only change themselves. You can point out areas where they might want to explore, and having explored will decide to see things differently, but I cannot make that decision for them.
>
> (Respondent 1)

Of central importance within a normative-re-educative approach is how the client understands his or her problem. With this strategy the change agent works with the client to discover the client's attitudes, values and opinions. The change agent seeks to avoid manipulating the client by bringing the values of the client, along with his or her own values, into the open and by working through value conflict responsibly. The motivational approach appears to have the greatest correspondence with Romantic and Reflective Practitioner orientations. 'There's an important distinction between *imposed change* and *self-identified change*', suggests an experienced developer working at national level.

> The reactions to these two different kinds of change are quite different. People always see imposed change as something to be resisted but change that they have identified and chosen for themselves they get interested in and are keen on.
>
> *The Interviewer: It's to do with motivation?*
>
> Yes. I quite like the model of change put forward by Hersey and Blanchard [1988], basically saying that if change is imposed then it's perceived as being that you've got to do something differently, i.e it's about behaviour. But they point out that change is concerned with knowledge and understanding and attitude. You have to try working from both directions. It's the old idea of working *with* people, not working *on* people.
>
> (Respondent 28)

Power stances

The motivational approach may seem to have an effect on hearts and minds, but the timescale involved may be unacceptably long. A power-coercive strategy, on the other hand, seems, not surprisingly, to be adopted more by those of a Political orientation:

> And you work with them to engage the people who are in leadership positions. Because there's not much point in trying to work with the people that you know are going to be really hard to convert. So unfortunately – and this where educational development needs the support of champions in order at some point or other maybe to say to some of the die-hards: 'You gotta do this guys!' So I think that's overtly political, and I think that educational development has always been a political process.
>
> (Respondent 2)

It is also likely to appeal to those of a Managerialist orientation. Here another developer recognizes the coercive power of external 'imperatives':

> Now there's folk realise that you can try and change something but if your timing is wrong and people don't see the need to do it there and then, even though you might be right and you've diagnosed it absolutely 100 per cent, it'll not happen. They're busy, they've got a lot to do, and if they don't think it needs to happen tomorrow, basically they're not going to do it. You'll get enthusiasts doing it but you'll not get

> widespread change. You *can* get them to address it when they all kind of recognise it's now becoming an imperative. The obvious coming imperatives are the RAE [Research Assessment Exercise], and the new Quality Assurance arrangements. These are absolute coming imperatives. Everybody will focus their mind on those issues because they're up in big neon lights in front of them. (*laughs*)
>
> (Respondent 14)

In power-coercive strategies the change agent has power and is able to use it to coerce others into change. Things may get done to order with this approach, but colleagues may remain unpersuaded of the benefits, refuse to 'own' the innovation and harbour resentments which may surface later. The result might well be compliance, or a mimicry of change. Change without change.

There is a danger here, of course, of conceptualizing power as something essentially negative, and as uni-directional, exerted by those who have it over those who do not. The work of Foucault (1975, 1980), in particular, has problematized such notions of power and indicated its more complex and multi-directional nature.

> We must cease once and for all to describe the effects of power in negative terms: it 'excludes', it 'represses', it 'censors', it 'abstracts', it 'masks', it 'conceals'. In fact, power produces; it produces reality; it produces domains of objects and rituals of truth. The individual and the knowledge that may be gained of him belong to this production. Is it not somewhat excessive to derive such power from the petty machinations of discipline? How could *they* achieve effects of such scope?
>
> (Foucault 1975: 194)

The productive and multi-directional nature of power is reflected in the perspective of Respondent 21.

> I think the relations of power that exist in any educational development situation are enormously complex. Certainly as a developer I find myself in situations where I realise I am being expected, on the part of the organisation or its senior management, to try and bring colleagues 'on board' or 'into line' on some particular initiative, like getting them to use new technologies, or to assess differently, or to start using learning outcomes. Whatever. You find yourself getting involved in all kinds of normalising judgements here about 'quality', about 'excellence', about who are the innovators and, you know, who are the resisters, the dinosaurs and so on. And sometimes I find myself counselling colleagues like a therapist of some kind, or a priest in the confessional. And that's the exertion of another kind of power. But the power flows in so many directions and the practice and identity of colleagues is shaped by so many forms of power – the knowledge they have, their discipline, the discourse they use, the technologies they use, as well as the managerial and quality regimes they are subject to. And they always have the power

to resist and to subvert. And of course the power to construct identities for us, the developers. And that's as it should be of course. Without power there would be no reality would there? Nothing would be shaped or determined or get done. It's flowing in so many directions, and having so many effects, like energy. So I'm a bit wary of assumptions that power can easily be applied in educational settings, of developers as 'change agents'. It's much trickier than that. Look at all those big expensive projects that have virtually no effect!

(Respondent 21)

Dialectical stances

We recall from Section 1 the way in which certain developers, characterized there as of an Interpretive-Hermeneutic orientation, felt that development came about primarily through the workings of dialogue, through intelligent conversation and encounter and the process of interpretation required to gain an understanding (*Verstehen*) of the position of the 'other', in order to avoid the easy characterization of the latter as resistant. We referred there to the work of Webb (1996a), who emphasized the need for a conceptual and emotional shifting within the relationships in which educational developers engage, and a process of constant interpretation and re-interpretation, a moving back and forth between part and whole in order to gain fresh insights and new perspectives for all parties engaged in the development. Such approaches clearly draw on hermeneutical thought, but can also reflect the way in which change is conceptualized as mutually developmental through dialectical processes.

The notion of *dialectic* expresses the view that development depends on the clash of contradictions and the creation of a new, more advanced synthesis out of these clashes. The dialectical process involves the three moments: thesis, antithesis and synthesis. K.Marx used the notion to account for social and historical events, but Engels extended the scope of dialectical analysis so far as to establish it as a general law of development that applied equally in social, natural and intellectual spheres. He believed both that the real world, whether of society or nature, developed according to dialectical sequences of contradiction and synthesis, and that dialectical logic was the means by which one could comprehend this development.

(Abercrombie et al. 1994: 117)

The view that contestability is an important aspect of development has occurred at various points in the narratives of respondents within this study.

I suppose if I were to try and capture what I think is most important – and usually the most exciting bit of educational development – I suppose it's to do with the clash of ideas and perspectives and working that through with colleagues. That's the best bit when you get into really

> contested positions and really engaging dialogue and *everyone* moves on in their thinking somewhat and we all end up in some new place where things look different and people find that their defended positions and differences are less important than they thought they were and folks are ready to get on with it and start making things happen. I'm not saying that happens all the time but when it does that's just the best thing. Makes this job worth doing.
>
> (Respondent 34)

The dialectic might also operate between theory and practice.

> What happens when you work in my job is you look at what's happening in practice and you look at the theory that people are writing, and you say, 'Well that's nonsense, it just doesn't work'. There's always a dialogue between theory and practice. There is a dialectic. Maybe some people will say you can't have practice without theory and that's probably true as well. [. . .] Its all about creating dialogue. I mean I like that word because I think all of the whole process is about creating a dialogue with staff around some of these issues but it does help if you can talk knowledgeably and you have examples and experience helps.
>
> (Respondent 12)

Others feel, however, that as a professional community we're still waiting for the contestation to arrive.

> I'm wondering where the debate is going to come from within the ILTHE. That's what we need to see emerging. Different groups and perspectives emerging within the ILTHE with different ideas of how things might be done and some real debate and differences of opinion about the values of such approaches instead of all this luvvy stuff and stroking that we've had in the past.
>
> (Respondent 25)

The need for, and role of contestation has been a recurring theme within the literature on contemporary higher education and this is often linked to the uncertainties and anxieties of the postmodern condition. Barnett (2000: 68) sees the 'offerings' of the academic enterprise as 'tentative responses, possible readings and suggested ideas for action and intervention [. . .] Given the situation of utter contestability and uncertainty in which the university finds itself.' Webb (1996: 65), similarly, argues that 'if there are no solid foundations upon which to stand, how can social improvement and social justice, progressive educational practices and staff development be affirmed? . . . in a word, by contestation.' The notion of contestability and development through dialectical processes might appeal also to certain developers of a Political-Strategic orientation. But the notion of synthesis, of the reconciliation of contested positions around some new unified position, might not meet favour with all of an

Interpretive or Hermeneutic persuasion. For them it might still retain an element of linearity or foundationalism. As Webb suggests 'we should be looking for edification (enlightenment, knowledge, learning) – which are always in process – rather than closure upon a particular foundational position' (65).

Bricolage stances

Though a rational-deductive ideal, appearing systematic and comprehensive, might be attractive as an approach to organizational decision-making, the reality is perhaps more likely to be what Lindblom (1959) referred to, felicitously, as 'the science of muddling through'. The technical name he gave to the way he felt that decisions are *actually* made in organizations was 'disjointed incrementalism'. According to Lindblom's classic model of organizational decision-making, decisions tend to be:

incremental – taken a bit at a time, dealing in small changes to the existing situation and therefore easier to comprehend

serial – a series of attacks on problems, which are not usually solved but merely alleviated; decisions only move in the general direction of a solution

remedial – the marginal changes move away from the ills of the day rather than towards defined (strategic) goals

means-oriented – the means (i.e. strategies) are not adjusted to ends (i.e. goals) but often the objectives are redefined so that they can be brought within the cost of the means

restricted – only a restricted number of alternatives is considered, with only a restricted number of consequences for each alternative; in this way the task remains manageable through the exclusion of imponderable possibilities that might prevent any decision being made at all

disjointed – decisions are made by many people at scattered and unco-ordinated decision points.

As a variant on or development of disjointed incrementalism, Birnbaum (1988, 1989) proposes a *cybernetic* approach to decision-making as the most appropriate for higher education institutions. In this approach the institutional system as a whole is goal-directed, but its common purpose is not driven from the top but via 'multitudinous individual decisions' at the point of activity.

You've heard of the bidet and the shower approach? *(laughs)*. I think probably in my first couple of years here I was a bit too confident about the value of policies and guidelines and putting them through

> committees and then somehow thinking that would influence people. I've become much more sceptical about those although that's not to say occasionally we don't still do that.
>
> (Respondent 6)

This respondent has learned the value of not putting too much faith in top-down decision-making and engages rather in something more akin to 'multitudinous individual decisions'.

> This is not the kind of institution, as I said at the beginning, which really drives things from the top. So we can't really expect, unfortunately, any strong strategic direction. So in a sense we're forced to work the bottom-up. But it isn't entirely bottom-up in the sense we're not working only with lecturers, I mean, as I've said, we work at the Committee level, we work with Heads of Departments, with Deans.
>
> (Respondent 6)

'I think change is about complexity and interconnectivity' suggests Respondent 28, whereas Respondent 1, when asked if change is a rational process, replies 'I don't think it is. Well I think it's multi-layered isn't it?' Respondent 12, similarly, recognizes that change is not 'single-faceted':

> When you said where does the change come from I suppose I had something like yeah outside-inside, inside the institution. The change occurs from a variety of different sources. It's not single-faceted. You can see the government creates lots of pressures, TQA has had a big effect so there's all these things. Internally there are things too.
>
> (Respondent 12)

As Birnbaum points out, universities seem to have enjoyed a remarkably stable institutional history over many centuries without resort to tightly-coupled management structures. Elton offers an explanation for this:

> The stability of such a system depends on constant adjustments and responses through cybernetic controls, i.e. on self-correcting mechanisms at a micro level based on negative feedback, with information flowing freely vertically, both up and down, as well as horizontally. As Middlehurst and Elton (1992) have pointed out, it is the very diversity of sectional interests in a university that establishes the checks and balances which, within a common culture, make for a reasonably common purpose and it is the resulting self-correcting mechanism at a micro level which controls the large scale forces which are observable in change processes. It is therefore at this level that the large-scale forces must be influenced by the change agent, if they are to be influenced successfully.
>
> (Elton 1998b: 2)

Birnbaum's model accords well with Weick's notion of *loosely coupled* organizations (Weick 1976, 1980). This involves the concept that a flexible solution, where different elements can be loosely coupled for part of the decision-making process and can combine and re-combine for different functions, is much more highly generative as a means of decision-making than when one aspect of the situation is tightly and permanently coupled to another, stifling creativity and restricting room for manoeuvre. 'Change in loosely coupled systems', suggests Weick (1980: 78–9) 'is continuous, rather than episodic; small scale rather than large; improvisational rather than planned, accommodative rather than constrained and local rather than cosmopolitan [. . .] To construct a loosely coupled system is to design a system that updates itself.' Elton warns against the embracing by top management of misleading, deceptively transparent, 'simplistic cause and effect models' in hierarchically managed, tightly coupled systems. Cybernetic systems, he advocates, are more accommodative of innovation and do not have chaotic effects.

> In contrast, in a cybernetic system the many forces which impact on any change, as initiated by a change agent, combine in a non-chaotic manner and in their resultant effect are broadly predictable. It is this which makes it possible to develop change strategies which are based, not on the erroneous idea of a simple cause and effect model, but on a multi-force model.
>
> (Elton 1998b: 3)

The following respondent clearly shares this view:

> I think there's an increasing desire amongst senior officers in universities, particularly University Secretaries, but not solely University Secretaries, and lay members of Court, I may say, to have tidy pictures. Whereas my view is the world is messy and will always be messy and for the love of heavens will you learn to live with the fact that it is going to be messy? That doesn't mean you don't have some notion of what you're trying to do but it's always going to be messy. It's always going to be fluid and dynamic, changing. So there's no point in having this lovely tidy picture because it's never going to work that way. *That doesn't mean that you let it be completely senseless chaos.* So what you've got to do is try and have this notion of moving in a direction, that sometimes I think is a bit like crazy-paving. It's a slightly zig-zagging course that maybe allows for wind-changes and so on. You know essentially the direction you're trying to move in and you know essentially, at least for periods of time, how you're trying to move there, but the detail will change a great deal. Priorities shift about.
>
> (Respondent 14)

Influential though the three-stage systemic model of Lewin has been, not all developers subscribe fully to it. The following respondent considers that the refreezing stage is, given today's organizational complexity, more problematic.

> Lewis Elton uses a three stage model from an author whose name I've completely forgotten, which is embarrassing, because it will come to me. But it's the model where you unstick things, you change them and then you let them re-stick again. The author will come back to me.
>
> *The Interviewer: Lewin?*
>
> Kurt Lewin. Right. That's the one. Now. I suspect that model's probably two-thirds right. I think the last bit's getting less important. I think he's wrong. I think it's more than that. These visionary management text clichés about permanent white water, and so on, I think they're probably right, by and large. It's a long time since somebody said to me, when are things going to settle down? I think it's starting to dawn that they aren't going to settle down. And part of me's quite pleased actually, because some of the patterns we settled to in the past were pretty hideous and unproductive and wrong. So it's going to keep on changing. And one of the tricks is going to be to help people come to terms with that appalling prospect. Namely that things are going to continue changing. I embrace it. I welcome it. I love it.
>
> (Respondent 27)

The approach that this developer prefers is that of 'continuous improvement', associated with the Japanese industrial approach to quality improvement, Kai Zen. The approach also has affinities with the notion of the 'learning organisation' (Senge 1990) and the 'learning university' (Duke 1992).

> I used to think that change was about stopping things being wrong and getting them right again. But I've since abandoned the simplistic notion of getting things right. I'll settle for Kai Zen, for continued improvement. I mean I think that's what it's about. But in order to talk sensibly about continued improvement, in order to help people achieve it, first of all you've got to help them have the necessary courage, because it's bloody scary. So you've got to give them the courage. You've got to give them the resources, by which I don't mean money. I mean things as simple as thinking space, and things as important as expert colleagues, like educational developers with whom to talk things through. Things like a culture in which it's possible to talk sensibly about these things. Things like access to ideas and materials which are published somewhere – all of those things. These are all necessary conditions for continuous change. And there are many others besides. But that's the model I want to shoot to.
>
> (Respondent 27)

This developer does not see change as geared to increased efficiency ('doing more with less') but debate about the nature of quality – 'finding out which way's up'. As he points out 'Change is not the point. Improvement is the point.' The notion of continuous improvement within a learning organization can be seen as the institutional equivalent of reflective practice within the individual – an organization talking and listening to itself, evaluating itself, seeking to improve itself. In this regard this perspective on change would appear to be the most obvious to be embraced by developers of a Reflective Practitioner orientation.

> Underpinning the idea of continuing change, rather than getting it right, is there's got to be some agreement on which way is up. On what you mean by improvement. And that's where I think some leadership is needed on that, possibly following debate, because I don't think there is much agreement on what's better. Change is not the point. Improvement is the point. Change must be – going back to our Physics days – must be a vector quantity not a scalar quantity. It must have dimension and direction. And it's crucial. I think we're losing it a bit on direction at the moment. I think direction is . . . what is it? It's . . . Oh God . . . it's above all about doing more with less. That's about the only direction there is. And that's horrible. It's brutal. So finding out which way's up. And I hope that that's what the debates will lead to. And I hope that . . . Yes that's what I want to do. I want to help. I don't want to tell people which way's up partly because I don't know and partly because that's not a model of development I subscribe to. As a developer I would want to help institutions and disciplines and courses and individual teachers – different constituencies, right – to work out which way's up. It's coming a bit. The Funding Council's saying take teaching more seriously. That's not exactly saying which way's up, except to say that teaching's important. It's a start! (*laughs*). It's a great start. But it's not enough. And some, just some debate about that. What would we mean by things getting better? If we can get that debate kicked off, educational development will get easier and more highly valued.
>
> (Respondent 27)

Ambiguity stances

One influential view of universities was offered by Cohen and March who characterized university modes of governance as 'organised anarchies' (1986: 197). They based this assumption on three factors: the ambiguity of goals, the lack of clarity about purposes, and the transient character of many participants' involvement. This view sees correspondences between the academic freedom found in collegial cultures and the lack of centralized government, and preference for voluntary cooperation that characterizes the political version of anarchism. It similarly recognizes in the two scenarios a concern for responsible individual and collective decision-making. Their view developed from the earlier work of Cohen, March and Olsen (1972) that employed a 'garbage can' metaphor to describe the processes of decision-making that occur in universities. In this perspective the relationship between problems and solutions in organizations is usually not clear. The 'garbage can' metaphor disengages them completely from each other. Each 'choice opportunity' (an occasion on which a decision is expected) is a garbage can 'into which various problems and solutions are dumped by participants' (Cohen and March 1986: 195). This is at the centre of Bush's (1986) ambiguity perspective on educational management, and anarchic culture, discussed in Section 3.

Garbage cans can have 'streams' of problems, solutions, participants and choice opportunities, and these provide opportunities for analysis of situations. 'A solution,' suggest Cohen, March and Olsen (1972: 3), 'is an answer actively looking for a problem.' Within a garbage can there is no easy causal relationship between problems and solutions, or questions and decisions. 'Despite the dictum that you cannot find the answer until you have formulated the question well, you often do not know what the question is in organizational problem-solving until you know the answer' (3).

The interesting aspect of Cohen and March's analysis is their disengagement of problems and solutions. In their garbage can analysis a decision is an outcome (or an 'interpretation') of several relatively independent 'streams' within an organization. Though 'problems' affect everyone in the organization, and stem from such things as job frustration, family, lifestyle, career, relations with colleagues, money and so forth, they are, however, distinct from 'choices'. Problems 'may not be resolved when choices are made' (3).

> University decision-making frequently does not 'resolve' problems. Choices are likely to be made by flight or oversight. University decision processes appear to be sensitive to changes in load. Active decision-makers and problems seem often to track one another through a series of choices without appreciable progress in solving problems. Important choices seem particularly likely not to solve problems.
>
> (Cohen and March 1986: 201)

What is also interesting in Cohen and March's analysis is the three ways in which they claim that decisions are made in organizations – by oversight, flight and resolution. 'Oversight' implies that if a particular choice is taken when the other available choices have problems attached to them, and if there is energy available to make the new choice quickly, it will be made without any attention to existing problems and with a minimum of time and energy. 'Flight' suggests that in some cases, solutions to problems are considered (unsuccessfully) for some time until a solution which is 'more attractive' to the problems comes along. 'The problems leave the choice, and thereby make it possible to make the decision. The decision resolves no problems (they having now attached themselves to a new choice)' (197–8). 'Resolution' implies that some choices resolve problems after some period of working on them. The length of time may vary greatly, depending on the number of problems. 'This is the familiar case that is implicit in most discussion of choice within organisations' (198). Their findings have the following important implications for the higher education environments in which educational developers find themselves having to encourage innovation or implement policies:

- Organisational decision making frequently does not 'resolve' problems.
- Important choices are much less likely to resolve problems than are unimportant choices.
- Important choices are made by oversight and flight. Unimportant choices are made by resolution.
- Problems, choices and decision makers arrange and rearrange themselves.
- Problems are often solved, but rarely by the choice to which they are first attached.
- Much of the process violates standard notions of how decisions ought to be made.

(199–200)

The authors acknowledge that their findings appear to be complex, paradoxical and capricious, yet at the same time appear to be a convincing explanation of 'how organizations survive when they do not know what they are doing' (200). They point out that:

> A major feature of the garbage can process is the partial decoupling of problems and choices. Although we think of decision making as a process for solving problems, that is often not what happens [. . .] It is clear that the garbage can process does not do a particularly good job of resolving problems. But it does enable choices to be made and problems sometimes to be resolved even when the organisation is plagued with goal ambiguity and conflict, with poorly understood problems that wander in and out of the system, with a variable environment and with decision makers who may have other things on their minds. This is no mean achievement.
>
> (202)

A developer recognizes the application of this perspective to his own practice in a large university organization.

> I don't know if you're familiar with what Americans call a 'garbage can' model of how things [. . .]
>
> *The Interviewer: Cohen and March?*
>
> Right! Well it's not far off the mark here. This place is definitely a garbage can. There's all kinds of stuff swilling around in here, in [name of senior committee] and no-one seems ever to link up solutions to what we're meant to be solving. And then things move on and other stuff keeps coming over the horizon, every bloody day, it seems, and when stuff does get decided it's usually because the big players have lost

interest or it's just got derailed by something else and things get settled . . . by default I suppose.

The Interviewer: Organized anarchy!

Yes! Absolutely. But don't get me wrong. If you asked me whether I'd want the culture to be different I'd probably say no. In many respects it suits. There are opportunities. Gaps open up. People's eye goes off the ball and things can 'happen' (*laughs*). I mean I remember quietly squeezing through a module on Independent Learning. Colossal precedent! Students could design their own learning! Not a squeak. Committee were obsessed with some other daft thing about APEL that didn't matter a hoot as it turned out.

(Respondent 21)

This recalls Cohen and March's reference to 'the phenomenon in complex organisations of "important" choices that often appear to just "happen"' (Cohen and March 1986: 200). Another developer notes how, as Cohen and March would put it, 'Problems, choices and decision makers arrange and rearrange themselves'.

You know for all the world the senior managers and deans in this place remind me of little kids at Christmas. They've got all these projects and initiatives and corporate objectives all over the floor like toys at Christmas. And they get excited because they've just unwrapped one present but then they get another and now they're confused because they don't know which one to play with first and they keep picking them up and putting them down and then another shiny toy appears, so they chuck the others aside. It's really like that! They just don't know what they're doing. Then another kid comes in and thinks 'Ooh I like that one too, I think I'll have that!'

The Interviewer: It'll end in tears!

Oh, it always does! (*laughs*)

(Respondent 32)

Contingency stances

Unlike Respondent 27 above, who argued that 'change must be a vector quantity' and that 'It must have dimension and direction', Taylor (1999: 142) contends that change does not always have 'dimension and direction'. It requires a disruption of familiar contexts, a discontinuity and loss of meaning. Taylor distinguishes between 'plan-driven change', which he associates with managerialism, and 'action-driven change', the flow of which, he argues, most academics are willing to go along with, and, he suggests, is a more effective strategy within academic cultures.

> Problem solving is focused on sources of uncertainty which are everyday yet unpredictable, even random. Uncertainty generated by organisational change is different from more 'natural' causes in at least two senses: it implies an intention; and it involves a disruption of familiar contexts. When universities change their practices, most academics tend to assume that there are good reasons underlying the decisions – that the need for the change and the processes by which it will be achieved have been considered carefully. Thus, there is a sense that change is imposed in an intentional and reasoned way. But change-focused decision making is made necessarily under conditions of uncertainty.
>
> (142–3)

As academic managers have to grapple with uncertain external factors it is therefore inevitable that their decision-making includes 'elements of ambiguity, and 'the outcomes cannot be predetermined' (143). Academics should not therefore attribute certainty 'where uncertainty is the case'. Academics need to be wary of misrecognizing the 'best guesses' of their managers as informed 'solutions' (143). Such a situation, argues Taylor, is 'an emulation of certainty, when much more tentativeness is called for [. . .] The expectation of leadership generates both leaders and followers' (143). He advocates that academics adopt a practice of 'self-interested self-management' (7) based on critical reflection.

But whereas garbage can and cybernetic approaches were seen earlier to be highly complex but 'non-chaotic', Taylor (1999) and Fullan (1993) envisage notions of change which are non-linear and with chaotic tendencies. Fullan enumerates what he calls the 'Eight Basic Lessons of the New Paradigm of Change' which is, in effect, a chaotic non-linear view of change based on a postmodern perspective:

> 1. You Can't Mandate What Matters. (The more complex the change the less you can force it.)
> 2. Change is a Journey not a Blueprint. (Change is non-linear, loaded with uncertainty and excitement and sometimes perverse.)
> 3. Problems are our friends.
> 4. Vision and Strategic Planning Come Later.
> 5. Individualism and Collectivism Must Have Equal Power.
> 6. Neither Centralisation Nor Decentralisation Works. (Both top-down and bottom-up strategies are necessary.)
> 7. Connection with the Wider Environment is Critical for Success. (The best organisations learn externally as well as internally.)
> 8. Every Person is a Change Agent. (Change is too important to leave to the experts, personal mind set and mastery is the ultimate protection.)
>
> (Fullan 1993: 21–2)

Respondent 21 seems well aware of the chaotic nature of change and the need for 'personal mind set and mastery':

> I don't think my Assistant Principal would be too happy to hear this but I'm not sure that you can manage change in an institution like this. The operational environment is too complex. It's chaotic. I don't think you can be like a railway signalman pulling levers and changing the direction of things. I see it more that you have to be like one of those Hawaiian surfers. You've got one big wave behind you and another coming in from a different angle and there's a point that you can see you want to get to but the wind's blowing you away from that point so you twist and turn to try and keep going where you want to get to but then you're getting closer and closer to those rocks! (*laughs*). It really feels more like that! I think you have to surf change these days.
>
> (Respondent 21)

Whilst Respondent 30 recognizes the role of coincidence and contingency.

> I think it's really hard to make change from the bottom, I think it's really hard. I think you can try and this Centre is proof that you can do it, but you have to work really hard and a lot of it is just coincidental.
>
> (Respondent 30)

This non-linear conception of change would seem to be that most likely embraced by developers of an Opportunistic or Entrepreneurial orientation on the one hand and Interpretive-Hermeneutic on the other.

Change and acceptance

It must be realized, argues Elton, that all the phases of change, but especially the initial unfreezing phase, require time and patience. 'Change agents tend to be impatient and they risk failure through overhastiness' (1998b: 4). One respondent sees this as a slow 'chipping' process:

> The whole focus is very much, as I say, educating the individual then accepting that there will be a culture change over one period of time. And the notion that it is a long period of time that it might be fifty, eighty years, a couple of generations or three generations for me is more of a 'chipping' technique.
>
> (Respondent 18)

A number of commentators have attempted to conceptualize the stages of mental development that the client must go through to accept change. Rogers (1967) suggests a five-stage model of *awareness, interest, evaluation, trial* and *adoption.* Lloyd (1996) offers the more complex sequence of cognitive and social processes illustrated in Fig. 3.

However we conceptualize the process of acceptance, rejection is possible at any stage, suggests Elton. 'Change agents have to allow time for their clients to go through each stage if they want to avoid rejection, which is usually irreversible' (Elton 1998b: 4).

Social Processes

↑

COMMITMENT
- trust
- loyalty
- partnership
- altruism
- unsolicited effort
- generosity

INVOLVEMENT
- consultation
- participation
- contributions
- engagement
- recognition of input
- listening and responsiveness

SUPPORT
- acceptance/acknowledgement
- compliance/coercion
- conviction/endorsement
- acceptance
- logic and relevance established
- favourability

Cognitive Processes

↑

UNDERSTANDING
- clarification
- explanation
- edification
- appreciation
- enlightenment
- contextualisation
- association/ connectedness

AWARENESS
- recognition
- visibility
- acknowledgement

Figure 3 Cognitive and social processes in strategic change (adapted from Lloyd 1996)

Development and 'progress'

The interrelated connotations of the terms change, development and progress are problematic for educational developers. There is a wider philosophical issue here in terms of the nature and purpose of agency. 'What characterises human beings,' suggests Ignatiev (1996: 1), 'apart from being self-reflexive and reflective, is their dynamic intervention in their environment.'

> They don't just live in and use their environment they want to change it. They are continually striving to improve it. Christianity gave us the myth of progress to channel this striving, which was later developed in the Enlightenment as the idea of a more rational world, and through Marxist notions of destiny to an economically fairer world, and then in the nineteenth and twentieth centuries the notion of a technologically more efficient world. But now in the late twentieth century all these myths of progress are no longer sustainable. The holocaust put paid to that, particularly, Winston Churchill said, because it came about through 'the lights of perverted science'. We dropped the myth but are left with the continual striving.

In many respects the myth of a technologically more efficient world is mirrored in the faith held by many developers in a more effective, and in some cases, more efficient educational practice, particularly by those of a Managerialist, Reflective Practitioner or Educational Researcher orientation. But where does Ignatiev's argument leave us in late modernity with notions of development and betterment? Giddens (1991) has spoken of the 'ontological insecurity' experienced by many professionals in relation to their practice in late modernity where the myths that have upheld much professional behaviour heretofore begin to be contested and appear less sustainable.

But the binary opposite of progress is not necessarily nihilism or despair, suggests Ignatiev (1996: 1). 'It can be a healthy realistic acceptance of our human and earthly predicament. A preparedness to accept the here and now and to make a go of it.' Perhaps notions of 'development' are more appropriately translated into a concept of 'support' (Respondent 25), or 'engagement' (Respondent 21), or Respondent 28's idea of 'basically getting from where you are now to where you need to be' at any given time.

> Development mainly implies change, but you need to consider the term from the perspective of both its denotations and its connotations. In its denotative sense it means change towards something, but in its connotative sense it implies change for the better, that progress is being made. But I think I would define development as transition management, basically getting from where you are now to where you need to be. And that's a cycle that will need to be repeated over and over again as time goes on.
> (Respondent 28)

Change and eclecticism

One senior developer suggests that a prerequisite for transformative change is a capacity for eclecticism on the part of educational developers:

> The other thing is Dearing, Government Green Paper, Learning Age. You know, all of that sort of stuff. Behind all of that is essentially the argument that we're looking at transformative change. That is a phrase that has little attractiveness inside the institution to individuals. Certainly here, I, senior managers in the institution and so on, may well be driving for transformative change but we don't call it that. And I think folk make a big mistake if they try and load it that way round. Another thing is that people object if we say things like 'the lecture is useless, you shouldn't have the lecture, you shouldn't be teaching that way at all.' You mustn't knock down their prevailing paradigm. It's OK inside a discipline for that to happen but if we come to a discipline and start to attack what is their prevailing paradigm you will inevitably meet resistance. So you've really got to be very, very sensitive about how that territory is explored. One of the things that most practitioners in educational development and staff development and organisational development are nothing like sufficiently pragmatic about is that actually most of the time you will be dealing with *eclectic* situations – or diverse situations if you don't like the word eclectic. Only some of the time will you have a really clean paradigm operating. Most of the time you will have some diversity operating when it's bits of a variety of things. And some of these, potentially, are not totally compatible. But people make them work, just the same as students can actually go to lectures from A who adopts this style or lectures from B who adopts that style and the students can cope with the fact that actually they may be in complete conflict with each other. And students are extremely shrewd and always have been at handling that, and they know that they write this way for A and they write that way for B and they may think this is a piece of bloody nonsense but they do it. And they play the game. And we have to recognise that this is the reality we operate in. Sometimes because some of our colleagues are over-evangelical, sometimes because they're over-purist – and the rest of the world is not interested in us being either purist or evangelical. They want us to be helpful. We say as part of our strategy, we say that one of the things we want is to provide a helpful expert service. I think that is worth bearing in mind. *A helpful expert service.*
>
> (Respondent 14)

The need for eclecticism should be complemented by a realistic acceptance of the need for indicators of the nature of change and development achieved.

> It's an extremely challenging job. And part of the problem is if you don't work in this type of area it's extremely difficult for people to truly

> understand what you do. Secondly it's extraordinarily difficult to prove what you have achieved. But then that's true of all teaching and learning. It's extraordinarily difficult to prove that actually what you did caused a student to learn. Could they have achieved the same thing quite independently of what you were trying to do? Any lecturer would be in that position. You don't know because you can't re-run it again, independently. They're taking indicators of outcomes and just assuming that there's a cause and effect relationship between what they were trying to do, the indicator, and what happened. Which is not, I'm afraid, completely proven. And we have the same problem but one of our snags is maybe we don't pay enough attention to the indicators. And I do think we have to pay a bit more attention to the indicators. To be honest I think [name of Vice-Chancellor] has sometimes been a bit mystified as to why we keep getting very, very considerable praise in Quality Assessment reports and Quality Audits and so on, when he also seems to hear from people inside the place, you know, lack of conviction about exactly what we're doing. And it's because we're trying to work this very, very complex chemical change, not run a tight managerialist thing.
>
> (Respondent 14)

Correspondences between orientations to educational development and conceptions of change

We might now see possible correspondences between the orientations to educational development identified in Section 1 and the conceptions of change discussed in the present section. Again, as with the proposed model of orientations to educational development, this model is not intended to be in any way prescriptive, comprehensive or overly causal, bipolar or hierarchical. Some of the interrelationships represented in the model below are closer than others and it is important not to stretch the analogies further than they can go. The model is intended to suggest a reasonable and illuminative set of correspondences between orientation and conception.

Whatever change strategy a developer might adopt, he or she should not expect too much recognition for their effort. As Respondent 14 wryly observes:

> It's all ultimately about the management of change. I am absolutely certain that we are in the business of the management of change. I'm absolutely certain that is so. But what we have to do is to make that change palatable as well as achievable. If we just go in as evangelicals we'll fail. If we go in as instruments of government or the management or whatever else it is, we'll fail. So the trick is actually facilitating this

Orientation to educational development	**Conception of change**
Opportunist Entrepreneurial	chaotic/complexity (Fullan) non-linear, multi-perspectival 'cracks' theory (Berg and Östergren) garbage can (Cohen and March) ACORN model (Hawkins and Winter) cybernetic (Birnbaum) loosely coupled systems (Weick)
Reflective Practitioner	Kai Zen, continuous improvement (Senge), normative re-educative (Benne and Chin)
Interpretive-Hermeneutic	dialectical (Marx, Webb) chaotic/complexity (Fullan) cybernetic (Birnbaum) loosely coupled systems (Weick)
Romantic (Ecological Humanist)	personal growth (C.R. Rogers) self-identified (Hersey and Blanchard) normative re-educative (Benne and Chin) biological/progressive cybernetic (Birnbaum) loosely coupled systems (Weick)
Professional Competence Modeller-Broker	stepping stones/interconnectivity (Havelock) diffusion (E. Rogers) tightly coupled systems
Political-Strategist (pragmatist)	power-coercive (Benne and Chin) force field (Lewin) unfreezing/refreezing (Lewin) street-level bureaucracy (Lipsky)
Consultant Researcher	rational-empirical (Benne and Chin)
Provocateur (Disciplinary)	dialectical (Marx, Webb) diffusion (E. Rogers) ACORN (Hawkins and Winter) stepping stones (Havelock) cybernetic (Birnbaum)
Managerial / HRM	unfreezing/refreezing (Lewin) strategic leadership transition management (management by objectives) progressive/linear power-coercive (Benne and Chin)

Figure 4 Possible correspondences between orientations to educational development and conceptions of change

> change without people thinking we did it. Now of course the rub about doing that is, the better you do that, the less they think you had any part in doing it. So if you're really superb at doing it they don't think you did it! (*laughs*) It's true. It's absolutely true. So if you're really, really good at it, they don't even realise that you were instrumental in that happening. They think they did it. (*laughs*)
>
> (Respondent 14)

History, too, can be illuminative:

> It must be remembered that there is nothing more difficult to plan, more doubtful of success, nor more dangerous to manage than the creation of a new system. For the initiator has the enmity of all who would profit by the preservation of the old institution and merely lukewarm defenders in those who should gain by the new ones.
>
> *The Prince*, Niccolo Machiavelli (1469–1527)

3

Strategic Terrain: The Educational Developer and Academic Cultures

' "Culture",' Alvesson (2002: 22) reminds us, 'easily refers to everything and nothing'. As an anthropological metaphor to describe higher educational organizations and communities, and the ways of thinking and practising within them, it is potentially highly generative. It can be particularly illustrative of the feelings, normative values and decision-making processes to be found within the disciplinary 'tribes' and other groupings to be found within the academy (Becher and Trowler 2001). However, the metaphor is a very broad one and hence potentially vague. We will need later in this section to revisit the complex and multiple meanings that 'culture' might hold in order to gain a more nuanced view and a sharper focus. Given the endless play of signification within language, of course, this is likely to draw in further metaphors for culture! Meanwhile, this proviso notwithstanding, let us start with Hewton's observation that:

> the notion of organisational cultures, and particularly dominant cultures, within an institution, or within a department, is a useful way of clarifying the complex mixture of factors which together give rise to a 'normal' way of doing things and offer some clue as to the reaction which might be expected to attempts by outsiders to introduce change. The importance of this to the adviser in working towards a strategy for change is clear. The kind of strategy he must choose, or not choose, will be determined, in part at least, by the kind of culture he is dealing with.
> (Hewton 1986: 259)

Following from Machiavelli's stern caution at the end of the preceding section, Hewton's advice here is apt for those educational developers who assume to effect some kind of change within higher education organizations. Hewton's conclusion that matters of organizational culture 'should be of concern to an outsider intent upon introducing change into a culture' is predicated on the observation that 'Each culture offers to the outsider different kinds of opportunity and different forms of resistance' (259). But if organizational cultures are the strategic terrain which developers have to traverse, how do we recognize and understand them in order to best negotiate them? The following sections consider a number of ways of representing organizational and academic cultures and from these we might derive a provisional eclectic model to characterize the 'strategic terrain' within which educational developers conduct their practice. We will then be in a position to relate this terrain to the orientations to development discussed in Section 1.

Identifying organizational cultures

Schein offers the following pragmatic definition of organizational culture:

> A pattern of basic assumptions – invented, discovered, or developed by a given group as it learns to cope with its problem of external adaptation and internal integration – that has worked well enough to be considered valid and, therefore, to be taught to new members as the correct way to perceive, think, and feel in relation to those problems.
>
> (Schein 1985: 5)

At one level this definition offers a provisional adequacy for our purposes in that it is broad enough to accommodate all sizes of organizational unit, it acknowledges the existence of subcultures and is not predicated specifically on the idea of overt behaviour which could be interpreted as a function of personal attributes, cultural predisposition or situational contingency. We can further differentiate this notion to consider both *organizational* cultures and more specific *academic* cultures. However, the notion that there might be a 'correct way to perceive, think, and feel' within organizational culture remains problematic.

Van Maanen and Barley (1985) conceptualize organizational culture somewhat differently. They see it as a product of four attributes. The first two, *ecological context* and *differential interaction*, are structural prerequisites insofar as cultures only develop where actors are in proximity to one another and interacting with one another. The third, *collective understandings*, is considered to be the central attribute.

> Only when members of a group assign similar meanings to facets of their situation can collectives devise, through interaction, unique responses to problems that later take on trappings of rule, ritual and value.
>
> (Van Maanen and Barley 1985: 34)

The fourth attribute, *a reproductive and adaptive capacity*, emphasizes that cultures are necessarily neither fixed nor immutable. The manner in which Van Maanen and Barley conceptualize culture suggests that it is unlikely for an organization to maintain a unified culture. A fissiparous tendency is seen as more usual, with sub-units likely to develop distinctive subcultures over time. This is consonant with Smith and Peterson's somewhat Hobbesian view

(1998: 102) that 'the normal state within most organisations is some degree of conflict and difference in perceptions and priorities rather than consensus.' Hewton (1986: 257) suggests that, for the outsider, a cultural perspective 'offers some preliminary insights into a number of questions which will be of concern in deciding policy and strategy'. Though the perspective offers only partial answers it nonetheless 'opens some windows on the insiders' world and identifies certain patterns of thinking and acting which may have some explanatory power when the outsiders – assuming the role of diplomats – approach the culture with a view to negotiating change'. Within educational institutions he sees both organizational characteristics and subject discipline as 'major factors in shaping the practices of insider groups'.

> Culture offers a unifying concept, insofar as it assumes certain similarities and a degree of consensus between members of a particular group, but, at the same time, it indicates the diversity which can be found between groups [. . .] For instance, if faced with an attempt to introduce change, might a technical college react differently to say a college of education or a university? Or, might the approach needed to ensure the co-operation of a Physics department in a polytechnic be different to that needed for, say, a Law or History department? Or might the procedures and results which an Electrical Engineering department would expect from allowing outsiders to evaluate their courses or introduce changes into their teaching or courses differ from those expected by say a Sociology or an English department?
>
> (257)

This provides a helpful perspective from which to consider educational development practice within its strategic context or 'terrain'. It is a very similar kind of cultural reading of diverse contexts undertaken by Hewton's 'diplomats' that educational developers must undertake daily 'with a view to negotiating change' (257). They too have to adapt their practice to accommodate such cultural and subcultural diversity in their attempts to foster innovation and improved practice across disciplines.

> An outsider intent on bringing about change will have to operate at various levels in seeking to understand the culture into which he [*sic*] seeks to introduce change. Overall, the organisation with which he is concerned may tend towards the acceptance of a certain kind of management style which affects the way in which control over members is exercised and the way in which they are formally required to relate to each other. But there may also be variations in management styles between departments which have different functions – administration and teaching units representing one obvious division.
>
> (257)

Hewton's analysis draws heavily on the influential organizational theory of Handy (1976). Handy, developing an earlier categorization by Harrison (1972), identifies four main styles of organization as *power, role, task* and *person*. In *role culture* 'Position power (the power which stems from the role description) is the major source of authority and clearly defined rules and procedures relating to job specification, limits of authority, settlement of disputes, etc., are the major form of influence' (Handy 1976: 260). In *task culture*, emphasis is on action and getting things done. Roles are fuzzier, power stems rather from personal expertise, skill and influence than any formal authority derived from office. Symbolized by a net, in this culture power and influence are located at the interstices of the strands. 'Influence is more widely dispersed than in the role culture and tends to shift according to the job in hand. The organisation seeks to bring together the appropriate resources at the right time in order to complete a specific task or project' (260). *Person culture* is centred upon the individual and any structure exists only to serve those persons in the culture. The organization has no external objective other than to serve the needs of the members, who tend to be a group of individuals banding together to share common facilities or provide mutual support but ultimately pursuing their own goals and ideas. 'In such organisations influence is generally shared and based upon expertise. Individuals do what they are good at and are listened to on appropriate topics. They are free to give up their membership but the organisation seldom has the power to evict them' (261). Handy's final culture, *power culture*, is represented by the image of a web. Control emanates from the centre, usually dominated by a powerful central group, and is mediated through key actors dispersed to strategic points in the web. Rules, procedures and rationality remain minimal, with emphasis mainly on decisions resulting from power struggles. Resource power is the major power base in this culture, with some elements of personal (charismatic) power at the centre. Emphasis is upon results and the means are less important. The culture therefore has a tough and abrasive side which creates a highly competitive atmosphere. There will be concern for the individual only insofar as they produce results. Such organizations may well suffer low morale and high turnover.

These cultures, suggests Handy (1976: 177), 'profoundly affect atmosphere, morale, communications, efficiency, adaptiveness and innovativeness within an institution'. The cultures manifest themselves through a broad range of indicators.

> In organisations there are deep seated beliefs about the way work should be organised, the way authority should be exercised, people rewarded, people controlled. What are the degrees of formalisation required? How much planning and how far ahead? What combination of obedience and initiative is looked for in subordinates? Do work hours matter, or dress, or personal eccentricities? [. . .] Do committees control or individuals? Are there rules and procedures or only results? These are all parts of the culture of an organisation.
>
> (177)

The four cultures are of course organizational stereotypes, ideal forms, unlikely to be encountered in their ideal form in practical contexts. They serve however as useful simplifications and it is likely that academic organizations will show tendencies towards one type or another. 'It is important', Hewton advises, 'for the outsider involved in educational change to recognise this' (1986: 262). He also reminds us that within the larger academic organization individual sub-units (departments) may well develop their own cultural style. The nature of such subcultures may well be determined by factors such as size, purpose, personnel, research interests, wider environment. Each case is likely to be a distinctive blend of 'mixed cultures and contrasting subcultures' (262). This cultural and subcultural terrain is the strategic context in which educational developers will ply their trade.

Academic terrain

Studies of organizational culture have generated further analyses more specifically focused upon academic institutions. The most well known of these is probably Becher's (1989) examination of university culture. Becher stresses the complexity of universities as organizations and characterizes the following models of organizational behaviour:

Organizational Pattern	Characteristic Features
Hierarchical	Authority conferred from above. Recognizable chains of command. Pre-determined regulations and procedures. Specified roles.
Collegial	Authority ratified from below. Equality of rights in decision-making Decisions exposed to dissent. High personal discretion.
Anarchical	Authority eroded by personal loyalties. Emphasis on individual autonomy. Ambiguous goals; pluralistic values. Influence based on expertise.
Political	Authority deriving from personal power. Conflict as basis for decisions. Policies based on compromise. Influence deriving from interest groups.

Figure 5 Becher's four main patterns of organizational behaviour (from Sawbridge 1996: 9)

The first category in Becher's typology, *hierarchical* forms, refers to an organizational culture predicated on recognizable lines of command, predetermined bureaucratic procedures and clarity of role. However, Sawbridge (1996: 5), in her study of employment-led staff development, concluded that 'hierarchy, in the form that would be recognizable in the civil service, the army or in many industrial and commercial enterprises, is not evident in universities in spite of distinct trends towards a more sharply defined post-Jarratt Report (1985) role for vice-chancellors and immediate seniors.' What she did conclude was that hierarchical decision-making was more prevalent in the ex-polytechnic institutions, where staff developers were found by Sawbridge to refer to the vice-chancellor as a significant figure far more than in older universities.

'The counter-balance' she argues, '(some would argue that it is a barrier) to more centralised control systems is because of other organisational forms at work. Of most significance in academic folklore and tradition, is the question of collegiality, sometimes embraced in the concept of a community of scholars' (5). In this she draws on Becher's view that hierarchical forms tend to be compromised in academic institutions because 'there remains a fundamental value in the academic community that the trade in ideas should be free [. . .] the result is a strong sense of collegiality in which scholars are called upon to respect each other's intellectual independence regardless of age and position. Authority is, in this tradition, always subject to ratification from below' (Becher 1989). However, if *collegialism* is a constant counterweight to hierarchy within academe, then Sawbridge recognizes that a threat to the collegial ideal may still arise from a newer post-Jarratt *managerialism*:

> It would appear to be the case that the increased focus on employer-led initiatives in the last decade, appraisal, performance-related pay, increasing casualisation of the workforce, trends towards massification and more pro-active staff development to name but a few, is different in character than in the post-1960s. Then the major concerns were about growth within an elitist structure and perceived problems about how to deal with staff, many with unfamiliar pedigrees and / or disruptive and unsocialised students. In this sense one can see employer initiatives, including the growth of interest in staff development, as intervening in the collegial culture because it leaves too much to chance at a time of institutional challenge.
>
> (Sawbridge 1996: 6)

This is a theme to which Halsey (1992) drew attention in the early 1990s. Halsey argues that the fragmentation of the academic workplace is one of a number of material and ideological conditions which, taken together, are transforming university teachers into a new proletariat whose relative class and status advantages are being significantly eroded:

> Managerialism gradually comes to dominate collegiate co-operation in the organisation of both teaching and research. Explicit vocationalism displaces implicit vocational preparation, as degree courses are adapted to the changing division of labour in the graduate market. Research endeavours are increasingly applied to the requirements of government or industrial demands. The don becomes increasingly a salaried or even

> a piece-work labourer in the service of an expanding middle class of administrators and technologists.
>
> (Halsey 1992: 13)

Halsey argues that university teachers lack 'ideological' control over their work in the same way that nineteenth century textile workers came to lose such control. Miller suggests this loss of control is in relation to their 'raw material', the students:

> Through their command of discrete expertise, academics can still largely influence the processes of both their research and teaching, but the raw material (students or problems to be investigated) is increasingly determined by the combined influences of the state, institutional managers and the market.
>
> (Miller 1995b: 56)

This tendency has continued throughout the nineties and into the new century with a drive for expansion – up to 50 per cent age cohort participation by 2010 in the UK – and the increasing diversity and widening participation of the student intake. Dummett (1994) talks of the 'principles' of insecurity, competition and surveillance.

> [. . .] each task must be done at the least possible cost; that people work effectively only if they know their jobs are insecure, and if they are lured by increases of salary or of status to be obtained in competition with their colleagues; and that no institution can be trusted to evaluate its own or its employees' efficiency, which must be estimated by having each employee assessed by other employees or by the 'customers', by objective performance indicators or, best of all, by the reports of external inspectors.
>
> (Dummett 1994: 1269)

However, a countervailing tendency might be observed in relation to *anarchical* forms of organizational behaviour, in that academics in some respects are able to retain an arm's length independence from their employing institution. 'Because their reference group is national and international, they are more able to resist managerial pressures,' suggests Sawbridge (1996: 7). 'In any event their subject expertise makes it difficult for managerialist interventions to succeed without their co-operation.' Becher concludes that the anarchic tendency of some academic organizations, which are 'more anti-managerial than managerial, concerned with dis-organisation rather than organisation [. . .] stems from the high degree of autonomy enjoyed by academics.' However Gouldner (1979) reminds us that there remains an important difference between 'cosmopolitans', those more entrepreneurial academics whose status allows them a privileged role and greater autonomy within managed organizations, and the less privileged, more managed and put upon 'locals'.

Becher's identification of *political* forms within academic organization draws attention to the personal and professional power of individuals and groups in decision-making processes. Birnbaum (1988) points out that the most powerful departments are those generating the greatest income through research or fees and in turn attracting the best students, enhancing their status and power further. But political cultures are, according to Becher (1989) usually conflictual cultures and resolution of such internecine strife often amounts to political expediency, compromise and short-term vision. 'It means that decision-making within the institution will rest on the degree to which it is seen to be in the political interests of influential people in departments and faculties' (Sawbridge 1996: 8–9). Such political punching has also been found to be a prerequisite of the effective functioning and even survival of educational development units. Elton suggests that it depends on:

> how politically effective they could be in their negotiations with senior staff dependent on the strength of the constituency they could gather around them. It underpins the concern about the status of staff development and its structural location within the university in which it operates, some seeing that there is a need to pull one's political weight by being a department with the same kind of remit as other departments.
>
> (Elton 1995, cited in Sawbridge 1996: 9)

A similar typology is offered by Bergquist (1992) who also identifies four broad institutional cultures as *collegial, managerial, developmental* [approximating to autonomy] and *negotiating* [political]. Hooijberg & Petrock (1993) have a fourfold 'competing values' model set against a vertical axis differentiating between flexibility /individuality and stability /control, and a horizontal axis differentiating between an internal focus and an external focus. Against these axes their cultural typology takes the form of *clan* culture, *adhocracy* culture, *hierarchy* culture and *market* culture. For an elaboration of this model see Fig. 6. Finally, McNay suggests the four cultures of *collegium, bureaucracy, corporation* and *enterprise.* Some of these labels, he suggests, may carry pejorative connotations. However that is not his intention, as he believes that all can be justified: 'what is crucial is the appropriateness of the "fit" with circumstances. All four co-exist in most universities, but with different balances amongst them. These differences depend on a range of factors including traditions, mission, leadership style and external pressures' (McNay 1995: 105–6). He is particularly interested in the emergence of the enterprise culture, and also in the changing role that administrative staff play in such cultures, a hitherto neglected area.

> such staff have a key role in mitigating potential conflict between practices and procedures which differ by culture. Research preferences in the collegial units may not fit with corporate priorities: decision processes and 'norms' of the bureaucracy may not be flexible enough for an enterprise in a competitive market.
>
> (106)

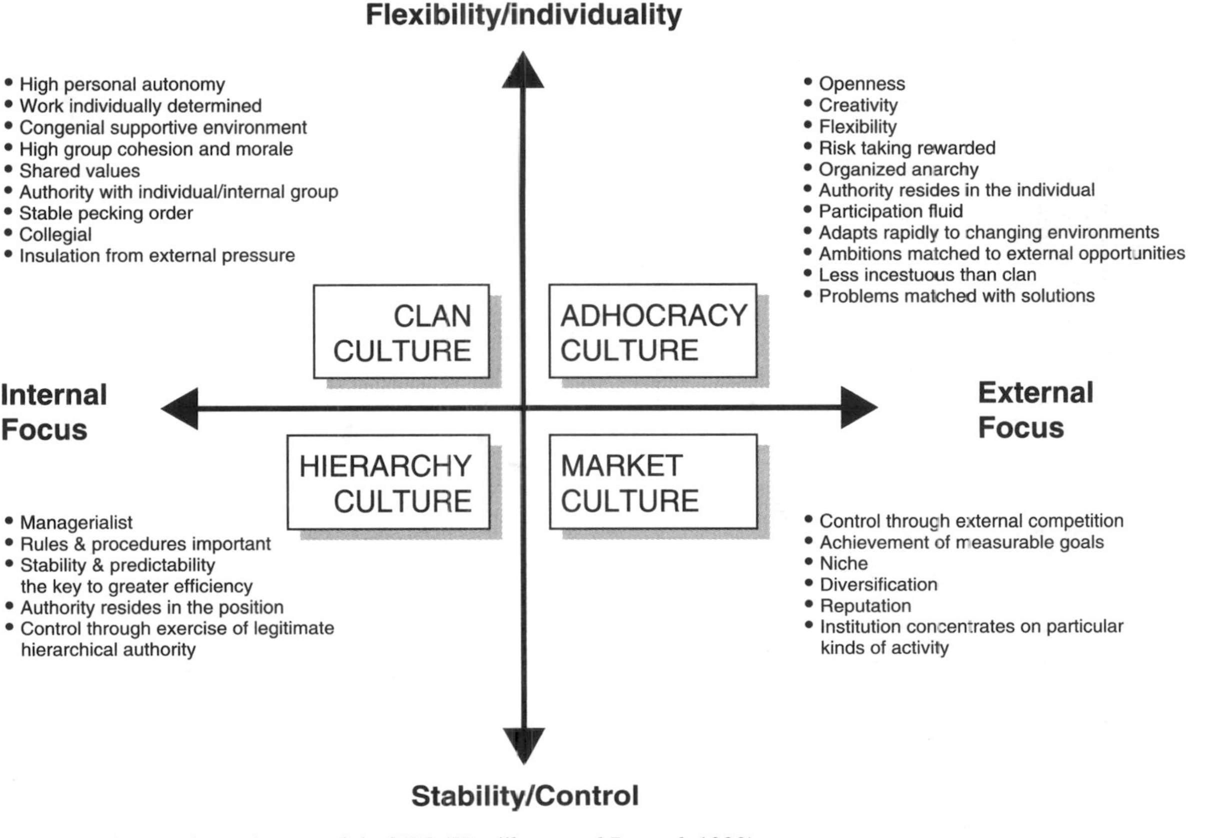

Figure 6 Competing values model of HE (Hooijberg and Petrock 1993)

McNay provides a diagrammatic representation of how the four cultures relate to tight or loose coupling in relation to policy definition and control of implementation.

The key word for the collegium, suggests McNay, is 'freedom'. For bureaucracy it would be 'regulation', though this can have 'many positive objectives: consistency of treatment in areas such as equal opportunities or financial allocations; quality of activities by due process of consideration; propriety of behaviour by regulatory oversight; efficiency through standard operating procedures' (106). In the corporation culture the key word is 'power' and in the enterprise culture 'my choice of key word would be "client" '(107).

> That carries with it connotations not only of the market, where customers would be more appropriate, but of professionalism where the knowledge and skills of experts, and the needs and wishes of those seeking their services, come together. In organisation terms, it means that key decisions should be located close to the client, within a well-defined general policy framework, and that the good of the client should be the dominant criterion for decision-making.
>
> (107)

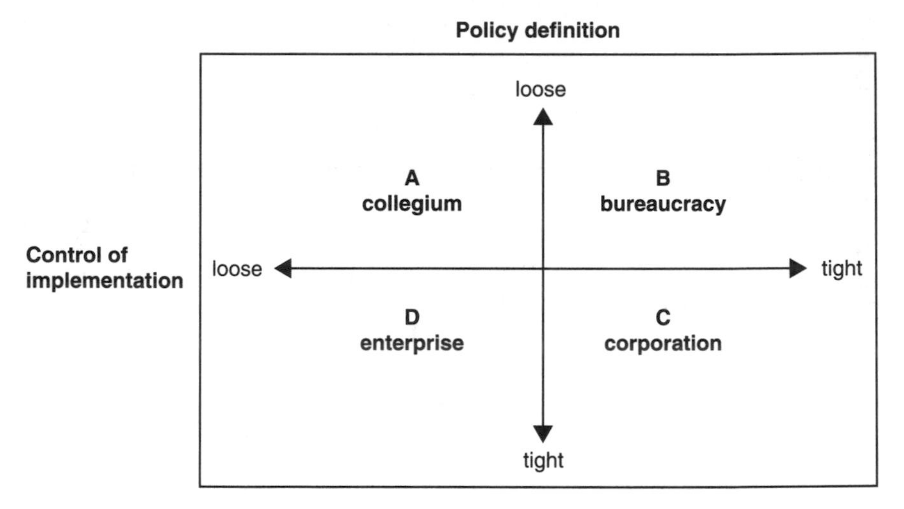

Figure 7 McNay's representation of universities as organizations

Having considered various theoretical 'takes' on organizational culture as a contextual factor of which educational developers must take account, we should consider also the related notions of models of management and organizational structure.

Management and organizational structure

Styles of leadership inevitably reflect the particular features of the diverse models of management we find in institutions. Bush (1986) has identified five different styles: *formal*, with the official leader playing a key role in decision-making, determining goals and formulating policy; *democratic*, with policies emerging from complex processes of discussion at committees and other settings, both formal and informal; *political*, with leaders actively participating in processes of bargaining and negotiation; *subjective*, de-emphasizing the concept of leadership, stressing instead the personal attributes of individuals rather than their official positions in the organization; and *ambiguity*, pointing to the uncertainty facing leaders and the difficulties associated with the management of unpredictability. It is interesting to note how these competing management perspectives give rise to different understandings of the nature of organizational *structures*. Bush's formal and democratic models, for example, imply, in fairly modernist fashion, that structures are 'objective realities' which exert strong influence via the 'defined positions' that individual actors hold within the organization, whereas other perspectives present the notion of structure as less 'fixed', more 'unstable', 'problematic' or 'conflictual' (Bush 1986).

> Formal models treat structures as hierarchical with decisions being passed down from the leader. Democratic models present structures as lateral with all members taking part in the decision process. Political models portray structure as one of the unstable and conflictual elements of the institution. The design of the structure is thought to reflect the interests to be served by the organisation. The elements within the structure may become the settings for conflict between interest groups anxious to promote their policy objectives.
>
> (2)

Subjective and ambiguity models give rise to notions of structure that are more in keeping with postmodern theories of the organization. Subjective models, for example, suggest that organizational structure arises from relationships between individuals rather than being a 'fixed entity which constrains the behaviour of its participants'. How members of the organization interact determines its structure, 'which is valid only as long as it accurately represents those relationships'. Ambiguity models likewise render structure problematic 'because of the uncertain relationships between loosely coupled sub-units'. The significance of structure is further compromised by 'the fluid participation of members in committees and other forums' (2).

These structures provide one way of representing the strategic terrain which educational developers must negotiate on a daily basis in their practice of seeking to transform or develop prevailing approaches to teaching and learning in higher education institutions. Turner (1982) provides an alternative representation of structure, also a five-part typology, though differently categorized as *hierarchical*, *collegial*, *matrix*, *family* and *autonomous*.

The *hierarchical* structure is unquestionably the most common structure found in large organizations and is the basis of bureaucratic systems of operation. It provides the basis of the traditional university structure of departments and sections and both reflects and is reinforced by academic salary agreements. Its strength would appear to be the clear, usually pyramidal, lines of accountability in terms of who is accountable *to* whom and *for* whom. It enables the division of academic work into specialist departments and centres (such as educational development units), permitting the creation of smaller sub-units and restricting the 'span of control' or number of people for whom any one actor has responsibility. This in turn allows control and monitoring activity to take place at all levels – of central importance in a quality-driven culture – and facilitates the coordinating and planning activities of senior managers. From an educational development perspective such structures can be seen on the one hand as a useful guarantor of quality and accountability, but on the other as impeding innovative activity, new thinking and creative response. The following respondent in the study complained of the 'increasing distance' from management felt by colleagues in his institution.

> There is a concern that an increasingly managerial style removes influence over important decisions. Now in the past it's never been very clear how this influence has made itself felt but you got the sense that people in senior positions were more amenable to direct questioning or to people raising problems with them on an individual basis, and were more willing to consider views being expressed to them – feedback from staff – and therefore amend policies accordingly. And you don't get that sense any more.
>
> (Respondent 2)

Interestingly, in terms of attitudes to innovation, the institution under discussion here was one which saw the abrupt closure of its large educational development unit.

> I think there's an increasing distance. I think that you've seen the distance increase ultimately between the level of the Head of Department and their staff, and that kind of 'separation out' of managers from managed. And that's where the separation is the most evident, and whether or not there will ever be much grounds for common understanding between managers and managed remains to be seen. Now I know that it depends at what level you look at this. People who are managed by their Head of Department might manage people who help teach their courses, even in the course leader role, but I think it's true to say that course leaders are seen largely as foot soldiers, members of the infantry, and it's that level of the Head of Department and above who are seen as being increasingly dragooned into a certain style of operating and a certain kind of what sometimes looks like – this is probably unfair – a stimulus / response way of conducting affairs (*laughs*).
>
> (Respondent 2)

Such hierarchical, subject-based departmental systems tend to operate as semi-independent units. They often become characterized as 'baronial' fiefdoms of significant power, protective of their own staff, students and courses, and acting in fierce competition with other baronies over the allocation of resources. Other kinds of structure tend to curb such baronial hegemony and hence are less popular with heads of department.

Collegial structures are often idealized as communities of scholars drawn into common purpose by the pursuit of learning and shared professional interests. Decisions are made collectively, on a corporate basis, informed by rationality and civilized discourse. Collegial organizational culture is by necessity 'flat', permitting collaborative action and decision-making, and fostering the growth of interpersonal relationships and encouraging strong group interaction. One head of educational development, working in a new English university, observes of the culture of her own organization:

> It's essentially voluntaristic in its approach – well, not imposed from the Centre. I think it will need to restructure certain areas. The power is devolved and there's been no wish to impose from the Centre. It has espoused a collegial model and celebrated the independence and different characteristics of each of its faculties. Now whether that is only another way of expressing a weak management style is debatable.
>
> (Respondent 5)

The collegial ideal tends to be compromised, as is perhaps implied in this comment, by the weak definition of precise responsibility of individuals and by the obligation for all individuals to accept group decisions, even though they may disagree. The management of potentially intense interpersonal and group behaviour (often in committees) can be problematic, as can the dominance of strong personalities in small group settings. Moreover the legal responsibility held by the Principal or Director, despite communal decision-making, cannot be delegated.

Turner's third category, the *matrix* structure, has much in common with Handy's task culture. It would appear, from an educational development perspective, to allow a higher education institution more room for innovative manoeuvre insomuch as it permits the institution to respond more easily and swiftly to fast-changing environmental conditions. The model of organization, which arose from technological development, mainly on a project basis, in the aerospace industry, is designed to bring together two essential dimensions of work, namely resourcing and the project or programme. Within higher education settings this translates into the separate alignment of *academic staff* from *courses* or projects. A matrix system disrupts the 'ownership' of staff and students by subject departments and frees them for activity in other domains. It encourages lateral communication, which is weak in departmental hierarchies where (usually downwardly) vertical communication is the norm, and often obliges teachers from different disciplinary specialisms to work together. It can be seen to foster interdisciplinarity at the expense of the traditional departmental or disciplinary stronghold and is often accompanied by the rise of a new breed of project managers, course-team leaders or cross-institutional co-ordinators. The latter become significant players within the middle management team. Given the use of funded educational projects as one strategic approach popular with certain kinds of educational developer, it is not surprising to find developers responding positively to the flexibility offered by matrix-type structures. A head of a development unit in a new university in the English Midlands is describing the main roles in her job description:

> One is to run a task force and I have twenty-six half-time seconded people. They're seconded for two or three years so they're a big substantial project. They are change agents inside the subject area. They are the spokes. I manage that project. My job really is to make more out of that than just a series of projects. They've all got individual projects which are subject-based. I'm increasingly trying to push them towards staff development inside the subject area and working together on thematic issues. They are quite a powerful group.
>
> (Respondent 17)

The matrix structure has its drawbacks like any other, however. There is a danger of two hierarchies emerging instead of one. Academics in higher education matrix structures such as modular schemes may feel concern that their subject expertise is being eroded through their assumption of dual roles, often in interdisciplinary teams, and that career opportunities, particularly those associated with research activity, might be restricted as a result. The matrix is essentially a political structure requiring skilful liaison between subject heads and course or project directors. There is a danger too of powerful interest groups establishing themselves in either course or subject divisions leading to intense competition for resources and influence.

What Turner characterizes as a *family* structure is usually found in smaller organizations and would be found more typically in colleges or, perhaps, research units, though it can be found in sub-units such as departments. There is little hierarchical structure and scant bureaucratic apparatus. Members tend to act informally but are governed by strong organizational norms and *modi operandi*. As in Handy's power culture the working environment is one of dependency on the leader, the boss. The strength of the boss gives the organization its strength. The security provided by the structure might suit some staff but from an educational development perspective such structures tend not to be innovative unless this is sanctioned by the leader. The following respondent describes a clash of structures arising from merger within his organization.

> I remember when the University 'merged' with the teacher training college – everybody knew it was really a take-over – and we became this one big Faculty. And the Principal of the College became the Dean but it was quite clear that he couldn't – or wouldn't – adjust to the new culture he found himself in. He'd been used to running his little set-up

like some Victorian paterfamilias, with his two sidekicks, not consulting with anyone else and everything, but *everything*, went through him. And then when he'd become Dean he'd make decisions in the way he'd always done, before committees met, and then when the committee decided something else he'd say 'Well we can't have that!' And when it was tactfully pointed out to him that, well, we *would* have that because that's the way the University works, he'd go off his trolley and then go behind everyone's backs and start doing deals so that he'd get his idea through. And so for a long time basically we had two systems operating in the Faculty.

(Respondent 21)

Turner's final category, *autonomous*, assumes that academics are more or less left to their own devices and self-organization as far as is possible. The assumption is that academics are trained professionals, do not require supervision or overt checks on their activities and can be relied upon to know what is required of them. They are specialists who tend to work independently of others and the decisions of any individual actor do not greatly impact on other members of staff. There is a climate of trust; good government is seen as virtually no government and administrative activity is restricted to the absolutely essential.

I call this place a 'benign anarchy' (*laughs*). There is a lot of respect here for the expertise of individuals and for the right of everyone to have their say. But it's considered to be somewhat of a breach of manners, rather indelicate, to tell anyone else what they should be doing. People have all kinds of opinions on everything, even when they don't really care about something they'll still argue heatedly in committees just for the sake of it, but most of them don't like taking responsibility for getting anything done in the institution. Outside's a different matter of course. And if someone's got a three million quid contract from GlaxoKlineSmith to work on some drug or other, no-one's going to tell him or her where they should be or what they've got to attend. You asked whether people at the top know what we do here. No I don't think they do really. But it works on the whole. Whether it will continue to long term I just don't know.

(Respondent 21)

Of course one of the implications of this pattern of organization is that although there are few regulations to restrict these autonomous specialists there are also few rules to protect them. They may well find themselves subject to the whim and caprice of powerful managers. Indeed this proved to be the experience of one respondent.

Now the problem – part of the reason for which we were closed – was that we played the role of honest broker and in that sense no one had a stake in us. We were kind of independent, largely. We had one champion who was then the Deputy Vice-Chancellor, who retired, and

> we had talked for many years that if he were to go we'd be wide open. And it so happened that he went just after the new Vice-Chancellor had arrived, just after the University's concern to cut the staffing budget had come through, and we were just sitting ducks. And so although it may be that at grassroots level there was quite a lot of support, there were always critics who were complaining about the topslice. Nonetheless, regardless of the expression of support, at the end of the day we had no champion. And so without that you're just too vulnerable.
>
> (Respondent 2)

A final model we may wish to consider is that of Becher and Kogan (1992) who analyse what they term a 'quadrilateral of interests' in higher education, each emphasizing their own *value positions.* Higher education, they argue, must negotiate with each of these interests and find its own path within them. In this respect we may regard higher education as meeting the needs of various stakeholder interests at any given time. The four interests identified are *professional* (the academy), governmental or *managerial* (the state), the *market* (wealth producers) and *social utility* or welfarism (the public).

> One group of values is professional and derives from academic norms and aspirations. Another is governmental and is concerned with the demands of the state, which can range in different times from those of theocracy to those of the economy. A third is that of the market as it seeks particular skills in its workforce and particular forms of knowledge for conversion into wealth production. And, finally, there is that of public and social utility at large, whose interests may lie both in increased educational opportunities and in the maintenance and enhancement of a civilised society.
>
> (Becher and Kogan 1992: 177)

Orientations to educational development and academic cultures

There would seem to be an observable degree of thematic convergence across the models, structures and sets of values we have considered. If they are presented as a list we can see the cultural contours emerging:

power, role, task and person (Handy)
hierarchical, collegial, anarchical, political (Becher)
managerialism, collegiate cooperation (Halsey)
collegial, managerial, developmental [approximating to autonomy] and negotiating (Bergquist)
collegium, bureaucracy, corporation and enterprise (McNay)
formal, democratic, political, subjective, ambiguity (Bush)
hierarchical, collegial, matrix, family, autonomous (Turner)

professional (the academy), governmental or managerial (the state), the market (wealth producers) and social utility (Becher and Kogan)
clan, adhocracy, hierarchy, market (Hooijberg and Petrock)

For purely illuminative purposes of the present analysis, and without any overly simplistic assumption of closure or definitiveness in this respect, we could construct a provisional eclectic framework from the models discussed. Re-organized in this fashion, six prevalent cultural forms would seem to emerge as follows.

Managerial (managerial, corporation, governmental)
Political (power, political, negotiating)
Anarchic (person, anarchical, developmental [approximating to autonomy], subjective, ambiguity, autonomous, adhocracy)
Hierarchical (bureaucracy, role, formal, hierarchical, family)
Enterprise (task, matrix, the market, enterprise, social utility)
Collegial (collegium, collegiate cooperation, democratic, collegial, professional, the academy, clan)

This choice of representative cultures is inevitably a simplification for the sake of greater clarity, and is merely a proxy for what in reality would be a more complex and nuanced typology of academic cultural forms and structures. As a simplified representation of 'strategic terrain' it permits us, however, to demonstrate (Fig. 8) how the various orientations to educational development might be located in relation to these prevailing cultures. An Interpretive-Hermeneutic or Researcher orientation, for example, would, it is suggested, be a more likely feature of agent conduct, to use Stones' term (1991, 1996) when the agent context is a mainly anarchic culture, just as a Managerialist (Human Resource) orientation would be more likely to characterize agent conduct when the agent context and strategic terrain is predominantly a managerial culture. The diagram is an attempt to indicate the variation within orientations, and the *ecological* nature of the environment in which educational developers operate – a notion pursued with more sophistication in the work of Frielick (2004).

The orientations to educational development can be further positioned in relation to two axes each representing polarized tendencies. The vertical axis charts the extent to which educational development practice might be seen as focused more directly towards meeting the personal needs of individual practitioners (academic staff or students) as opposed to being oriented more towards the requirements of the institution and its functioning at a systemic level. A concern with the efficient implementation of a system of modularization, for example, might be considered as demonstrating a systems orientation whereas concern with helping a junior member of staff cope with the stress levels engendered by burdensome assessment loads might be deemed more of a person orientation. The horizontal axis again measures polarized tendencies. A domesticating tendency indicates practice that is principally concerned with encouraging or developing behaviours both in self and

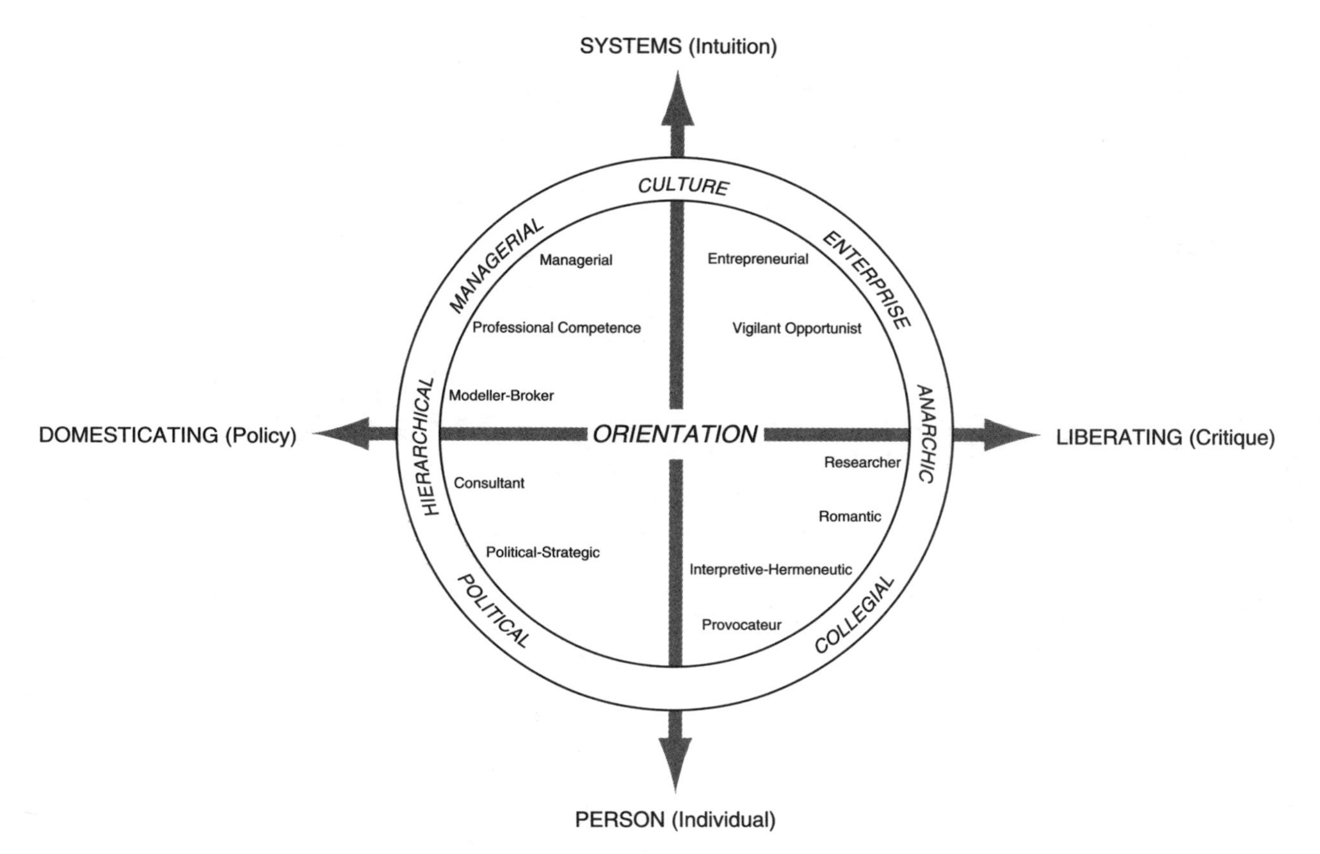

Figure 8 Towards an ecological paradigm of educational development

others that conform with the expressed 'official' or explicit purposes or mission of the institution or its prevailing and influential normative culture(s), which may be either explicit and overt or implicit and covert. A liberating tendency on the other hand would indicate practice that ran counter to such prevailing purposes and cultures and sought to transform them. These tendencies have been adapted from a conceptual model originally proposed by Wellington and Austin (1996) in relation to differences in orientation to reflective practice. It is suggested here that these tendencies have equal validity in relation to how orientations to educational development might be plotted against these differing values. Fig. 8 elaborates the model by suggesting that a systems orientation implies the meeting of institutional needs as opposed to the meeting of individual needs through a person orientation. Similarly it is argued that Wellington and Austin's domesticating-liberating axis can be interpreted as marking a spectrum which emphasizes adherence to expressed policy at one extreme and commitment to 'emancipatory' critique at the other. It might of course be argued that not all educational research activity should be construed as offering critique and that educational research can be deployed to support an existing policy stance. Such policy-oriented research would of course be plotted further towards the domesticating end of the horizontal axis. This is omitted on grounds that the model is acknowledged as demonstrating an inevitably simplified view.

The usual caution would apply against reading too much prescription, closure, or foundationalism into this representation. It is intended to be a useful heuristic at a given point of time, and is meant to serve as a useful and illuminative simplification only. Two particular complicating factors would remain to be taken into account in any interpretation of such a pattern. The first of these is the notion of tribalism and the second that of 'cultural traffic', with its implication of 'multiple cultural configurations'.

Tribalism

The concept of *tribalism* has proved influential as an explanatory concept to characterize the behaviour of actors within higher education settings. Becher's (1989) classic account of *Academic Tribes and Territories* has drawn attention to the tribe-like allegiances encountered within disciplinary groupings in universities, and the specific cultural pressures that arise within those tribes.

> Any systematic questioning of the accepted disciplinary ideology will be seen as heresy and may be punished by expulsion; any infiltration of alien values and practices will be appropriately dealt with [. . .] Thus, within economics, those who question the basic axioms of the subject are regarded as deranged if not positively dangerous, and are liable to find themselves cast into a wilderness of their own; deviants in other

marginal fields, such as statistical areas of mathematics, may be cut off and left to form an independent self-sufficient community.

(1989: 37)

Evans (1988, 1993) has described the interior cultures of language teachers and English teachers within higher education from a quasi-anthropological ethnographic perspective. Badley (1996: 63, after Biglan 1973) presents 'the four domains of the tribal university' as follows:

	Abstract	Concrete
Reflective	(Hard pure) Natural sciences Mathematics	(Soft pure) Social sciences Humanities
Active	(Hard applied) Science-based professions e.g. engineering	(Soft applied) Social professions: social work, law, education

Figure 9 Badley's four domains of the tribal university

Badley points out that traditionally universities have tended to privilege the hard pure knowledge domains over the soft applied ones. He sees educational development, in this perspective, as a *nomadic* tribe, 'with no fixed abode' (64), occasionally inhabiting 'the obscure and ill-favoured hinterland of application' (Becher 1989: 57). Badley characterizes the ways in which the different tribal cultures within the university have differential expectations of educational development and make different demands upon it. Whilst, in his opinion, the collegial academic more or less ignores educational development altogether – 'after all Oxford managed to do without an educational development service for the best part of a millennium and survived' (Badley, 1996: 65–6) –'the managerial university on the other hand wants the educational development centre to do its bidding. It pays the piper and it calls the tune and the tune had better be a hymn to corporate excellence' (66). Badley refers to McNay's provocative description of staff development as 'management propaganda'. Entrepreneurial university cultures on the other hand prefer to have enterprise units rather than educational development units, though 'their staff tend to go native and turn into educational developers' (66).

In the tribal university the various tribes want different things from educational development. The so-called hard disciplines often want clear answers to pedagogical questions. They may be irritated by the educational developers' vagueness and their inability to give simple answers to straightforward problems. The soft disciplines, occupying much the same tribal domain as the educational developers themselves, may be more understanding because they recognise the subtleties and

> difficulties of educational practice and the lack of clear-cut answers. However there is a widespread perception that the real trouble with these educational developers is that when you ask them to tell you how to do something they organise a 'bloody workshop'.
>
> (66)

One obvious caveat for developers working in the tribal domain is to be aware of the tribal taboos, the deep-seated cultural or discursive predispositions which are transgressed at one's peril. Taylor (1999) has called for greater 'inter-tribal understanding' within universities as a means of providing greater security for a profession under economic threat. Within this present study it is interesting to note how respondents identify the tribal characteristics of their own professional grouping. One respondent makes the following observation.

> I think it's fair to say that there *is* a sense of a staff development community, both internally within the UK but also internationally with staff developers in other countries such as HERDSA in Australia. And that's a rather unusual thing, and interesting, compared with other professions. What it suggests is that the sense of community is more about 'HE-ness' than about being a staff developer. But I think there are different neighbourhoods in the [educational development] village. Some are seen as being a bit posher than others, and some as being a bit more 'desirable.' I think it is probably a natural thing where you have practitioners who have a very varied set of backgrounds and routes into the career. I think if normative entry requirements were to be made mandatory then the sense of being part of a 'tribe' would grow. Again I think it comes back to the issue of accreditation. At the moment anyone can enter into educational development because there are no accreditation requirements.
>
> (Respondent 28)

He points out that there are different types of practitioner within the tribe.

> There are people like [X], and [Y]. They are respected by other practitioners because they've thought hard about what they're doing. They've contributed to knowledge about practice. I would call them *knowledge-led practitioners*. Then there are what I would term as *practice-led practitioners*. People such as [Z] at [a new university] come to mind. Their work is mainly about *performance*. We need both kinds. I would say there are:
>
> 1. the thinkers about practice
> 2. those who use the knowledge about practice
> 3. those practising
>
> (Respondent 28)

Cultural traffic

Alvesson (2002) has warned against oversimplification and promises of quick fixes in relation to organizational culture. He cautions against 'premature normativity' as well as the 'trivialisation' and 'managerialisation' of culture (43–7). Instead of a functionalist and instrumentalist notion of 'good culture', or pointing culture in the 'right' direction, he suggests that 'Learning to "think culturally" about organisational reality might inspire enlightened managerial everyday action rather than unrealistic programmes for culture change or bending patterns of meaning, ideas and values to managerial will' (47). He points up the importance of the 'complexity, variation and tolerance for incoherence of cultural values, ideas and meanings' and introduces the concept of 'cultural traffic' (192). This might be *media-carried*, through ideas and meanings communicated across distances by mass media, books, Internet and Web technologies, consultants, political movements and so forth, or *group-carried*, through the flows and movements of people in and out of organisations and communities, with ideas conveyed on the back of geographical and social mobility, increasingly on a global scale. This suggests that we would do better to think in terms of 'multiple cultural configurations'.

> Related to these multiple 'cultural movements' where ideas and meanings originate in institutions and communities and then put imprints in a particular organisation, but of great significance in itself, are the groupings and regroupings around various issues that trigger different social constellations and cultural orientations. We can thus talk about dynamic cultural repositionings, fuelled by the multitude and dynamics of social and ideational sources of meanings, ideas and identifications. Here we have a cultural traffic between the multitude of meanings and values made possible between the ideologies and discourses that are or can be made present in an organisation.
>
> (192)

Metaphors for culture

As we noted at the outset of this section, the use of 'culture' as a broad metaphor is potentially problematic. Since Morgan's (1980, 1986) influential writing on organizations, the use of metaphors has been very much in vogue to describe organizations as pyramids, organisms, machines, ecologies, garbage cans, traffic, and the like. Indeed this book on educational development is 'littered' with metaphors. Since empirical data never speaks for itself, research can never fully avoid the use of such tropes. Of course, they draw in subjective association, the fanciful, even the absurd, but the purpose of this is to defamiliarize, to provide an altered perspective. Brown (1976: 173) describes metaphors as 'category errors with a purpose, linguistic madness with a method'. However the use of metaphor can be seductively playful, or fashionable, leading to superficiality or over-simplification. As Alvesson (2002: 23) argues,

> Complex understanding is perhaps more often derived from a synthesis of different metaphors than from a single sharp-profile picture. This problem arises partly from the limitations of current metaphors and partly from the complexity of the phenomena we deal with. For example, it is unlikely that any researcher sees an organisation exclusively as a machine or exclusively as an organism [. . .] There is also the problem that language is restricted. The words which we have at our disposal do not always adequately signify just what we want to pinpoint.

Hence, in order to gain a more sophisticated perspective on the metaphor of organizational culture, Alvesson (31–6) offers us a further series of metaphors *for* culture. These involve considering culture as 'exchange-regulator', as 'compass', as 'social glue', as 'sacred cow', as 'affect-regulator', as 'blinkers', as 'world-closure' and as 'disorder'. It is worth considering, from the developer's perspective, the applicability of these metaphors to the academic cultures which the developer has to negotiate.

In the first of these metaphors, culture as *exchange-regulator*, culture is seen as 'a control mechanism that can handle complex exchange relations' (31). It provides members of the organization with 'intellectual tools and a long memory' to enable them to evaluate 'fair rewards in the long run'(31). In this view culture would socialize academics into accepting that over the long term their interests are congruent with those of the senior management (the employer) and would suppress 'short-term opportunistic behaviour' (31). One can see how this might fit with domesticating purposes of development, in reaching trade-offs with academics in terms of their willingness to enter into new developmental transactions. Such trade-offs might, for example, be recognition that engagement with new technologies and pedagogies might meet the needs and study preferences of students from diverse backgrounds. This in turn might increase curriculum flexibility, improving retention and hence safeguarding courses and academic jobs 'in the long run'. Or there may be other, less tangible rewards. As a respondent in a European development project recently remarked, 'This takes a lot of time; it is fortunate that I enjoy it, because I have spent holidays, weekends and entire evenings working at this' (Cousin et al. 2004: 138). Though an obvious conclusion might be that such a cultural interpretation might suit the perceptions of developers with a predominantly managerial orientation, one could also see such a negotiating position being adopted by developers of other orientations discussed earlier, such as the Romantic orientation or even the Interpretive-Hermeneutic.

When culture is envisaged as a *compass* it is seen as pointing to the desirable direction (or set of values) towards which the organization should aspire (or where the management wishes it to go). This has much to do with the image or brand that the institution wishes to maintain. An older university might set its compass to collegiality, individual autonomy and scholarliness. A newer institution might point more to serving the needs of regional industry, meeting the needs of a diverse local student population, and offering innovative marketable courses. In relation to the compass direction of the departments they are dealing with developers might be advised to heed Alvesson's observation that 'Traditional values are anchored in history and are persistent, while leader-induced values are less stable. An idea of product durability and reliability apparently governs the argument [. . .]'(32). Caught as they often are between competing discourses and influences within the organization, there may be a cautionary note emerging here for developers about promoting, or even just backing, 'leader-induced values' that are in contradistinction to traditional values that are seen to preserve continuity and unity, regardless of whence they might have been derived. Where the financial solvency of the organization enters as a factor however, the developer may need to judge whether culture is acting as compass or exchange regulator, or, of course, both.

Considering culture as *social glue* is probably the most common way in which culture is envisaged within organizations, as a set of shared values and beliefs which helps to integrate and stabilize organizations, reduce conflict and tension, and create a sense of order, purpose and harmony. However Alvesson talks of two versions of the glue metaphor, one emphasizing integration, with consensus seen as 'natural' and 'something organically produced', and the other seeing corporate culture as 'the last frontier of control' and as 'a strategy for achieving social-glue-like effects' (32). The former would seem to be consonant with Wenger's (1998) notion of the community of practice, with its normative capacity and its powerful role in the identity formation of participants. There are implications for developers, acting as 'legitimate peripheral participants' (Wenger 1998: 100–1) in, for example, discipline-based communities of practice with strong social and cultural 'glue', to recognize the importance of dialogue and participation in the early stages of encouraging or implementing any innovation, the better to foster an acceptance culture. Such a view might well be in keeping with developers of a Romantic or Hermeneutic orientation who would be likely to adopt such a line. Developers of a Managerialist or Political orientation, however, might well feel the need to apply a little corporate glue in the form of mission statements, corporate objectives, departmental awaydays and other 'bonding' activities. In academic organizations where policy definition and control of implementation are loosely-coupled 'the glue is viewed as fragile, in need of maintenance work, and not always capable of holding the organisation together' (Alvesson 2002: 33). Cousin et al. (2004: 138), analysing participation in an e-learning project involving universities from several European countries, caution against any attempt at imposition of cultural norms.

> The conversations amongst the group of innovators in the institution developed into a community of practice where participation was as

> much an indicator of success as reification in the form of published outputs. An important factor here also seems to be that individuals or groups can find their own measure of participation and therefore remain within a personal comfort zone. Our data suggests that participation needs to be encouraged on whatever terms actors feel comfortable. As Wenger argues, participation is a condition of learning and the institution must acknowledge that this learning and creativity cannot be imposed.

An implication for developers here is, perhaps, the sometimes uncomfortable, almost collusive, position of having to manage meaning(s) between such 'organic' communities and senior management wishes to 'develop a corporate culture functioning as a social-integrative force' (Alvesson 2002: 33).

Developers will be familiar with the various *sacred cows* that culture might enshrine within their organization. The notion of the 'sacred' in culture, derived from Gagliardi (1986: 123), refers to 'the deeper levels of culture and members' internalisation of certain ideals and values' (33). There is a strong emotional identification with, and ontological dimension to, these values. They may take the form of academic freedom or the primacy of research, widening participation and access, learning for learning's sake, vocational relevance, the founder's original vision, or they may reside within the discipline and be related to particular standards of practice or notions of truth. These ideals and values will very probably be manifested through discourse. Hence, tensions and divergence will also be signalled discursively. Gagliardi argues that the priority for every organization is to maintain its cultural identity and that the 'sacred' values and ideals serve in a powerful way to sustain this identity, hence imposing very real limits on change, indeed suggesting that they are nigh on impossible to change. The implication here for developers is that because these sacred cows have a self-evident, taken-for-granted quality amongst academics – who are deeply committed to them – it might be an act of folly to attempt to counter them. Of course the sacred cows might not, from the managerialist perspective, make sense in terms of *realpolitik* and organizational survival, in which case the developer might again find him or herself managing meaning, and engaging in some cultural exchange-regulation as described earlier. But, as Alvesson points out (2002: 33), such deeply held cultural commitment is not easily amenable to negotiation.

> The sacred-cow view of course can be seen as referring to similar functions as the compass or the social-glue idea – the metaphors are in no way contradictory – but it does not clearly show the direction of concrete behaviour, nor can it be regarded as a control strategy. Rather, what the sacred-cow metaphor refers to is value commitments than control strategies. It differs from other metaphors in referring to much deeper and more affective aspects of culture.

A different way of conceptualizing organizational culture is to see it as an emotional arena in which the strengthening of the culture requires 'the subtle (or not so subtle) control of employee emotions – or at least those emotions expressed in the work place' (Van Maanen and Kunda 1989: 52). Alvesson refers to this disciplining of the emotions of organizational members in terms of 'culture as *affect-regulator*' (2002: 33). This is one of the trickiest aspects of the developer's work, negotiating spaces in which colleagues may consider revising their existing practice, and in doing so, tolerate shifts, however minor or subtle, in their professional identities and feelings. Consider for example, the developer confronted with the response of this young, research-minded, overworked lecturer attending an induction workshop:

> We've given up three precious days of research for this. There is frustration and resistance among us, and most certainly considerable levels of suspicion. We've already heard that this is a waste of time, from those who have passed through this phase of development before us and returned with this as settled news. Most of us haven't had a chance to do any research at all during the course of this term. It's been just too overwhelming. We are anxious about this. We have book proposals to write, articles to finish, and untold piles of marking to get through before the end of the week. Our discussions are not on the subject of teaching and learning, but on whether we have found somewhere to live, on mortgages, house prices, and the wages paid to us as academics. We also talk of our partners, the miseries and freedoms of the separations that academic life inevitably brings, however temporarily. 'What are you working on?' is the question between us. The question is never 'What courses do you teach?' Not here, not now, not at the beginning. The stakes are too high. This is not the game we are in.
>
> (Ashworth et al. in press)

The transformation that the developer might be wishing to undertake in such situations can be viewed in terms of what Meyer and Land (2003, 2004) have described as a 'threshold concept'.

> in certain disciplines there are 'conceptual gateways' or 'portals' that lead to a previously inaccessible, and initially perhaps 'troublesome', way of thinking about something. A new way of understanding, interpreting, or viewing something may thus emerge – a transformed internal view of subject matter, subject landscape, or even world view.
>
> (2004, in press)

Such transformations, they go on to argue, entail both epistemological and ontological considerations. The transformed way of thinking will often involve 'the indissoluble inter-relatedness of the learner's identity with thinking and language (reading, writing, listening, talking). Threshold concepts lead not only to transfigured thought but to a transfiguration of identity and adoption of an extended or elaborated discourse' (2004, in press). One such transformation is often that characterized by Biggs (1999) in terms of a shift in level on the part of teachers in higher education when they move from considering their practice in terms of their own teaching performance to that of the understanding and achievement of their students. The ontological shift and *affect-regulation* involved in such a transformation is not inconsiderable. The developer is required, with considerable skill and judgement, to create an appropriate developmental space, or 'holding environment' (Winnicott 1971), within which this transformation might be effected. Meyer and Land (2004, in press) offer a further example which illustrates the discursive and often 'troublesome' nature of such affect-regulation and shift in identity:

> Similarly, educational developers who provide accreditation programmes for academics in higher education report the troublesome nature of 'reflection' for academic colleagues, such as engineers, who hold quite different understandings of scientific knowledge and who initially find the now well-established discourse of professional reflection both alien, inaccessible and unnecessary, though a facility with such discourse is increasingly deemed *de rigeur* by various quality regimes. Again, from the teacher's perspective, 'they just don't get it'. From the learner's perspective there is an unwelcome power relation deemed to be in operation in which one academic tribe is seen imperialistically to be colonising the discursive space of other tribes.

A more unusual perspective on culture, but one with resonance for the experience of educational developers is that of culture acting as *blinkers*. In this Alvesson draws on the Jungian approach of Krefting and Frost (1985) who argue that organizational culture is channelled through the unconscious, and hence members of the organization have only partial access to it, and understanding of it, and 'easily become victims of shadows, archetypes, and fantasies' (Alvesson 2002: 35). Whereas much writing on organizational culture emphasizes *organization* and its emphasis on orderliness, order-creation and the systematic, this approach suggests that this emphasis can produce only blinkered understanding, a blind eye, and hence conformity and compliance. Considering alternative, even deviant and subversive perspectives of the organization ('unincorporated shadows'), might be healthy, constructive and emancipatory.

> Effective cultures need a balance, which requires the incorporation of shadows or other less dominant elements. Such cultures must also deal with 'problems posed by life-situations' (Turner) in complex and realistic ways rather than at the idealised, archetypal level. When organisational culture goes awry, blockage may well result from unincorporated shadows or unresolved archetypal conflicts; hence, exploring the problem in terms of shadows or archetypes may well be the way to approach it.
>
> (Krefting and Frost 1985: 156)

As part of their practice developers often find themselves obliged to deal with such unincorporated shadows and unresolved conflicts. In terms of archetypes, the developer's role might at times be conceptualized as Court Jester, Fool or tribal Witch Doctor. Such motifs capture the paradoxical status of the developer, influential but vulnerable, the harbinger of troublesome change, the agent of transformation, but often ridiculed and seen as of inferior status to the 'true' academic. The developer is seen as a potential stressor, the lackey of management, but also as comedic, ludic, the eternal flipchart-bearing facilitator, the 'looney in the portacabin' (Respondent 33). But as with all ludic and carnivalistic activity, inversions and subversions are permitted. The cliché of 'thinking outside the box' in development sessions might occasionally mean that the unincorporated shadows are allowed, briefly, to be rendered visible. In this way developers become the catalysts of troublesome knowledge, providing glimpses of alternative futures and practices, in a position to speak truth to power, even though it may incur a whipping subsequently. Such engagement with the unresolved, with the problematic, can be the spur of change, and draw members of the organization (tribe) into a state of liminality (Meyer and Land 2004) in which previous learning is rendered less certain, more fluid, and open to transformation. As Meyer and Land's work on threshold concepts indicates, grasping a new concept – in this case in terms of professional practice – is never just a cognitive shift. It involves a repositioning of self in relation to the subject. From the viewpoint of educational development this implies that some attention has to be paid to the discomforts of troublesome knowledge, or else resentment, anxiety or mere 'mimicry' and compliance may ensue. Moreover this view of culture should serve to remind the developer that despite their own, sometimes evangelistic commitment to teaching and learning enhancement – their own sacred cows as it were – they can be viewed in some quarters of the organization with mistrust, and seen as collusive or complicit with authority.

> we should not forget that the metaphor of the Jester also implies the use of indirect and subtle ways to achieve desired results. There is a clear idea on the part of the Jester of which results are important to achieve and there is a definite element of hiding the real message so that the receiver is not aware of what is really happening. This element of deception, possibly of manipulation, is one that we find it difficult to combine with the ethos of the academy and the value of open argumentative discourse.
>
> (Ashworth et al. in press)

Another way in which culture might serve to impose a form of blindness on the organization is through what Alvesson calls *world-closure*. Whereas the previous metaphor of 'blinkers' emphasized psychological factors, this notion stresses sociological factors. In this view he argues (2002: 35) that, though social reality is potentially open and negotiable, 'culture makes it appear given, natural and, when it comes to basic premises, impossible (or at least very difficult) to question.' There is a strong discursive effect here. Alvesson provides an example (36) of the way in which the discourse of 'teamwork' or 'community' can be used in organizations in ways which do not actually describe the organizational situation but *define* it. In this way such discourse has a normative effect, naturalizing and legitimizing a particular way of seeing the organization, and using cultural means to sustain existing power relations within the organization. 'This effect may be produced by traditions or other impersonal forces or by the more or less conscious influence of powerful actors using cultural and ideological means' (35). Of course educational developers may operate on either side of this cultural closure. They may themselves serve to bring about a degree of world-closure in order to foster perspectives relating to, say, learning, or quality, in the wider interests of the student experience or organizational effectiveness and survival. The promotion of outcomes-based approaches to learning, notions of deep and surface learning, adherence to quality assurance precepts, access, student enterprise or employability, for example, could be construed as versions of 'world-closure', with benign intent. Developers with Managerialist, Political, Entrepreneurial or Professional Competence orientations might be characterized as more likely to operate in this fashion. They might be seen, too, in this regard, as serving a domesticating function within the organization. On the other hand developers might wish to challenge what they see as unhelpful forms of world-closure, critiquing, for example, the very notions just mentioned, from the emancipatory end of the axis. This might be more typical (stereotypical?) behaviour of those with Romantic, Research, Consultant or Interpretive-Hermeneutic orientations. Here the concern may be to provide for colleagues different ways of seeing, and new avenues for movement. Again we are reminded of the developer in Section One who saw development, in chess terms, as 'unblocking', as the removal of closure and provision of new spaces.

> I see development as 'opening up' so that people's potential could be fully realised. You haven't got this powerful queen . . . you don't want to move really. Open spaces really. Of course the point is when you've opened it up the queen can go straight, left, all sorts of places. It just doesn't open up one single channel which is pre-determined as the queen's route. It means that the queen is able then to go in five different directions, backwards even. It's an unblocking.
>
> (Respondent 8)

The final metaphor Alvesson provides is that of culture as *disorder*. This cultural perspective on the organizations of today assumes that they, like the societies in which they are situated, are characterized by ambiguity, uncertainty, multi-facetedness, fragmentation, confusion, risk and dissensus. 'The concept of disorder' he suggests, 'may be the best choice to mark the non-systematic, fluid and contradictory character of cultural manifestations in organisations [. . .] even though it can be argued that it moves on the border of where a culture concept is meaningful' (34). Such a view, of course, contrasts sharply with the notion of culture having an 'ordering' function, and even with the notion of 'organisation' itself. However, as Martin (1987) has pointed out, cultural diversity, fragmentation and multi-facetedness in societies or organizations does not render them 'non-cultural' or pre-cultural. The metaphor accords well with Fullan's (1993) notions of non-linear change discussed in Section Two. One can see its appeal to certain developers of a postmodernist persuasion and to certain of those of an Interpretive-Hermeneutic or Researcher orientation. It might also accord well with the theory-in-use, if not always the espoused theory, of certain developers of an Opportunistic or Entrepreneurial orientation. We recall Respondent 21 observing, in Section Two, that 'I'm not sure that you can manage change in an institution like this. The operational environment is too complex. It's chaotic.' Let us bring this section on culture to a close with the difficulties for management that this respondent identifies.

> Obviously we have to make plans in our organisation, and we have to plan for change, though we know three or five year plans never really reach fruition. They are always provisional imaginings of ways to go, of possible futures. But given the *very* varied nature of the constituencies within this university – socially, culturally, politically, in terms of disciplines and discourses and multiple meanings and so on – it's hard, very hard – to imagine what particular vantage point in terms of management would give you that kind of purview that would allow you to make sense of the place, and the directions in which it should go and the best way it should be organised. It needs very skilled insight to get that sort of understanding and I think management need more, really, to go *with* the different cultures in the Departments here, to navigate them, rather than try and *create* a 'university culture' whatever that would be. And that has very complex implications for management.

Postscript

To 'conclude', or offer some other form of closure on the community at this stage in its own development would seem inappropriate and premature. Educational development as it has been represented here appears as a problematic enterprise and a fractured community within higher education, growing in influence though paradoxically still vulnerable and marginal. It is shown as occupying a variety of educational spaces within the academy, being caught up in competing institutional narratives and shot through with conflicting value positions. The question remains as to whether development is best seen as a historical phase or likely to become a permanent feature of the higher education landscape, with a growing body of professional knowledge and a more secure research base. Recent research indicates a growing plurality of ways of fostering educational development (McArthur et al. 2004).

This study has sought to clarify what educational developers consider their role to be, both operationally and strategically, how they make sense of their practice, characterize it and explain it to others, and what their priorities and preferred ways of working are. In response to these questions the study has produced a number of theoretical representations or artefacts to explain the relationships between educational development practice, notions of organizational change and its context of action or strategic terrain. It is hoped that the development of these theoretical representations might aid future discussion of the nature of educational development practice and provide possible insight and direction for further practice-related research in this area. These theoretical constructs point to the evident complexity of the educational development role. There can be no definitive valorized approach to effective practice as chosen strategies must be appropriate to, and are to considerable extent determined by, specific operational contexts and terrain. These latter include such variables as the structure, culture and size of institutions, the nature and conventions of disciplines, the expectations and needs of particular stakeholders and the remit of development units. The terrain and responses to it are rendered more complex by the fact that both continue to change as the wider higher education environment continually changes, often in non-linear fashion.

Educational development and modernism

In the light of this, educational development is becoming a contested notion, value-laden in terms of implied import and outcome and subject to constant review and negotiation. That notwithstanding, it would appear from accounts in this study that a good deal of the thinking of respondents in relation to their practice takes place within a modernist perspective. Educational development, as currently practised, remains, on the whole, a modernist project. It is often informed, for example, by conceptualizations, such as those derived from managerialist notions of organizational change, which valorize benign ideas of progress. Alternatively, other orientations are informed by conceptualizations such as 'deep' and 'surface' approaches to learning which, like the ideas of Marx, Freud, Saussure and other powerful influences on the modernist period, are derived from notions of *structuralism* which are often seen to underpin the modernist project. The massification of higher education which, as discussed in the introduction, has so exercised educational development, and its accompanying patterns of modularization can themselves be seen as modernist tendencies.

> Modernism equates change with progress, which is defined as increasing control over nature and society. Perhaps the most important means for understanding and carrying out the modernist project is education. Higher education is deeply embedded in the ideals, institutions and vocabulary of modernism.
>
> (Bloland 1995: 523–4)

When modernist assumptions of progress come under scrutiny and challenge, the modernist educational development project is rendered problematic.

> Concepts that lend credence to faith in reason, science, progress, and the Enlightenment are privileged in the modernist world, and especially in the university and college. Once their legitimacy is called into question, all sorts of hierarchies become suspect in the university.
>
> (527)

Certain orientations, principally the Interpretive-Hermeneutic, the educational Researcher and the Political-Strategic, seem to accommodate understandings which recognize that higher education institutions, as 'institutions of modernity', (525) are vulnerable to critical scrutiny from postmodernist perspectives, which, when directed towards higher education 'provide a powerful delegitimating lever that interrogates the purposes, structure, and activities of higher education as it now operates in its modernist context' (528).

> Postmodernism interrogates the modern system, which is built on continuing, persistent efforts to totalise or unify, pointing out that totalisation hides contradictions, ambiguities, and oppositions and is a means for generating power and control. Institutions of modernity come under critical postmodern scrutiny, and among the primary institutions open to questioning are the college and university. To see postmodernism as a way of understanding the limits of modernism is to view our world in the midst of profound change and to concentrate on the disillusionment we are experiencing with some of our deepest assumptions and cherished hopes relating to our most important institutions. We seek rational solutions in a world that increasingly distrusts reason as a legitimate approach to problem solving. We try to move forward in our lives and through our institutions in a milieu of declining faith in the possibility of progress.
>
> (525–6)

Such is the challenge facing educational developers at the start of the twenty-first century. Whilst Readings (1997) has spoken of the 'University in ruins,' with the implication for developers that the lot of academics increasingly will be to manage and live with dissensus, Delantey (2001) suggests that a future purpose of academies in a state of postmodernity will be able to act as nodes of interconnectivity in a knowledge society, a role perhaps not entirely unfamiliar to educational developers.

Community, diversity and fracture

Modernism, and higher education, have also always celebrated community, but community as inclusive, the *universitas.* Postmodernism, however, would seek to organize a politics of difference.

> Deconstruction celebrates differences, but refers not to the difference of heterogeneity, which is intrinsic to modernism, but to the difference of disruption, tension, and the withholding of closure. The modernist idea of community also celebrates difference, but emphasises that which unites people, smooths over disruption, and places limits on the depth and intensity of differences.
>
> (529)

The very idea of a community of practice includes within it, paradoxically, the notion of *exclusion.*

> The creation of community generally is a process of setting boundaries, and this means that communities always have those excluded and those created as marginals.
>
> (529)

The orientations that have been described within this study can be seen as representing forms of *heterogeneity* within a community. However, it may be that, in a coming century defined more by postmodern notions of change, a development community based on the 'intensity of *differences*' (529), rather than heterogeneity, might be more effective, if not essential. Young (1990: 301) speaks of the need for 'inexhaustible heterogeneity' and 'openness to unassimilated otherness' as an alternative system to that of a community which, in defining itself, simultaneously excludes. At the time of writing there is clearly a tendency to encourage 'otherness', unassimilated or not, in the promotion of discipline-specific subject centres, devolved and distributed, under the aegis of the Learning and Teaching Support network (LTSN).

The community of practice of educational development emerges from this study as diverse and fractured. In relation to a question about shared values in the community one respondent summarized the situation as follows:

> Up until about two years ago I'd have said yes. Accepting those lines of cleavage and the SEDA/UCoSDA split along the old and new university lines. Accepting that I would have said yes in general, if by values you mean what matters most, then I would have said yeah, you could have said there's a community of interest. That is, there are common values, and what mattered most to people were things like – well *profoundly* a preoccupation with student learning. And a view of students as being the real clients or beneficiaries of our work. A notion of pedagogic progress (that it's always possible to do things better) and that what we are striving to do is improve our thinking and practice around the pedagogic function. Some of the qualities, the personal qualities or behavioural styles that attached to those were things like sensitivity towards others' needs, listening skills when working with clients, maybe a quasi-counselling relationship almost, a determination to share good practice, a clear support for innovation, creativity, new thinking, new ideas, new techniques, fertile ground for innovation, the sense that when you met educational developers at conferences or elsewhere, you've kind of come home. A like-mindedness. It was comfortable. It was easy. It was one of those cases where you meet someone for the first time and within ten minutes it's as if you'd met them ten years ago, kind of thing. I think we've seen so many changes that educational development is undergoing a fracture or series of fractures.
>
> (Respondent 2)

This fracture can be detected at the level of individual practice. 'There are a number of sets of people who I see personally as relevant but none of them do the whole thing,' suggests Respondent 14. 'They do bits of the thing. There is a set of good higher education researchers, also a set of education philosophers, a set of teaching and learning researchers and people who have done work on staff development – assessment initiatives, teaching initiatives, student satisfaction stuff, management.' Respondent 3 describes a supportive community but one riven by petty feuds.

> I think it's also a bit like living in a village where rifts and feuds occur. I think it's also a bit like being in a village in which when somebody's in trouble a lot of people rally round and help. We may all bitch about each other, but we do actually help to sort people out, I think. I think certainly we're a world full of gossip. We're a world full of petty rivalries and bitchinesses but I would say that if you name any university of Britain – we can test this out later – I would normally be able to name somebody who worked in our field in it and I would normally have had some kind of contact with them.
>
> (Respondent 3)

It is from such fracture that the different orientations emanate. But a fracture can also be identified at the level of national organization, which goes deeper than the UCoSDA/SEDA fault line already mentioned:

> In the USA POD – an excellent network. 500 folk at this year's conference. They've been terrific at taking on board new people. They're superb at helping to induct new people, and help them. The best analogy the UK had was when SRHE had its staff development group, which then merged with SEDA. In some ways I think that was an error of judgement. It some ways it wasn't but in some ways it was. I think there were some things that that group did which SEDA have never really taken on board terribly seriously, in terms of organisational development, institutional development, that sort of stuff. SEDA's had a different sort of focus and then been opportunistic about other sorts of things, and that's been very good and they've done many good things. I think they're about to now face a major crisis, if HEA comes into being, as it will, about how does that change SEDA's role. And I don't think some folk high up in SEDA have come to terms with that as yet, frankly. Over time HEA will become infinitely more independent of SEDA than some of them think. It must . . . must. To be healthy it must. It can't be in the pocket of another organisation. It's a must.
>
> (Respondent 14)

The community, like the sector whose transformation it seeks to encourage, is itself in process of transformation. The establishment of ILTHE/HEA posed a paradox for the educational development community. In many respects the creation of the ILTHE/HEA owed much to the ceaseless lobbying activity of the community over many years. In the same moment, however, it took much of the accreditation (professional competence) and possibly practice-related research function away from established educational development organizations such as SEDA and HESDA, whose roles must now be reviewed and redirected. Moreover since its inception it has strongly emphasized the importance of the roles of learning technology and discipline-specific approaches. These development groupings represent major sites of turbulence within the future direction and growth of the educational development community. It is not clear at present whether either of these newly developing communities will wish to be identified as part of the educational development tribe or whether they will remain discrete communities. What is possible is that the next generation of *de facto* developers will draw on both groupings, particularly as there is no obvious sign that the current community, the first generation of its kind, is self-replicating.

Vocation and professional status

This raises issues about entry to the community, regulation and its professional status or aspiration.

> I'm just wondering what a profession is. Is a professional somebody who has a professional body? Because if you do say that I'm not sure we have. Is a professional someone who has to undergo a formal training? Well there isn't formal training for educational development. Nobody leaves school or University and says 'I know what I want to be. I want to be an educational developer!' We're all second career people, if not third or fourth. So I'm not sure we are what you might call a profession. I think we might be more what you might call a *vocation*. Because a lot of us have joined this through passion and commitment and involvement. And if you compare that to a profession like Medicine, or Law – maybe they're vocations as well, I don't know – but certainly if you think about the kind of people who work in our field, we're not doing it for the money. You look around at the originating disciplines of people who are staff developers, which is a very interesting question – quite a few Psychologists, quite a few people from Literature, a smallish number from Education, and the rest come from absolutely everywhere.
>
> (Respondent 3)

However, certain developers would celebrate this inclusiveness, seeing the regulation of entry as potentially stifling a culture of innovation. The lack of formal recognition can be seen as the source of aspiration:

> I think it's basically a philanthropic culture. I think it's quite a supportive culture. Relatively supportive. I think we're aspirational. Certainly the grouping I belong to *long* to be taken seriously, *long* to be on the big national committees. Long to be somebody the Times Higher Education Supplement rings up, rather than the other way round. Some of us break through and some of us don't. But we are aspirational. Partly because we're *not* a recognised profession.
>
> (Respondent 3)

The craving of recognition, of academic respectability is something that has long exercised the reflections of educational developers. But the colonizing or assimilation of existing disciplinary ground by a new field can prove counter-productive.

> I would think that one of the dangers that any area like ours can have is that it dives into other disciplines for theoretical respectability and goes for sociological theories or psychological theories and the snag with that is self-evident, in that in picking one set you tip the thing apparently that way. So you have a kind of semi-psychologist's eye of the world. The other snag is invariably you're a fraction out of date with that discipline so you're half a step behind that discipline itself. So then you become known as second-rate sociologists or second-rate psychologists and that's just not a clever move. And you're back to the jargon thing anyhow. You've almost won nothing out of your bid for respectability. But it's been done in different disciplines before, so it's not original to say that that has been tried. It's a slightly dangerous tactic, is probably the fair way to capture it. And it's not always a terribly productive tactic which is even more to the point. It's a crisis of confidence one. And people retreat to what they see as the temples, the academic temples, as a way of getting greater security. I think we have to try and find more productive devices than that.
>
> (Respondent 14)

The 'crisis of confidence' may also be seen to manifest itself in what some developers have identified as a lack of the contestation that seems to characterize other, more mature, professional or disciplinary communities of practice.

> I'm wondering where the debate is going to come from within the HEA. That's what we need to see emerging. Different groups and perspectives emerging within the HEA with different ideas of how things might be done and some real debate and differences of opinion about the values of such approaches instead of all this luvvy stuff and stroking that we've had in the past.
>
> (Respondent 25)

The newly formed successor organization to the ILTHE, the Higher Education Academy has indicated its intent to foster the development of a substantial research base at the interface of higher educational theory and practice. If a more rigorous research knowledge base is established it remains to be seen whether the culture of confidence and contestation that Respondent 25, and others, identify as a mark of a vigorous and effective practice, comes into being. Alternatively the torch of educational development in higher education may pass more into the hands of discipline-specific practitioners if funding imperatives continue to steer activity in that direction, or into a hydra-like proliferation of the practices of what Gornall (1999) has termed 'new professionals'. This latter group might indeed become much more a 'community of difference', including Web-based designers, flexible learning advisers, learning technology support staff, instructional designers, work-based learning advisers, study development professionals, academic writing advisers, key skills developers and others, many of whom lead a precarious existence at present in the somewhat twilight world of funded-project culture. This study has not had the scope to research the practice of such new professionals, or the practice of discipline-specific educational developers and the academic and pedagogic discourses that they might use or develop. It would however seem timely for such research initiatives to get under way. (A helpful contributory factor here would be an acknowledgement within the Research Assessment Exercise that educational development-related research within disciplines is meritable.)

The next decade will be a pivotal and perhaps defining period in the short history of educational development. There is no doubt of the continuing nature of change within higher education during this period, but whether educational development will become an established tribe within the higher education community, or come to be seen as having been a catalytic process within a specific historical period, later transmogrified into myriad other developmental agencies within a massified industry – 'other workers in the vineyard' – remains to be seen. One developer envisages a more central role for the community:

> The picture will be much different in 10 years I'm absolutely certain of that and I think that really because what is going to happen in higher education is much more of an *Americanisation*, if you like, that we are going to actually have a more important role. It may not be bigger because we don't know how much it will grow, but I do think that our role will become more of a fundamental role in the universities. To me it's becoming much, much more obvious we're shifting, we're really shifting from the margins and I think of that as tremendously hopeful because whatever the discipline and with mass higher education I think that if I don't enable learners to learn you know if we don't sort of take them through these processes and support their personal and professional development then we all may as well go home. Because I think that the massification hasn't even finished yet. That is quite clear. And people out there in the disciplines are on their knees. I know that they are on their knees. They're trying to cope and I think that what we're going to see is much more like core development for students in the earlier years and that their specialisation, their primary degree, may even be like they've learned how to learn, and their specialism actually comes in postgraduate Masters courses. It [going into educational development] was an enormous risk to take at that particular time as a reasonably successful scientist and I now feel that with the Academy and all sorts of things that, you know, taking a risk and coming in to what had almost an immature feel, if you like, but we've grown up!
>
> (Respondent 19)

However, certain misgivings remain.

So that's how I would see the big picture. Maybe it's an incredibly optimistic picture but there is a touch of pessimism there as well because I worry about the mass higher education and how we're actually going to manage it all. How the students are going to handle this. The pedagogical skills associated with new technologies are a big bugbear of mine. Yes we've got the tools but do we understand online environments? Do we understand the skills that students are going to need to be able to develop learning processes which are appropriate to that kind of medium? So while I have a lot of optimism, I also have a lot of worries that there's just not enough of us to handle that process.

(Respondent 19)

Vocation, self-belief and passion seem appropriate grace notes with which to close. As Respondent 3 observed.

Well I suppose the word passion popped up a bit ago, and I think educational developers as a breed tend to be quite *driven.* If you think of the great charismatic educational developers in this country, some of whom I've named and some of whom I haven't, these people are quite evangelical. We have to believe in what we do. And I think a passion for good learning is what drives us. Now where we get that from is another matter.

References

Abercrombie, N., Hill, S. and Turner, B.S. (1994) *Dictionary of Sociology*, 3rd edn. Harmondsworth: Penguin.

Altbach, P.G. (1997) An international crisis? The American professoriate in comparative perspective, *DÆDALUS*, 126(4): 315–38.

Alvesson, M. (2002) *Understanding Organisational Culture.* London: Sage Publications.

Ashworth, P., Handal, G., Hole, C., Land, R., Orr, M. and Phipps, A. (2004) Who are 'we'? Who are 'you'? Who are 'they'? Issues of role and identity in academic development. Elvidge, E. (ed) *Exploring Academic Development in Higher Education: Issues of Engagement.* Cambridge, Jill Rogers Associates.

Atkins, M.J., Beattie, J. and Dockrell, W.B. (1993) *Assessment Issues in Higher Education.* Sheffield: Employment Department.

Badley, G. (1996) Educational development in the managerial university, *Journal of Education Through Partnership*, 1(1): 53–70.

Ball, S.J. (1990a) *Politics and Policy Making in Education.* London: Routledge.

Ball, S.J. (ed.) (1990b) *Foucault and Education: Disciplines and Knowledge.* London: Routledge.

Barnett, R. (1992) *Improving Higher Education: Total Quality Care.* Buckingham: SRHE and Open University Press.

Barnett, R. (1994) *The Limits of Competence: Knowledge, Higher Education and Society.* Buckingham: SRHE and Open University Press.

Barnett, R. (2000) *Realising the University in an Age of Supercomplexity.* Buckingham: SRHE and Open University Press.

Barton, L. (1996) A policy statement, *Teaching and Learning in Higher Education*, 1(1): 1–6.

Becher, T. (1989) *Academic Tribes and Territories: Intellectual Enquiry and the Cultures of Disciplines.* Buckingham: SRHE and Open University Press.

Becher, T. and Kogan, M. (eds) (1992) *Process and Structure in Higher Education*, 2nd edn. London: Routledge.

Becher, T. and Trowler, P.R. (2001) *Academic Tribes and Territories*, 2nd edn. Buckingham: SRHE and Open University Press.

Bender, T. (1997) Politics, intellect, and the American University, 1945–1995, *DÆDALUS*, 126: 1–37.

Benne, K.D. and Chin, R. (1969) General strategies for effecting changes in human systems, in W.G. Bennis, K.D. Benne and R. Chin (eds) *The Planning of Change*, 2nd edn. New York: Holt Rinehart.

Berg, B. and Östergren, B. (1979) Innovation processes in higher education, *Studies in Higher Education*, 4: 261–8.

Bergquist, W.H. (1992) *The Four Cultures of the Academy: Insights and Strategies for Improving Leadership in Collegiate Organisations.* San Francisco: Jossey-Bass.

Bergquist, W.H. (1995) *Quality through Access, Access with Quality: The New Imperative for Higher Education.* San Francisco: Jossey-Bass.

Biggs, J. (1999) *Teaching for Quality Learning at University: What the Student Does.* Buckingham: SRHE and Open University Press.

Biglan, A. (1973) Relationships between subject matter characteristics and the structure and output of university departments, *Journal of Applied Psychology*, 57(3): 204–13.

Birnbaum, R. (1988) *How Colleges Work: The Cybernetics of Academic Organisation and Leadership.* San Francisco: Jossey-Bass.

Birnbaum, R. (1989) The cybernetic institution: toward an integration of governance theories, *Higher Education*, 18: 239–53.

Bloland, H.G. (1995) Postmodernism and Higher Education, in *Journal of Higher Education*, Vol. 66, No 5.

Bonamy, J., Charlier, B. and Saunders, M. (2001) 'Bridging Tools' for change: evaluating a collaborative learning network. *Journal of Computer Assisted Learning*, Vol. 17, No. 3: 295–305.

Booth, C. (1998) *Accreditation and Teaching in Higher Education* (The Booth Report). London: Committee of Vice-Chancellors and Principals (CVCP).

Boud, D. (1999) Is problem-based learning sufficiently robust to meet the new challenges of professional work? Paper presented at *Advancing Learning Communities in the New Millennium*, 8th European Conference for Research on Learning and Instruction, 24–28 August, Göteborg, Sweden.

Bourdieu, P. (1977) *Outline of a Theory of Practice*, trans. Nice, R. Cambridge: Cambridge University Press.

Brookfield, S. (1986) *Understanding and Facilitating Adult Learning: A Comprehensive Analysis of Principles and Effective Practices.* Milton Keynes: Open University Press.

Brookfield, S. (1996) Fostering critical conversation in the learning university, *International Journal of University Adult Education*, 25(1): 48–60.

Brown, R.H. (1976) Social theory as metaphor, *Theory and Society*, 3: 169–97.

Bush, T. (1986) *Theories of Educational Management.* London: Harper and Row.

Cameron, K. and Tschirhart, M. (1992) Postindustrial environments and organisational effectiveness in colleges and universities, *Journal of Higher Education*, 63(1): 87–108.

Carr, D. (1999) *Professionalism and Ethics in Teaching.* London: Taylor and Francis.

Carr, W. and Kemmis, S. (1986) *Becoming Critical: Education, Knowledge and Action Research.* London: Falmer.

Clarke, J. and Newman, J. (1997) *The Managerial State: Power, Politics and Ideology in the Remaking of Social Welfare.* London: Sage.

Codd, J.A. (1988) The construction and deconstruction of educational policy documents. *Journal of Education Policy*, 3(3): 243–7.

Cohen, M.D. and March, J.G. (1986) Leadership and ambiguity, in O. Boyd-Barrett, T. Bush, J. Goodey, I. McNay and M. Preedy (eds) *Approaches to Post-School Management: A Reader.* London: Paul Chapman Publishing.

Cohen, M.D., March, J.G. and Olsen, J.P. (1972) A garbage can model of organisational choice, *Administrative Science Quarterly*, 17(1): 1–25.

Cousin, G. (2004) Learning from cyberspace, in R. Land and S. Bayne (eds) *Education in Cyberspace*. London: RoutledgeFalmer.

Cousin, G., Deepwell, F., Land, R. and Ponti, M. (2004) Theorising implementation: variation and commonality in European approaches to e-learning, in S. Banks, P. Goodyear, V. Hodgson, C. Jones, V. Lally, D. McConnell and C. Steeples (eds) *Networked Learning 2004*. Lancaster: Lancaster University and University of Sheffield.

Craib, I. (1994) *The Importance of Disappointment*. London: Routledge.

Darby, J. (1995) Education in the year 2000: will we recognise it? in F. Percival, R. Land and D. Edgar-Nevill (eds) *Computer-Assisted and Open Access Education*. London: Kogan Page.

Day, C. (1993) Reflection: a necessary but not sufficient condition for professional development, *British Educational Research Journal*, 19(1): 83–93.

Dearing, R. (1997) *Higher Education in the Learning Society*. Report of the National Committee of Inquiry into Higher Education. London: Department for Education and Employment. http://www.leeds.ac.uk/educol/ncihe.

Delantey, G. (2001) *Challenging Knowledge: The University in the Knowledge Society*. Buckingham: SRHE and Open University Press.

Deleuze, G. (1992) Postscript on the societies of control. *October*, 59: 3–7.

Dewey, J. (1922) *Human Nature and Conduct. An Introduction to Social Psychology*. London: Allen and Unwin.

Duke, C. (1992) *The Learning University: Towards a New Paradigm?* Buckingham: SRHE and Open University Press.

Dummett, M. (1994) Too many cooks and a capitalist flavour, *The Tablet*, Educational Supplement No 71 (8 October): 1268–9.

Ellis, R. (1993) *Quality Assurance for University Teaching*. Buckingham: SRHE and Open University Press.

Elton, L. (1994) *Management of Teaching and Learning: Towards Change in Universities*. London: Committee of Vice-Chancellors and Principals (CVCP) / Society for Research into Higher Education (SRHE).

Elton, L. (1995) An institutional framework, in A. Brew (ed.) *Directions in Staff Development*. Buckingham: SRHE and Open University Press.

Elton, L. (1998a) Managing new ways of learning: people, problems and practicalities – Paper 1, SRHE / CVCP / THES Seminar (Change), 30 April.

Elton, L. (1998b) Managing new ways of learning: people, problems and practicalities – Paper 2, SRHE / CVCP / THES Seminar (Change), 30 April.

Engestrom, Y. (1991) Activity theory and individual and social transformation, *Multidisciplinary Newletter for Activity Theory*, 7: 6–17.

Entwistle, N., Hanley, M. and Hounsell, D. (1979) Identifying distinctive approaches to studying, *Higher Education*, 8: 359–63.

Entwistle, N.J., Thompson, S.M. and Tait, H. (1992) *Guidelines for Promoting Effective Learning in Higher Education*. Edinburgh: Centre for Research on Learning and Instruction, University of Edinburgh.

Eraut, M. (1994) Schön shock: a case for reframing reflection-in-action, *Teachers and Teaching: Theory and Practice*, 1(1).

ETL (2004) *Enhancing Teaching-Learning Environments in Undergraduate Courses*. Economic and Social Research Council Teaching and Learning Research Programme. http://www.ed.ac.uk/etl

Evans, C. (1988) *Language People*. Milton Keynes: Open University Press.
Evans, C. (1993) *English People: The Experience of Teaching and Learning English in British Universities*. Buckingham: Open University Press.
Fenstermacher, G.D. (1988) The place of science and epistemology in Schön's conception of reflective practice, in P. Grimmett and G.L. Erickson (eds) *Reflection in Teacher Education*. New York: Teachers' College Press.
Foucault, M. (1975) *Discipline and Punish: The Birth of the Prison*. Harmondsworth: Penguin.
Foucault, M. (1980) *Power/Knowledge*. New York: Pantheon.
Frielick, S. (2004) *The Zone of Academic Development: An Ecological Approach to Learning and Teaching in Higher Education*. Unpublished PhD thesis, University of the Witwatersrand.
Fullan, M. (1993) *Change Forces: Probing the Depths of Educational Reform*. London: The Falmer Press.
Fulton, O. (ed.) (1989) *Access and Institutional Change*. Buckingham: SRHE and Open University Press.
Gagliardi, P. (1986) The creation and change of organisational cultures: A conceptual framework, *Organisation Studies*, 7: 117–34.
Gibbs, G. (1996a) Who shall teach the teachers? *Managing HE*, Issue 3, Summer.
Gibbs, G. (1996b) Supporting educational development within departments, *International Journal of Academic Development*, 1(1).
Giddens, A. (1979) *Central Problems in Social Theory*. London: Macmillan.
Giddens, A. (1991) *Modernity and Self-Identity: Self and Society in the Late Modern Age*. Cambridge: Polity Press.
Giesen, B. and Schmid, M. (1989) Symbolic, institutional and social-structural differentiation: selection-theoretical perspective, in H. Haferkamp (ed.) *Social Structure and Culture*. Berlin and New York: De Gruyter.
Goodlad, S. (1995) *The Quest for Quality: Sixteen Forms of Heresy in Higher Education*. Buckingham: SRHE and Open University Press.
Gordon, G. and Partington, P. (1993) *Quality in Higher Education: Overview and Update*. USDU Briefing Paper Three. Sheffield: Universities Staff Development Unit.
Gornall, L. (1999) 'New professionals' – changing organisational roles in HE learning and teaching. Paper delivered at 6th Association for Learning Technology Conference (ALT-C), Bristol, 21–23 September.
Gosling, D.W. (1996) What do UK educational development units do? in *The International Journal for Academic Development*, 1(1): 75–83.
Gosling, D.W. (1997) Educational development and institutional change in higher education, in K.M. Gokulsing and C. DaCosta (eds) *Usable Knowledges as the Goal of University Education*. Lampeter: The Edward Mellen Press.
Gosling, D. (2001) Educational development units in the UK – what are they doing five years on? *The International Journal for Academic Development*, 6(1): 74–90.
Gouldner, A. (1979) *The Future of Intellectuals and the New Class*. London: Heineman.
Green, D. (1994) *What is Quality in Higher Education?* Buckingham: SRHE and Open University Press.
Grimmett, P.P., Mackinnon, A.M., Erickson, G.L. and Riecken, T.J. (1990) Reflective practice in teacher education, in R.T. Clift, M.C. Houston and Pugach (eds) *Encouraging Reflective Practice in Education*. New York: Teachers' College Press.
Habermas, J. (1970) *Towards a Rational Society*. London: Heinemann Educational Books.
Habermas, J. (1978) *Knowledge and Human Interests*, 2nd edn. London: Heinemann.

Halsey, A.H. (1992) *The Decline of Donnish Dominion.* Oxford: Oxford University Press.

Handy, C. (1976) *Understanding Organisations.* Harmondsworth: Penguin.

Harrison, R. (1972) Understanding your organization's character, *Harvard Business Review,* May–June: 119–28.

Havelock, R. (1973) *A Change Agent's Guide to Innovation in Education.* Englewood Cliffs, New Jersey: Educational Technology Publications.

Hawkins, P. and Winter, J. (1997) *Mastering Change: Learning the Lessons of the Enterprise in Higher Education Initiative.* Sheffield: DfEE and Whiteway Research International.

Hayles, N.K. (1999) *How We Became Posthuman: Virtual Bodies in Cybernetics, Literature, and Informatics.* Chicago: University of Chicago Press.

Hewton, E. (1986) Inside knowledge, in O. Boyd-Barrett, T. Bush, J. Goodey, I. McNay and M. Preedy (eds) *Approaches to Post-School Management: A Reader.* London: Paul Chapman Publishing.

Hooijberg, R. and Petrock, F. (1993) On cultural change: Using the competing values framework to help leaders execute a transformational strategy, *Human Resource Management,* 32(1): 29–50.

Hounsell, D., McCulloch, M., Scott, M., Burley, E., Day, K., Falchikov, N., Haywood, J. and Land, R. (1996) *The ASSHE Inventory: Changing Assessment Practices in Scottish Higher Education.* Sheffield: UCoSDA, with the University of Edinburgh and Napier University, Edinburgh.

Ignatiev, M. (1999) Contribution to BBC Radio 4 discussion programme, 8pm, 10 January.

ILTHE (1999) *Guidelines on Institutional Programme Accreditation.* York: Institute for Learning and Teaching.

Jackall, R. (1988) *Moral Mazes. The World of Corporate Managers.* Oxford: Oxford University Press.

Jaques, D. (1989) *Course Design,* Module 10, Certificate in Teaching in Higher Education by Open Learning. Oxford: Oxford Centre for Staff Development.

Jarratt Report (1985) *Report of the Steering Committee for Efficiency Studies in Universities.* London: Committee of Vice-Chancellors and Principals (CVCP).

Jarvis, P. (1985) *The Sociology of Adult and Continuing Education.* London: Routledge.

Jary, D. and Parker, M. (1994) The McUniversity: Organisation, management and academic subjectivity, *Organization,* 2(2): 319–38.

Jenkins, A. (1996) Discipline-based educational development, *International Journal of Academic Development,* 1(1): 50–62.

Jenlink, P. and Carr, A.A. (1996) Conversation as a medium for change in education, *Educational Technology,* 36(1): 31–8.

Kearsley, G. (2000) *Situated Learning (J. Lave),* Explorations in Learning and Instruction: The Theory into Practice Database. The George Washington University. Published online at: http://www.gwu.edu/~tip/lave.html

Knowles, M.S. (1978) *The Adult Learner: A Neglected Species.* Houston: Gulf Publishing Co.

Knowles, M.S. (1980) *The Modern Practice of Adult Education.* Chicago: Association Press,

Kolb, D.A. (1983) *Experiential Learning: Experience as the Source of Learning and Development.* New York: Prentice Hall.

Krefting, L. and Frost, P.J. (1985) Untangling webs, surfing waves, and wildcatting: A multiple-metaphor perspective on managing organisational culture, in P.J. Frost et al. (eds) *Organisational Culture.* Beverly Hills: Sage.

Land, R. and Bayne, S. (eds) (2004) *Education in Cyberspace.* London: RoutledgeFalmer.

Laurillard, D. (1979) The processes of student learning, *Higher Education*, 8: 395–409.
Lave, J. and Wenger, E. (1991) *Situated Learning: Legitimate Peripheral Participation.* Cambridge: Cambridge University Press.
Lewin, K. (1952) *Field Theory in Social Science.* London: Tavistock.
Lieberman, A. (1989) *Staff Development in Culture Building. Curriculum and Teaching: The Next 50 Years.* New York: Teachers' College Press.
Lindblom, C. (1959) The science of muddling through. *Public Administration Review*, 19: 78–88.
Lipsky, M. (1980) *Street-Level Bureaucracy: Dilemmas of the Individual in Public Services.* New York: Russell Sage Foundation.
Lloyd, P. (1996) *Enhancing Communication – Communicating Strategy and Change.* Office for Public Management. Napier University Strategic Change Initiative Conference, Edinburgh, 1–2 November.
MacIntyre, A. (1985) *After Virtue.* London: Duckworth.
Martin, J. (1987) The black hole. Ambiguity in organisational cultures. Paper presented to the 3rd International Conference on Organisational Symbolism and Corporate Culture, Milan, June 1987, cited in M. Alvesson (2002) *Understanding Organisational Culture.* London: Sage.
Marton, F. (1999) *Variatio est mater studiorum.* Opening address, 8th Conference for Research on Learning and Instruction (EARLI), Gothenburg, Sweden, 24 August.
Marton, F. and Säljo, R. (1976) On qualitative differences in learning – I: Outcome and process, *British Journal of Educational Psychology*, 46: 4–11.
Maxwell, N. (1987) *From Knowledge to Wisdom.* Oxford: Blackwell.
McArthur, J., Land, R., Earl, S., Elvidge, E., Juwah, C. and Ross, D. (2004) *PROMOTE – Alternative Ways of Fostering Educational Development.* Edinburgh: Napier University and LTSN Generic Centre.
McNay, I. (1995) From the collegial academy to corporate enterprise; the changing cultures of universities, in T. Schuller (ed.) *The Changing University?* Buckingham: SRHE and Open University Press.
Meyer, J.H.F. and Land, R. (2003) Threshold concepts and troublesome knowledge (1) – Linkages to ways of thinking and practising, in C. Rust, (ed.) *Improving Student Learning – Ten Years On.* Oxford: Oxford Centre for Staff and Learning Development.
Meyer, J.H.F. and Land, R. (2004) Threshold concepts and troublesome knowledge (2): epistemological considerations and a conceptual framework for teaching and learning, *Higher Education*, special issue (in press).
Mezirow, J. (1981) A critical theory of adult learning and education, *Adult Education*, 32(1): 3–24.
Middlehurst, R. and Elton, L. (1992) Leadership and management in higher education, *Studies in Higher Education*, 17: 251–64.
Miller, H. (1995a) *The Management of Change in Universities.* Buckingham: SRHE and Open University Press.
Miller, H. (1995b) States, economies and the changing labour process of academics: Australia, Canada and the United Kingdom, in J. Smyth (ed.) *Academic Work: The Changing Labour Process in Higher Education.* Buckingham: SRHE and Open University Press.
Morgan, G. (1980) Paradigms, metaphors and puzzle solving in organisational analysis, *Administrative Science Quarterly*, 25: 606–22.
Morgan, G. (1986) *Images of Organisation.* Beverly Hills: Sage.

Naidoo, R. (2003) Corroding relations: The impact of student consumerism on teaching and learning in higher education, *SRHE Annual Conference, Research, Scholarship and Teaching: Changing Relationships?*, 16–18 December, London: Royal Holloway University of London.
Nixon, J. (1996) Professional identity and the restructuring of higher education, *Studies in Higher Education*, 21(1): 5–16.
Parker, S. (1997) *Reflective Teaching in the Postmodern World.* Buckingham: Open University Press.
Philp, M. (1985) Michel Foucault, in Q. Skinner (ed.) *The Return of Grand Theory in the Human Sciences.* Cambridge: Cambridge University Press.
Polanyi, M. (1983) *The Tacit Dimension.* Magnolia, MA: Peter Smith.
Pollit, C. (1993) *Managerialism in the Public Services.* Oxford: Blackwell.
Power, M. (1994) *The Audit Explosion.* London: Demos.
Price, S., McAndrew, P., Cuttle, M., Rist, R., Mayes, T., Bonharme, E., Land, R., Haywood, J. and Macleod, H. (1997) The MARBLE Project: A collaborative approach to producing educational material for the Web, *International Journal of Educational Telecommunications*, 3, (2/3).
QAA (1998) *Quality Assurance in UK Higher Education: A Brief Guide.* Gloucester: QAA.
Ramsden, P. (1979) Student learning and perceptions of the academic environment, *Higher Education*, 8: 411–27.
Readings, B. (1997) *The University in Ruins.* Cambridge, MA: Harvard University Press.
Reynolds, J. and Saunders, M. (1985) Teacher responses to curriculum policy: Beyond the 'delivery' metaphor, in J. Calderhead (ed.) *Exploring Teachers' Thinking.* London: Cassell.
Rogers, C.R. (1942) *Counselling and Psychotherapy.* Boston: Houghton Mifflin.
Rogers, C.R. (1961) *On Becoming a Person.* London: Constable.
Rogers, C.R. (1969) *Freedom to Learn.* Columbus, Ohio: Merrill.
Rogers, E. (1967) *Diffusion of Innovations.* New York: Free Press.
Rorty, R. (1979) *Philosophy and the Mirror of Nature.* Princeton, NJ: Princeton University Press.
Rowland, S. (1996) Relationships between teaching and research, *Teaching and Learning in Higher Education*, 1(1): 7–20.
Salter, B. and Tapper, T. (1992) *Oxford, Cambridge and the Changing Idea of the University.* Buckingham: SRHE and Open University Press.
Sawbridge, M. (1996) *The Politics and Organisational Complexity of Staff Development for Academics: A Discussion Paper.* Sheffield: UCoSDA Occasional Green Paper No.14.
Schein, E.H. (1985) *Organisational Culture and Leadership.* San Francisco: Jossey-Bass.
Schön, D.A. (1983) *The Reflective Practitioner.* New York: Basic Books.
Schön, D.A. (1987) *Educating the Reflective Practitioner.* London: Temple Smith.
Scott, P. (1995) *The Meanings of Mass Higher Education.* Buckingham: SRHE and Open University Press.
Scott, P. (ed.) (1999) *The Globalisation of Higher Education.* Buckingham: SRHE and Open University Press.
Senge, P.M. (1990) *The Fifth Dimension.* London: Random House.
Smelser, N.J. (1998) The rational and the ambivalent in the social sciences, *American Sociological Review*, 63: 1–16.
Smith, P.B. and Peterson, M.F. (1988) *Leadership, Organisations and Culture.* London: Sage.

Smyth, J. (1991) *Teachers as Collaborative Learners.* Milton Keynes: Open University Press.
Stones, R. (1991) Strategic context analysis: a new research strategy for structuration theory, *Sociology*, Vol. 25, No. 3: 673–95.
Stones, R. (1996) *Sociological Reasoning: Towards a Past-modern Sociology.* London: Macmillan.
Taylor, P.G. (1999) *Making Sense of Academic Life: Academics, Universities and Change.* Buckingham: SRHE and Open University Press.
Trow, M. (1974) Problems in the transition from elite to mass higher education, in *Policies for Higher Education,* OECD, Paris.
Trow, M. (1993) *Managerialism and the Academic Profession: The Case of England.* Stockholm: Council for Studies of Higher Education.
Trowler, P. (2002) The nature of things: change and social reality. Paper presented at the 3rd Education Doctorate Colloquium, Managing Educational Change, 4 April. Edinburgh: University of Edinburgh.
Trowler, P. (1997) Beyond the Robbins Trap: reconceptualising academic responses to change in higher education (or . . . Quiet Flows the Don). *Studies in Higher Education,* 22: 301–18.
Trowler, P., Saunders, M. and Knight, P. (2003) *Change Thinking, Change Practices.* York: LTSN Generic Centre.
Turner, C.M. (1982) *Structure of Organisations.* Further Education Staff College Information Bank Working Paper IBN 1768, Bristol: Coombe Lodge.
Tutt, N. (1985) The unintended consequences of integration, *Educational and Child Psychology,* 2: 30–38.
Usher, R. and Edwards, R. (1994) *Postmodernism and Education.* London: Routledge.
Van Maanen, M. (1977) Linking ways of knowing with ways of being practical, *Curriculum Inquiry,* 6(3): 205–28.
Van Maanen, M. and Barley, S.R. (1985) Cultural organisation: Fragments of a theory, in P.J. Frost, L.F. Moore, M.R. Louis, C.C. Lundberg and J. Martin (eds) *Organisational Culture.* Beverly Hills: Sage.
Van Maanen, J. and Kunda, G. (1989) Real feelings: Emotional expression and organisational culture, in B.M. Staw and L.L. Cummings (eds) *Research in Organisational Behaviour,* Vol. 11. Greenwich: JAI Press.
Webb, G. (1993) Announcing the death of development, again, in G. Ryan, P. Little and I. Dunn (eds) *Research and Development in Higher Education, 16.* Campbelltown, New South Wales: Higher Education Research and Development Society of Australasia.
Webb, G. (1996a) Theories of staff development: Development and understanding, *The International Journal for Academic Development,* Vol. 1, No. 1, May: 63–9.
Webb, G. (1996b) *Understanding Staff Development.* Buckingham: SRHE and Open University Press.
Weick, K.E. (1976) Educational organisations as loosely coupled systems, *Administrative Science Quarterly,* 21(1): 1–19.
Weick, K.E. (1980) Management of change amongst loosely coupled elements, in P. Goodman et al. (eds) *Change in Organisations.* Thousand Oaks, CA: Sage.
Weick, K.E. (1995) *Sensemaking in Organisations.* Thousand Oaks, CA: Sage.
Weiner, M. (1981) *English Culture and the Decline of the Industrial Spirit 1850–1980.* Harmondsworth: Penguin.
Wellington, B. and Austin, P. (1996) Orientations to reflective practice, *Educational Research,* 38(3): 307–16.

Wenger, E. (1998) *Communities of Practice: Learning, Meaning and Identity*. Cambridge: Cambridge University Press.

Williams, G. (1992) *Changing Patterns of Finance in Higher Education*. Buckingham: SRHE and Open University Press.

Winnicott, D.W. (1971) *Playing and Reality*. New York: Basic Books.

Young, I.M. (1990) The ideal of community and the politics of difference, in L. Nicholson (ed.) *Feminism/Postmodernism*. New York: Routledge.

Index

The Society for Research into Higher Education

The Society for Research into Higher Education (SRHE), an international body, exists to stimulate and coordinate research into all aspects of higher education. It aims to improve the quality of higher education through the encouragement of debate and publication on issues of policy, on the organization and management of higher education institutions, and on the curriculum, teaching and learning methods.

The Society is entirely independent and receives no subsidies, although individual events often receive sponsorship from business or industry. The Society is financed through corporate and individual subscriptions and has members from many parts of the world. It is an NGO of UNESCO.

Under the imprint *SRHE & Open University Press*, the Society is a specialist publisher of research, having over 80 titles in print. In addition to *SRHE News*, the Society's newsletter, the Society publishes three journals: *Studies in Higher Education* (three issues a year), *Higher Education Quarterly* and *Research into Higher Education Abstracts* (three issues a year).

The Society runs frequent conferences, consultations, seminars and other events. The annual conference in December is organized at and with a higher education institution. There are a growing number of networks which focus on particular areas of interest, including:

Access
Assessment
Consultants
Curriculum Development
Eastern European
Educational Development Research
FE/HE
Graduate Employment
New Technology for Learning
Postgraduate Issues
Quantitative Studies
Student Development

Benefits to members

Individual

- The opportunity to participate in the Society's networks
- Reduced rates for the annual conferences
- Free copies of *Research into Higher Education Abstracts*
- Reduced rates for *Studies in Higher Education*

- Reduced rates for *Higher Education Quarterly*
- Free online access to *Register of Members' Research Interests* – includes valuable reference material on research being pursued by the Society's members
- Free copy of occasional in-house publications, e.g. *The Thirtieth Anniversary Seminars Presented by the Vice-Presidents*
- Free copies of *SRHE News* and *International News* which inform members of the Society's activities and provides a calendar of events, with additional material provided in regular mailings
- A 35 per cent discount on all SRHE/Open University Press books
- The opportunity for you to apply for the annual research grants
- Inclusion of your research in the *Register of Members' Research Interests*

Corporate

- Reduced rates for the annual conference
- The opportunity for members of the Institution to attend SRHE's network events at reduced rates
- Free copies of *Research into Higher Education Abstracts*
- Free copies of *Studies in Higher Education*
- Free online access to *Register of Members' Research Interests* – includes valuable reference material on research being pursued by the Society's members
- Free copy of occasional in-house publications
- Free copies of *SRHE News* and *International News*
- A 35 per cent discount on all SRHE/Open University Press books
- The opportunity for members of the Institution to submit applications for the Society's research grants
- The opportunity to work with the Society and co-host conferences
- The opportunity to include in the *Register of Members' Research Interests* your Institution's research into aspects of higher education

Membership details: SRHE, 76 Portland Place, London W1B 1NT, UK Tel: 020 7637 2766. Fax: 020 7637 2781. email: srheoffice@srhe.ac.uk
world wide web: http://www.srhe.ac.uk./srhe/
Catalogue: SRHE & Open University Press, McGraw-Hill Education, McGraw-Hill House, Shoppenhangers Road, Maidenhead, Berkshire SL6 2QL. Tel: 01628 502500. Fax: 01628 770224. email: enquiries@openup.co.uk – web: www.openup.co.uk